Social Theory
A Basic Tool Kit

John Parker

with

Leonard Mars, Paul Ransome
and Hilary Stanworth

palgrave
macmillan

First published 2003 by
PALGRAVE MACMILLAN
Houndmills, Basingstoke, Hampshire RG21 6XS and
175 Fifth Avenue, New York, N.Y. 10010
Companies and representatives throughout the world

PALGRAVE MACMILLAN is the global academic imprint of the Palgrave Macmillan division of St. Martin's Press, LLC and of Palgrave Macmillan Ltd. Macmillan® is a registered trademark in the United States, United Kingdom and other countries. Palgrave is a registered trademark in the European Union and other countries.

ISBN 0–333–96211–7 hardback
ISBN 0–333–96212–5 paperback

This book is printed on paper suitable for recycling and made from fully managed and sustained forest sources.

A catalogue record for this book is available from the British Library.

Library of Congress Cataloging-in-Publication Data

Social theory : a basic tool kit / John Parker ... [et al.].
   p. cm.
  Includes bibliographical references and index.
  ISBN 0–333–96211–7 — ISBN 0–333–96212–5 (pbk.)
   1. Social sciences—Philosophy. 2. Social sciences—Research. 3. Culture.
4. Action research. I. Parker, John, 1946–

H61.S7746 2003
300'.1—dc21

                                   2003040529

Editing and origination by Aardvark Editorial, Mendham, Suffolk

10 9 8 7 6 5 4 3 2 1
12 11 10 09 08 07 06 05 04 03

Printed in China

Contents

List of Main Examples

List of Figures and Tables

Figures

Tables

Preface

This book offers an introduction to basic social theory for those who are curious about the social world and how they and the social sciences try to explain it. Written from a realist point of view, it insists that there is no great divide between how we ordinary people living social lives, and social scientists, explain our social experience. It encourages people to reflect on their existing explanatory practices, and helps them to see social theory as an important set of tools for thinking about the substantive and practical problems that everyone faces and in which social scientists specialise. It presents social theory as fundamental for making sense of social life and something relevant for everyone – a thoroughly practical business.

We suggest that as 'active theorists' we work with a basic social theoretical 'tool kit', a set of fundamental concepts, the equivalent of the DIYers' hammer, saw, screwdriver, pliers and drill, tools which, with a little luck, allow us to deal with most everyday problems because the functions they perform are universal and unavoidable. We introduce five fundamental social theoretical concepts: individuals; nature; culture; action and social structure, and use a wide range of everyday, and not so everyday, examples of puzzling social phenomena to reveal the strengths but also the limits of each concept. We argue that we need to take all of them into consideration to generate the most powerful social explanations. (The main examples we use are listed below.)

This book is for anyone interested in explaining social life. It tries to provide an efficient and distinctive route to understanding the basic structure of social explanation, taking readers rapidly to the heart of the matter. It does not presume any prior knowledge of social science theorists or theories, nor is it designed to teach you which theorists said what and when. Many other texts do that very well. However, it can be used as complementary reading to such texts and the 'standard' social theory courses built around them. To help perform this complementary role we provide strong hints, both in the text and also in the glossary, about how to link the discussion of the concepts and the examples to the ideas of important social theorists. However, the main way it complements teaching built around theorists and theories is by showing what it is that makes them worth learning about.

Acknowledgements

The origin of the book lies in an 'Introduction to Social Theory' module the authors have recently developed for students in sociology and anthropology at the University of Wales, Swansea, and we would like to thank colleagues and students for their support for this project. We have particularly benefited from the feedback from those who have contributed to teaching the module: Stephanie Adams, John Campbell, Charlotte Davies, Felicia Hughes-Freeland, John Hutson, Margaret Kenna, Mike Pany and Luis Valenzuela. Catherine Gray of Palgrave Macmillan, gave a swift initial assessment of the original teaching materials and then advice which has substantially shaped the purpose and design of the book. We would like to thank her for seeing its potential, as well as her efficiency and enthusiasm.

The Tool Kit

Being curious about collective phenomena

The social science disciplines such as sociology, anthropology and history have been developed to explain puzzling social phenomena. They particularly investigate 'collective' phenomena, that is, aspects of people's lives that are not unique to them, ones that they share with at least some others. These disciplines are founded on the ordinary common-sense recognition that the behaviour of individuals, and what happens in the social world, is powerfully affected by the way individual people are 'collectivised', that is, by the ways they come to be in similar circumstances of one kind or another. Everyone understands that how people are collectivised makes a difference to how they are likely to act and what they are likely to think, and that knowing these things helps us when we have to deal with them. Being able to give answers to questions such as 'Why do these people typically or regularly do that?' or 'Why did that event or kind of event happen when and where it did?' is a practical requirement of life for everyone.

To explain collective phenomena the social sciences use 'social theory', which may sound difficult or strange, but is merely a developed version of what we use all the time in our everyday lives whenever we try to explain some social phenomenon to ourselves or others. Our approach to social theory is built on the fact that everyone has an interest in explaining social phenomena and already does so with some practical effectiveness. Effective human beings must have a practical, sound grasp of the concepts needed to analyse social reality, concepts which social theory makes explicit for the social sciences.

Hypothesising and explaining

Our approach to social theory and explanation is a *realist* one. Realists hold that there is a real world existing independently of both our direct physical experience of it and what we can say about it. This objective reality is the ultimate test for explanations. When we try to explain our experience, we must talk about the way the world really is. What we say must refer to the reality of mechanisms and genera-tive processes, which pre-exist and cause what we experience and describe (Figure 0.1). As we will show in Chapter 11, where we will discuss how our position differs from others in more detail, not all social theorists are realists. Some give explanatory primacy to either experience or language, rather than to reality itself.

For the moment, however, all we need to do is claim that explana-tion requires us to refer to the mechanisms and processes operating in reality to produce what we experience and may want to explain. The key point is that realists hold that there are many different kinds of causes at work producing social phenomena. Thus realism provides a good basis for introducing the varieties of social theory which seek to understand the causes of social phenomena.

For realists, explanation begins by inventing relevant hypotheses, that is, speculations about the various processes and mechanisms, which, in combinations and sequences, might produce the phenom-ena we want to understand. This is why explanation of recurrent phenomena involves more than making accurate predictions. We must also discover and understand the real mechanisms which produce what we may have successfully predicted. To predict that the sun will rise in the east and set in the west because it has always done so, is not the same as explaining why the sun rises in the east and sets where it does as the outcome of a mechanical process of daily rotation of the earth on its axis and its orbit round the sun.

From a realist point of view, theory's function is to contribute to the process of discovering real mechanisms and help to ensure that our hypothesising is relevant. We do not just suggest any old reasons for why things happen. Rather, we control our speculations by refer-ence to our general ideas about the kinds of thing we are trying to explain and the kind of real mechanism likely to have produced them. Realism merely sets the stage for arguments about what exactly the different kinds of reality are and the way they work. So, for example, if I want to explain why my bicycle tyre punctured this morning, I would hypothesise about likely causes such as broken glass

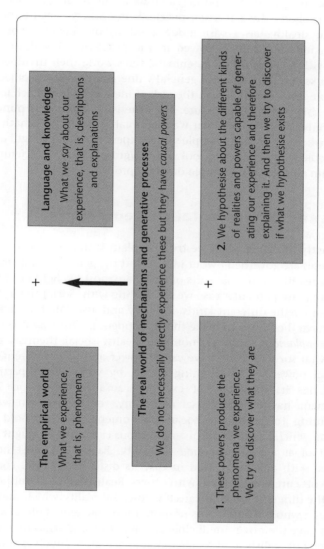

Figure 0.1 Relating experience and knowledge to reality

The empirical world

What we experience, that is, phenomena

Language and knowledge

What we *say* about our experience, that is, descriptions and explanations

The real world of mechanisms and generative processes

We do not necessarily directly experience these but they have *causal powers*

1. These powers produce the phenomena we experience. We try to discover what they are

2. We hypothesise about the different kinds of realities and powers capable of generating our experience and therefore explaining it. And then we try to discover if what we hypothesise exists

or drawing pins, rather than absurdly unlikely ones such as what I had for breakfast or the colour of my socks. We would be surprised if someone thought that hypothesising about breakfast and socks was useful in solving this particular puzzle. Why? Surely because (nearly) everyone already has a basic understanding, or 'theory', about the general kinds of reality involved in the problem being dealt with. Armed with a grasp of how pneumatic tyres work, their invulnerability to socks and breakfasts but general vulnerability to sharp objects, it is possible to focus quickly on the task of identifying the mechanisms causing this particular puncture. Hypothesising about this puncture will have been guided by what we might call general 'pneumatic tyre theory' (the fruit of many people's long experience and thought about such problems) to help us to look in the right places when attempting to explain this specific example of a tyre problem.

What the fundamental concepts do

It is exactly the same when we try to explain social phenomena. Our hypotheses are governed by our ideas about the general characteristics of social realities and what sorts of factor are most likely to be at work in shaping any particular case we are dealing with. Social theory's job is to identify the different kinds of reality and associated mechanism which have the power to make things happen. In this way it contributes to *explaining* social phenomena. Realist social theorists argue about what sorts of thing have causal power and how different sorts of causal power work. Anything which, by virtue of its particular nature, has its own way of exerting causal influence on social phenomena has its own causal autonomy, that is, its own way of contributing to producing social phenomena. Realists hold that anything which has this sort of autonomous causal power ought to be thought of as a particular *kind* of reality. Each kind must not be confused with any other kind in case its distinctive causal contribution is obscured or confused with others. Realists argue about how to define the different kinds of causally powerful reality which make up reality as a whole. There is lots of room for disagreement about which realities have their own irreducible causal nature and what their properties are, but realists tend to agree that explanation involves showing how their causal powers *interact*. For realists, explanation involves taking account of all the relevant causes and not trying to make only one of them do all the work. They are against assigning explanatory pre-eminence to any one kind of causation. The idea that there are many, real, causally autonomous mechanisms is of fundamental importance. Explanation involves showing the relations between the causal powers of a range of relevant, real mechanisms as they interact over time to produce what is being explained. We argue that all social explanations must use all the following five fundamental concepts denoting specific kinds with their own causal powers:

- individuals
- nature
- culture
- action
- social structure.

To help to convince you that these five concepts really are important, let's take an example of a 'collective phenomenon', and invite you to begin explaining it. Use your imagination to think of all the possible causes.

Why are children with working-class parents underrepresented among the educationally successful?

We guess, almost immediately, that you identified relevant causes which you reckoned were likely to affect achievement, such as access to relevant material resources (books, quiet, transport), individual motivation (emotional rewards, encouragement from parents and teachers, peer group support), cultural resources (language, world view, moral values), school organisation (selection criteria, streaming, discipline regime, performance indicators), and the curriculum (traditional knowledge hierarchies, political initiatives, local emphases). But *why* would you think these were relevant? We suggest that it is because, just as when explaining the puncture example, you understand the general kind of problem being dealt with.

You already know the sorts of consideration which are relevant. You have general ideas about the kinds of thing 'educational achievement' and 'social classes' are. 'Achievement' (an example of culture) requires an environment providing relevant material resources to enable individuals to act effectively within educational contexts, and 'social classes' (an example of social structure) function to distribute material resources and hence opportunities to 'achieve' educationally. Similarly, you have general ideas about what kind of thing 'individuals' are, that they are self-directed beings with rationality but who are socially and emotionally attached to members of their family, neighbourhood, peer group and so on and respond to the encouragement or discouragement of others. Again, you have general ideas about the kind of things 'institutions', and 'education systems' are. Thus you know that 'achievement' involves one's performance at specific tasks being evaluated by people who have the power to judge you by virtue of the positions they occupy in institutions. You know that institutions are organisations of social positions to which functions and powers attach – people in different positions have different powers of action.

Each of the five fundamental concepts denotes something which can make a difference to outcomes. Thus, although you know that individual ability and effort can contribute to success or failure, it cannot make all the difference by itself. You suspect that they have to be related to many other success-producing or inhibiting factors emergent from their social relations and institutional environments, of the kind we have just been discussing. Just as having ability cannot make all the difference, nor can going to a good school or having rich parents. It is the *interaction* of these and other variables which makes the difference. And you know this because you have an understanding of the mechanisms at work in social reality contributing to the formation and activity of individuals. You recognise that individuals are not self-created beings, but the products of socialisation and location within social worlds, which distribute access to resources and opportunities and which have consequences for what they are able to do and be. Hence the relevance of hypothesising about how position in social classes affects achievement.

In other words, ordinary thinking about this problem has been guided by an understanding of the relevance of considering the *interaction of the different kinds of real causes* involved, that is, by basic social theory. The social theory may not have been articulated before you started to think about this problem, but when you got going, your assumptions about the nature of individuals and collectivities, and how they are related, would have been brought into play, organising your hypothesising which would also structure any empirical enquiry you might subsequently make. If you don't believe that the brightest and most hard working inevitably do best (if you doubt that we live in a meritocracy), ask yourself why not. Is it because you believe that the powers of individuals are, to some degree and in various ways, effects of their being located in positions in organisations and structures of material inequality? Social theorising involves thinking about how such social phenomena are produced and how they affect individuals.

Different levels and kinds of theory, and creativity in social explanation

Perhaps, by now, you are asking: 'If I already hypothesise about social phenomena using social theoretical ideas, why do I need this book? Isn't it all just common sense?' What we hope we are offering, besides continual encouragement to be reflexive about your own social theorising, is an opportunity to learn what the most basic set of social theoretical concepts is, and why they are all necessary and unavoidable for social explanation. We will show you their logical properties and modes of relation using a wide range of concrete examples and puzzles. Armed with this small 'tool kit' of what we claim to be fundamental concepts, you should be much better placed to create valuable hypotheses, and understand what the major social theorists are up to. These concepts are fundamental to explaining social phenomena because social reality, as a particular type of reality, is the way it is. Thus they apply universally. No historical development can render them irrelevant; they will always provide the basis for explaining whatever does happen in social reality and whatever social experiences we have during our lives.

However, although these concepts are basic, that only means that they provide a sort of foundation upon which to invent other theoretical ideas (a glance now at the Glossary will show you many of them). These are equally necessary for social explanation – the basic concepts function to support an elaborate edifice of social theory and do not, and cannot, do all the explanatory work by themselves. Thus, for example, it is necessary to have the concept of 'social structure' before one can have a particular concept of a type of social structure, say a 'stratification system', and that concept is a precondition of being able to theorise different kinds of stratification systems, such as 'class' and 'caste' systems, which may be further refined by distinguishing between 'relatively open' and 'relatively closed' class systems. Here we see four levels of theoretical refinement. Similarly, it is necessary to have the concept of culture before one can have a particular cultural concept, for example 'gender' or 'religion' or 'social identity'. Or again, the concept of the human individual defines what can have a personality, and logically these concepts ('individual' and 'personality') must come before we can theorise different types of personality ('conformist', 'type A' or whatever).

Each level invites us to invent theories of how it operates. So, for example, the general theory of social structure supports theories of how class structures, in particular, are formed, develop and change. Such subsidiary theories (and their associated concepts) sometimes acquire their own momentum and autonomy. For example, Runciman (1966) (following Merton's theory of reference groups (1957)) developed the theory of relative deprivation to explain the willingness of some of the disadvantaged to accept their lot rather than struggle to change the class system. The theory suggested that people only object to the inequalities they actually perceive. This helps to explain Runciman's particular concern – which was why some working-class people can be easily mobilised against the system and others not. But the theory of relative deprivation can equally illuminate other problems such as the role of access to Western media in changing the aspirations of third-world populations and destabilising their societies.

Similarly, there are theories of specific historical phenomena which have wide application. A famous example is Weber's (1930) analysis of the consequences of the rise of Protestantism in the West. He developed this to account for the dominance of capitalism in Western societies but it has also been used to begin explaining the rise of science (Merton, 1957), the character of American urban development (Sennett, 1990), and Swedish environmentalism (Stanworth, n. d.). There are theories of slavery in general, and of the particular varieties found in ancient Greece and Rome, in Asia, Africa, the Middle East and America (Westermann, 1955; Davis, 1966; Watson, 1980; Pipes, 1981; Patterson, 1982; Lewis, 1990; UN, 1991). Similarly there are theories of revolution in general, and of its historical varieties, English, American, Russian, Chinese and so on (Moore, 1967; Skocpol, 1979). Such special theories vary in their abstractness, generality and empirical scope. So it is in the sense of providing the conceptual umbrella under which the multitude of social theoretical concepts cluster that we suggest our concepts are primary for social explanation.

In the following chapters, we shall inevitably be considering these less basic, but equally necessary, levels of theorising to show how they depend on the basic concepts, but also to suggest that the social sciences are a huge resource of imaginative ideas and examples of effective explanation for us to follow. However, we can only provide you with a taste of what is available. Similarly, we do not address what is often referred to by the term 'social theory', namely a whole range of general interpretations of the meaning of contemporary social changes and speculations about possible futures. Social theory, in this sense, includes the macroscopic theories about different types of society and their historical development of Marx, Weber, Durkheim, Habermas, Giddens and Foucault (to name some of the most prominent). Their ideas are discussed repeatedly in the textbook literature about theories and theorists. We are using the phrase in a more limited (and precise) way to refer to the basic concepts required to conceptualise social reality for purposes of social explanation. The various 'grand' theories just referred to all use these more basic social theoretical concepts. The position of this book is that social theory at this basic level is important because explanation is important, and because it provides the wherewithal for constructing the various theories of particular social phenomena.

One of the reasons for the enduring significance of the classical social theorists – Marx, Weber and Durkheim – is that they all recognised these concepts as being fundamental, and made them the basis for the creative elaboration of extremely valuable theory at less general levels. We have already suggested that, as we proceed, we will inevitably be introducing a large number of important concepts for social analysis and explanation, but they will be secondary to the most fundamental ones used to organise the book. So this is not a work about theories and theorists, but about basic concepts for thinking about why social phenomena are the way they are.

How the book is organised

As we have said, these are the basic concepts: *individuals*, *nature*, *culture*, *action* and *social structure*. Each denotes a kind of causation which is relevant for social explanation. We will look at each in turn via five pairs of chapters. The first chapter of each pair will look at the general properties of the concept in question, beginning to show its usefulness with reference to short examples. The second chapter of each pair uses fewer, more detailed, examples to further reveal the explanatory strength of the concept under consideration, but also to show its limits and that it must be supplemented by the other concepts. This mode of presentation derives from our belief that *all* the concepts are necessary for social explanation and that each has its strengths but also its limits. As realists, we must resist theories which hold that any particular one or other of these concepts is more important than the others in all circumstances, or is capable of forming the basis of all social explanation. These positions, which we refer to as 'individual*ism*', 'natural*ism*', 'cultural*ism*', 'action*ism*', and 'structural-*ism*' (and their varieties, such as functionalism, a type of structural-ism, or ethnomethodology, a type of actionism), are or have been very influential in social theory. On the other hand, our realist position, is pluralist in the sense that, in contrast to, for example, individualism or structuralism (which claim that all social phenomena can be explained by reference to (respectively) individuals or social structures alone), we hold that all five concepts are necessary for social explana-tion but that none alone is sufficient (Table 0.1).

The distinction between what is necessary and what is sufficient for explanation is of fundamental importance. Which range of concepts is needed for any given explanation and which concept(s) have most strength will vary between cases. Being technical again, each concept has relative autonomy. It has 'autonomy' because it has its own irre-ducible, distinct capacity to exert a causal force. But it is a 'relative' autonomy because it always operates 'relative to', that is, in combina-tion with the other kinds of causal forces. Explanations achieve suffic-iency only when they specify the interaction among all the necessary causal mechanisms responsible for the phenomena being explained.

In Chapter 11, we extend the discussion and defence of the funda-mental theory of social reality underlying our approach to social explanation. It says why we think such explanation is scientific and compares our approach with others. Finally, in Chapter 12, we under-line how using the tool kit can help us understand our own and others' predicaments, as well as be more technically and politically effective when we try to change things.

Table 0.1 Realist and non-realist requirements for social explanation

Realism	Five basic concepts	Non-realisms	
All five concepts are necessary	**Individuals**	One concept alone has causal primacy and is necessary and sufficient	Individual*ism*
Each has relative causal autonomy	**Nature**		Natural*ism*
None alone is sufficient	**Action**		Action*ism*
	Culture		Cultural*ism*
	Social structure		Structural*ism*

Part I

The Concept of the Individual

CHAPTER 1

What Do Individuals Explain?

When people in their everyday lives try to explain social phenomena, social events and patterns, they often think whether the phenomena can be plausibly accounted for by the characteristics of the *individuals* involved in them. This is a reasonable first move, given that there are no social phenomena without the individuals who participate in them. All social collectivities such as classes, families, teams, groups, tribes, clubs, nations, queues are composed of individuals. Classes, families and so on, but also ranks, roles and statuses, relate to ways in which individuals can share characteristics and thus be described as being the same as one another. These concepts refer to an ordering of existence that overarches individuals. But there could be no ranks, roles, tribes or clubs without people to fill or join them. There could be no queue without all the individuals in line who make it up.

But can we explain everything in society simply in terms of the individuals who belong to it? Some people, often called methodological individualists, who believe in methodological individualism (MI), say that individuals are the only kind of reality with the necessary and sufficient causal powers capable of generating social phenomena. So, in this chapter, we will start by looking at some of the ways in which the attributes of individuals undoubtedly do have explanatory potential and are therefore necessary for explanation. But we will also begin to consider whether they really provide us with all that we need, that is, whether they are sufficient for social explanation, as the methodological individualists claim.

Before we get going, it will help to point out, firstly, that if we are to agree with MI, we will have to be convinced that the causally effective attributes of individuals are not themselves produced by social factors. These attributes must be innate, not socially derived, since MI demands that the social is derived from them. Secondly, if the pre-social and causally important attributes of individuals alone are to explain different patternings of phenomena, we will have to agree that individuals are differently endowed with these attributes in the first place. For, if individuals alone produce outcomes, how could people who were quite the same generate a variety of effects? Ultimately, if we support methodological individualism, we must believe that families, tribes, classes, clubs, queues, even societies are ultimately nothing more than, are reducible without remainder to, the sum of the physical individuals who belong to them.

Individuals as embodied objects

Bearing all this in mind, we can now begin to think about what kinds of attributes of individuals might be considered sufficiently important for explaining social phenomena, such as the course of events and patterned regularities. One obvious possibility is to consider the individual as a sort of physical, biological object, a body. Are any of the bodily properties of human individuals socially relevant? We can begin to answer this question by thinking about whether the course of history and the shape of the social world be the same if, for example, women were very much bigger and stronger than men, both sexes could get pregnant, babies were born able to walk and feed themselves, humans lacked tongues and the ability to speak and had dog-like paws instead of hands. The social arrangements we have, for example, for bearing and bringing up children, the shape and scale of social products, such as tools and the houses, furniture, clothes we make with them, are all the way they are, in part because individuals, as members of the human species, have the biological form they do.

Our bodies set all sorts of problems for human societies to deal with and set limits to how they can be solved. So, for example, given the facts of sexual reproduction and the lengthy dependency of children, there will always have to be institutions and roles to organise sexual relations and care for and rear the young in every society. The fact that we always find such institutions and roles can be explained with reference to the character of human bodies. But given these characteristics are universal, they cannot account for differences in child-rearing practices or ways of organising sexuality. The actual content of the varying traditions and institutions which interpret the universal biological imperatives, and devise practical methods of responding to them, cannot be entirely biologically determined.

But what of cases where such bodily attributes are distributed differently between individuals? Could these help us to explain different social outcomes? They might be part of the explanation of, let us say, one person and not another taking up a career as a Tour de France cyclist (racing cyclists tend to have exceptionally large hearts). Or think of the disadvantages and discrimination that may be inflicted on the disabled and the physically exceptional (very small, very large, with a different skin colour from the majority). All societies require individuals to possess a sufficient minimum of the culturally approved human characteristics, if they are to secure their moral status as worthy of respect. Bodily differences between individuals here contribute to understanding why this person is socially accepted and that one not. But again they cannot supply the full explanation, for cultures vary in where they draw the boundaries around the biological characteristics one must have to count as a proper human being. A physical feature which makes you an outcast in one society might be considered quite unimportant in another.

Thus reference to bodily differences in social explanation is useful, but is not sufficient. As with biological explanations in general, it also needs to be treated with care. This is because overextending their applicability can generate politically and morally vicious forms of thought, such as racism and sexism. These mistakenly account for what are in fact socially generated attributes of categories (men, women, 'blacks', 'whites') as if they were caused by innate, biologically given characteristics of category members. This is particularly pernicious since it implies, for example, that inter-category differences in educational or occupational success, or differences in cultural forms, cannot be altered without contravening the laws of nature. The result is hostility to egalitarian proposals and the recommendation to the disadvantaged that they accept their fate.

Individuals as (non-rational and rational) subjects

Are there other attributes of individuals, besides their physical embodiment, that we might think were relevant for social explanation? People are more than just bodies. They are also beings with minds and emotions, who think, feel and are capable of action. People are subjects, and not just objects trapped in a physical form. One common-sense way of looking at history, as a series of events caused principally by the crucially influential actions of exceptional men (and sometimes women), sees people in just this way. It suggests that the unique 'power of mind', 'clarity of vision', 'genius' 'determin-ation', 'strength of feeling' of key political, economic, religious and cultural figures (Hitler, Henry Ford, Gandhi, even Elvis Presley perhaps) lead them to make decisions and act in ways which are historically highly influential. And certainly we can agree that, in some contexts at least, the actions of exceptional individuals in the right (or wrong) place at the right (or wrong) time have been crucial for events turning out the actual way they did. When we are trying to explain what happened, it will always be worth considering whether outcomes were influenced by the decisions and actions of some key responsible individuals.

But can we ultimately explain all social phenomena only in terms of an understanding of individuals as thinking or feeling beings, and, moreover, as methodological individualism requires, as individuals whose capacities for and modes of thought or emotion are innate, that is, only cause social phenomena and are not originally generated by them? Some theorists think we can. They have tended to focus on models of the individual as either innately rational, or as the oppo-site, that is, as a non-rational creature fuelled by biologically given drives for sexual gratification, or power and the domination of others. Thus, for example, in the non-rational camp, Freud's famous psychoanalytic theory explains the action of individuals by reference to a universal process of personality formation in which biological instincts for sexual gratification motivate behaviour. Desire is held to be so strong that its self-destructive implications must be disciplined by mechanisms of repression and civilisation. Social orders are thus 'explained' as emerging to fulfil the function of organising and chan-nelling sexually motivated behaviour into productive rather than destructive activities.

There are interesting insights here. We might, for example, usefully consider various arts, drama, sports, popular entertainment, elements of religious practice, rites of passage and so on as means of providing psychological gratification in controlled forms. But there are overall problems with this kind of perspective; not least in resolving how there is such variation in forms of social life if they are all motivated originally by desires for sex (or power). Individual variations in the extent to which people manifest universal drives might help us to understand some differences in behaviour between members of the same society. But such individual variety does not easily account for differences in social institutions and practices between whole soci-eties, even if we believe that all these institutions and practices are ultimately linked to the need to control potentially destructive universal desires and dispositions. Even if we could show that the members of some societies were more strongly endowed with the drive for sex or power than those of some others, this could scarcely account for all the inter-societal variations of social institutions and culture that we find. Moreover, we would have to be careful to establish that the strength of drives was in fact differentially distributed, independently of the institutional and cultural phenomena which we are trying to explain by reference to such drives.

Rational choice theory

How do theorists who conceptualise the individual as essentially rational proceed, and do they fall into the same kinds of difficulties? Rational choice theory (RCT) provides us with a recent and popular version of this line of attack, sufficiently interesting to look at in some detail. It is a sophisticated updating of a longstanding theory which has tried to derive moral rules for action from knowledge about what makes people happy. This theory (called 'utilitarianism' and most famously represented by the British philosopher J.S. Mill) thought of individuals as all motivated to want the same thing, happiness, and that good actions and sound social institutions are those which give the greatest happiness to the greatest number. Individuals are essentially the same, rationally seeking their own interests, as they typically do in economic markets. Social phenomena are seen as the product of individuals trying to achieve their own happiness.

Rational choice theorists, with utilitarians, hold that interests (ends, goals, desires, purposes, call them what you will) can be shared, but are more usually selfish. Individuals seek to satisfy their interests through strategic action, that is, action designed to get what is wanted by manipulating the circumstances and controlling the means to achieve the desired result. This is where rationality comes into play. Decisions about what means to use to get what is wanted are rational to the extent that they involve objective evaluation of the different costs of alternative methods. From this perspective, for example, money can be thought of as a tool for rationalising economic exchange by making it possible to price everything. It is functional for the sort of rationality required to find the cheapest way to solve problems. RCT refers to 'instrumental', 'technical' or 'calculative' rationality. The crucial resources to calculate rationally the best available means are *logic* (for conceptual consistency), *measurement* (for descriptive precision), *technical knowledge* (for understanding how things work) and *information* (about the specific circumstances of the problem being dealt with). In sum, RCT sees individuals as disposed to seek their self-interests and as using their innate capacity for rationality to decide how to get what they want. Rational individuals acquire the relevant information and know what to do with it to construct their strategies to achieve their goals.

Differences between individuals: personalities and skill in settling a land dispute

So, under what conditions might this approach to social explanation be useful? What kind of phenomena might it explain? It might be helpful for understanding the differences in the success with which given individuals pursue their interests. Variations in individuals' logicality, knowledge, skill, imagination, practical experience and so on are all potentially relevant to whether or not they achieve their ends. Barth's classic study of *Political Leadership among Swat Pathans* (1959) perhaps provides us with an example.

These Pathans, although Muslims, are divided into castes, and live in the Swat valley in Pakistan. Barth describes one of their village assemblies, which met to decide a land dispute between two leading members of the Pakhtoun, land-owning caste, Rashid Khan and Abdul Khan. From time to time, each rival would disappear behind a haystack and have secret conversations with one or other of the assembly members to try and ensure they did not ally with their opponent. However, at one point in the general meeting, a minor supporter of Rashid began to speak and Abdul interrupted him, telling him to be quiet and not to contradict his betters. This violated the Pakhtoun ethic that all men are equal and have a right to speak and the meeting broke up in uproar, with Rashid's party eventually bringing a case against Abdul for contempt of the assembly.

Barth claims Abdul knew this would happen and strategically sabotaged the meeting, having calculated that the price of doing so was worth the gain of ending the assembly, which his secret conversations suggested was not going his way. In the end, his dependants continued to use the land and he retained his position as an effective political operator and patron. We could say Abdul won because he was more skilled than Rashid in sizing up the situation and quicker off the mark to implement the best means in the circumstances to achieve the outcome he wanted. Had Rashid been smart enough he might have been able to insist that the land issue was resolved before moving on to the case for contempt.

Pointing to the skill in strategic action and the calculative rationality of individuals like Abdul and Rashid can help to explain events, outcomes and patterns in contexts where the ends being sought, and the 'games' being played to get them, are given and can be taken for granted. The focus is on the calculating and not on the creation of the situation in which it is being done. *Given* a chess game, we can analyse how well or badly it is played and explain who won in terms of the different skills, or the degree of concentration of the players. RCT is a promising approach when the problem to be explained is differential outcomes for individuals participating in the limited interaction of end-seeking 'games'. These could range from winning at chess or maintaining one's position in a queue, to securing continuity of land tenure in the Swat village. These are all situations where the ends are pretty clear, what counts as success is relatively easy to determine and the relevant variables which actors need information about can be defined. Each is a setting in which the self-interest of, and knowledge available to, the individual can be identified in theory, and possibly in fact, if you can ask them.

For bounded situations such as games, markets, courts or ghettos, where a special sphere of conflict has been separated out and relatively insulated from external influence, one can attempt to create abstract models of possible lines of strategic action open to individuals. One can define the logic of the actor's situation, that is, the possible strategic alternatives open to them under the specific conditions, with given ends and access to certain information and resources. When one has asked oneself 'What else could Abdul have done to get what he wanted in the circumstances, assuming he was not misinformed about the level of support for his case and about the rules governing the conduct of assemblies?', then one may feel that one has a reasonable basis for retrospectively accounting for why he acted as he did.

Differences between collectivities, and the social patterning of action

Conceptualising individuals as (more or less) rational and knowledgeable decision-makers may help us to grasp, in particular situations, why this or that person acted as they did and why they succeeded or failed in getting what they wanted. But can we explain broader patterns and similarities and differences between collectivities in this way? There are three main possibilities.

Firstly, just as we might explain why one individual does better than another by revealing how they more rationally pursued their goal, so, in principle, we might be able to account for the success and failure of whole categories of individuals, in terms of all the members of one group having a greater capacity for rational action than all the members of another. But, just as we warned earlier, when looking at the possibilities of explaining societal differences in terms of varia-tions in the strength of their members' non-rational drives, so in this case we must not deduce differential degrees of rationality on the basis of a differential outcome, which might actually be due to quite different factors. As the next chapter will show in more detail, it is unwise, for example, to assume that the lack of economic success of the poor means that every poor person is insufficiently rational.

Secondly, without having to presume any differential distribution of rationality, we might be able to explain some recurring patterns as common solutions to common problems. Thus, if we all have an interest in solving technical problems using rational techniques, patterning may sometimes be the result of a convergence on the relat-ively few effective solutions to any given problem by many different individuals and cultures throughout history. Why do so many soci-eties develop or use written languages, bureaucracies, scientific medi-cine, for example? Isn't this because these are all extremely powerful technical or organisational solutions? People will keep on using or reinventing the wheel if it really is the most technically rational way of moving heavy objects along the ground!

Thirdly, 'game theory', a development of RCT, offers a possibility. Rather than suggesting that patterns are the outcome of different people arriving at the same solution in isolation, it tries to show how new collective patterns, including patterns of cooperation, emerge as often unintended consequences of interaction between self-seeking rational individuals. Here 'game' is, as in 'game plan', the strategy that individuals devise to achieve their goal. Students of markets, political selection processes like voting and the global balance of military power have all embraced game theory, but we will start with a very simple example taken from Baert (1998: 161–2). He gets us to think about what happens when two people simultaneously want to get into a lift, the door of which is only wide enough for one. If they both step forward together, blocking the door, or if they both stand back, neither gets what they want. We know the kind of thing that often happens. Each senses the problem, suggests 'You go', 'No, after you', until someone feels that enough has been done to allow them to enter first. The other quickly follows and the lift gets under way. A measure of cooperation has been achieved which benefits both self-interested individuals. Subsequently the problem might be solved for the same individuals by taking turns and acquires a high level of predictability – and there is our social regularity.

In seeking to identify the potential for continuous, more or less orderly interaction in a social world held to be populated by self-seeking, rational individualists, rational choice/game theory typically analyses hypothetical situations and works out how individuals devoted to their own best interests, and calculating what they should do on the basis of available information, could choose to coordinate and cooperate. Where, as in the lift example, everyone can get what they want by cooperating (there need be no losers), and the individuals involved are few, it is relatively easy to understand how actions can be coordinated. Relevant information can easily be shared, every one increases their capacity to get what they want and nobody has to sacrifice anything.

Explaining cooperation between many individuals with mutually conflicting interests is more problematic. To reach their goals, each rational individual must act against the interests of others, since there must be some losers. What then stops people relentlessly, rationally, trying any tactic to optimise their self-interest at others' expense? If most people in fact set limits to their 'nastiness', can rational choice game theorists explain why this is so? Their answer is that 'going it alone' is a high-risk strategy, especially where, because of the numbers involved, information about others' actions is imperfect. Thus most of us eventually learn that nastiness is a luxury available only to those who can rely on the future cooperation of others (by making them dependent, threatening them and so on) or who are able and willing to forgo it. For most of us selfishness is modified by dependence on others and the desire to be successful in the future. Rational Choice analysis shows that in the long run it is more productive to be 'nice', cooperate, compromise and accept less than optimum outcomes. Being altruistic is in fact self-interested. Being nice and cultivating trustworthiness lowers risk and increases certainty about the future. Rational self-seeking involves pursuing one's interests partly by investing in the willingness of others to cooperate in the future. That means that each has an interest in making sure that their potential partners in future action are sufficiently rewarded for their cooperation. The upshot is that we all have an interest in investing in the formation and maintenance of collectivities such as partnerships, teams, networks, unions, families, organisations and so on.

Despite its artificiality, RCT's explorations of the social consequences of rational self-interest have resulted in an intuitively plausible account of why and how rational self-seekers achieve long term cooperation. Most people, most of the time, need to enter alliances to secure the power to be gained through cooperation. But some people, sometimes, see opportunities to go it alone and maximise gains just for themselves and are tempted to defect from alliances. Stories about members of lottery syndicates decamping with the winnings come to mind! So the problem we all have is to stop our partners defecting when they are tempted and keeping the costs of our own contribution to alliances as low as we can get away with. We must look after our own interest but not so enthusiastically (by defecting) that our partners punish us. Usually the advantages we seek by being selfish are not so great as to allow us to make a clean break from being dependent on those we betray. Similarly, defectors are usually still valuable as future partners. So the RCT formula for social life is as follows:

1. cooperation is the original condition

2. defection is punished by refusing to continue cooperation

3. the first offer of cooperation from the defector is accepted and cooperation resumes.

The basic rule is 'respond to nice action with nice action and nasty action with nasty action.' This is called 'tit for tat' reciprocity. It shows that it is rational for individuals to cooperate, be intolerant of defection, but to forgive it.

Conclusion

This chapter has provided various examples of the ways we might gain from considering the attributes of individuals, when seeking to account for social events and regularities. But we have already begun to point to difficulties with the methodological individualists' claim that looking at individuals alone offers sufficient explanatory power.

Now we can add that there is a yet more fundamental issue, which the validity of their claim that individuals' powers of action rest on pre-social, innate characteristics. Even the most sophisticated forms of MI assume that these powers are given. There is no interest in wondering whether these powers are socially formed and might vary, not by individuals but by collectivities – as the later chapters on culture and social structure will suggest.

Moreover, there are further problems. Any methodological individualist reduction of the individual to one key kind of attribute loses sight of the explanatory role that other aspects of individuals might play. We have spent most time looking at RCT, which abstracts the contribution of rationality to individuals' action, ignoring other factors. This is certainly tempting, since situations of rational problem-solving are ones where the analyst can easily suggest what the actor is thinking and understand their reasons for acting. However, not all action which can be analysed as the conduct of rational, self-seeking individuals is necessarily action of this sort. We previously presented Abdul's disruption of the village assembly as a rational move following his careful calculation of various possibilities on the basis of available information. This seems plausible. But couldn't one equally interpret the break-up of the meeting as an unintended consequence of the insult to Rashid's supporter, occasioned by Abdul's emotionally motivated, unpremeditated anger and frustration mounting as he lost support? The whole episode can be modelled as rational, but perhaps it was not. In fact, what Barth tells us about Swat Pathan society suggests that the emotionally charged issue of personal honour was probably important, thereby also reminding us that, although it is individuals who experience emotion, what feelings they have and how they express them are culturally patterned and not just innate.

Rational choice theorists sometimes suggest we consider any action which achieves a desired end as 'rational', and retrospectively analyse it as though everything which led to that outcome was rationally chosen. Thus they would deem Abdul's actions rational simply because they produced the end he wanted. But this kind of move is hardly satisfactory. It illegitimately protects RCT from refutation, whilst simultaneously avoiding the necessary but difficult task of trying to understand the spontaneous, habitual or emotionally fuelled reasons that may be contributing to how people act. Conversely, of course, abstracting and focusing only on the non-rational elements of the individual is similarly restrictive, if we agree that individuals are, at least in part, rational actors.

We could say that the above difficulties for RCT connect to the fundamental problem of what rationality is. RCT requires rationality to be a universal capacity of individuals, sufficient to enable them to act. As a property originating in individuals, it cannot be socially, culturally or historically relative. Basically, this amounts to saying that, short of ignorance and lack of skill, everyone interprets the world in the same way. We might be willing to accept that the tools of rational thought, such as logic and measurement, are universal. But rationality implies more than these. It involves using ideas about what is in the world and how it hangs together. Not only does rationality operate on fields of conflicting and incomplete theories; it is profoundly dependent on actors making judgements about what is to count as 'sufficient evidence', relevance and consistency. And these judgements are fuelled by emotions and cultural commitments. The formal tools of rational calculation have to be supplemented by judgements about their applicability and what their results signify. For example, how do you choose between two equally technically feasible and cheap ways of getting what you want? Do you use non-rational methods for deciding? How rational is it to choose a bicycle because of its colour? In other words, rationality itself is not entirely clear-cut and is only part of what is involved in making up our minds and choosing. Rationality is a powerful capacity of humans, but it cannot be used without something else to fill the judgemental gaps. The question for rational choice theorists is 'how do individuals fill the gaps without recourse to non-rational elements of individuals, or existing collectivities?' We explore these themes further, especially in Chapters 7 and 8.

This also relates to another important problem hinted at earlier, when we suggested that RCT was well suited to situations (the chess game and the land dispute, for example) where the external parameters were already clearly set. It is suited because RCT simply assumes that individuals have interests and takes the ends they seek for granted. Once ends are given, it looks at the outcomes of individuals' rational attempts to reach them. But it does not offer a rational explanation for the choice of ultimate ends themselves, which therefore remain mysterious. Those who see the individual as fundamentally motivated by non-rational drives offer one possible way out of this dilemma, since the goal of satisfying the drives is seen as built into people. The other possibility again is to look at the role played by existing collectivities. Subsequent chapters suggest plausible, alternative non-individualist solutions to the problem of where goals and interests come from.

Thus we can see that confining social explanation to the effects produced by the innate social properties of individuals soon runs into a range of difficulties. It also closes off a range of useful possibilities. Methodological individualism claims that there are no non-individual forces or processes which contribute to the determination of social reality and could feature in our explanations. This amounts to denying that what individual actors produce, intentionally or unintentionally, becomes autonomous and has some causal force in its own right, conditioning the future action of individuals. It is these products of action which are referred to as 'culture' and 'social structure'. MI sees actors as constrained only by their innate dispositions in the present, by their 'human nature', however that is conceived. But is this true? Are there other forms of constraint? Do the consequences of action *now* acquire constraining power in the *future* independently of the individuals and their activity, which generated these consequences? Later chapters will begin answering these questions by considering the range of 'non-individual' forces constraining the actions of individuals, which, we argue, must play some role in social explanation. Before we do this, however, we will use the next chapter to further elaborate on the strengths and weaknesses of RCT by applying it in more detail to a particular puzzling situation. This will reinforce this chapter's claim that individuals are an important element in social explanation but they are not sufficient and must be supplemented by other, non-individual concepts.

CHAPTER 2

Testing the Explanatory Value of Individuals

The last chapter ended by outlining some of the generic difficulties of trying to explain social phenomena entirely as the outcome of the properties and actions of individuals. However, this book claims that while none of the key concepts examined are sufficient to explain social phenomena, all are necessary. This chapter further explores how far we can explain social phenomena by the properties of the individuals who participate in them.

To simplify the argument, we will confine ourselves to the utilitarian/rational choice account of the socially productive capacity of individuals. We have just seen that this pictures individuals as pursuing their interests by rationally choosing means. It is an approach which takes its inspiration from the behaviour of participants in markets, trying to make a profit through economic exchange. High (and possibly continuous) profits are regarded as the desired reward for being as rational as possible about one's choice of means – the deals one agrees to, the investments one makes, the decisions to cut one's losses and so on. Strategic action, driven by rational principles, seeks the best information and makes the most precise calculations. It also invests in the future, maintaining its potential for cooperation. It accepts there may be short-term losses. That is the method leading to long-term success. The implication is that the successful are experts at rational choice, the unsuccessful rationally incompetent.

Testing for the 'sufficiency' of the individual: making ends meet in the ghetto

One approach to testing the strengths of a theory and method of explanation is to examine it on ground of its own choosing where its relevance and necessity is unlikely to be questioned. But the issue here becomes one of its sufficiency. If it is shown to be insufficient to provide a complete explanation, even for phenomena to which it is best suited, we can be fairly confident that it will be insufficient elsewhere. We might call this a 'sufficiency' test. Since RCT is based in economic action, it should feel most comfortable explaining social phenomena with an economic character. Such a case is the existence, in capitalist societies, of large numbers of individuals in long-term poverty, a condition which is reproduced in families across several generations. People are born into poverty, rear children in poverty and die in poverty.

How might rational choice theorists explain this macroscopic fact? Surely it is one they ought to relish. Here we have a case of manifest lack of success in the economic market. The poor do seem unable to lift themselves out of poverty with the resources available to them. They are the 'losers' in the capitalist game. Surely here, if anywhere, we will find the failures of rationality which the theory predicts lead to economic failure? At this point, we can sense the theory facing a slightly paradoxical test. If the poor can be shown to be irrational, in ways which make them fail economically, all well and good. The theory is confirmed, or at least not refuted. But if the poor are shown actually to be rational, although this is uncomfortable for the theory's explanation of poverty, all is not lost because the method of analysis is still shown to be relevant, that is, although it is insufficient it is still necessary. RCT might at least offer the tools to help us to recognise the rationality of the poor, even though by doing so it undermines its own explanation of poverty. In this case, what would happen is that explaining poverty would be shown to need concepts and theories about socially productive mechanisms, *in addition to* the capacity for rational self-interest of poor individuals. We might also learn more about what the analysis of being rational involves.

What we need in order to decide if the poor are rational or not (as a precondition to considering if this explains their poverty), is a description of how they really think and behave. A frustrating aspect of rational choice theorists' actual theorising is its remoteness from real flesh and blood people in real circumstances. We need concrete evidence to test the predictions based on abstract theorising and that requires detailed ethnographic observation. Such research into ways of life offers invaluable opportunities to follow actors through the whole process of making choices. It makes it possible to identify meanings, reasoning, symbolisation, patterns, repetitions and socially reproductive effects. It provides the descriptive richness that forces the development of more sophisticated explanations and more careful generalisations. Detailed ethnographic studies take a long time to produce and are relatively rare. They tend to undermine facile generalisations, making it impossible to say what all the poor do. But, for our purposes, since it claims universal applicability, rational choice theory needs only to be shown to be insufficient, when tested against one reliable ethnographic description of those suffering long-term economic failure, to be rejected as a general basis for explaining phenomena such as poverty.

Fortunately, Carol Stack's *All Our Kin* (1997) a study of the poor in 'The Flats', a black ghetto in a small, affluent mid-west US city, is a gift to anybody testing the RCT of poverty. It is the kind of clearly expressed, politically engaged, influential analysis which our approach to practical social theorising intends to encourage. Read it to learn what constitutes good social research, theorising and writing.

Stack began her fieldwork in the 1960s as a single, expectant mother and it continued during her son's early years. This is unusual, but was crucial in securing acceptance as an educated white woman into the domestic world of poor blacks, particularly poor black women struggling to raise their children. She was in the same predicament, potentially dependent, needing help to make it with her child on her own (Stack, 1997: 14). She was well placed to discover the 'rules of routine behaviour' which individuals followed to cope with poverty. Because the ghetto-dwellers were descendants of black migrants from the rural south, their parents and grandparents had also been poor. This meant that little of economic value was transmitted from the past. Nobody inherited significant material resources. Everyone was dependent on what they could get in the immediate present. Although the American economy was generally buoyant in the 1960s, the black ghetto's unemployment rate was over 20 per cent for a variety of reasons, which included racist restrictions by the city's biggest employer (the hospital) and certain labour unions. What work was available to them was poorly paid and insecure. Social welfare (in the form of Aid to Families with Dependent Children – AFDC) was ungenerous and only available to women without a cohabiting male partner. This meant that it was impossible to accumulate surpluses of money and material goods to tide people over crises. Stack's respondents were 'forced to use most of their resources for major monthly bills, rent, utilities and food. After a family pays its bills they are penniless' (Stack, 1997: 29). In short, saving was not an option.

Poverty was 'perpetual' (Stack, 1997: 22). Everyday life was lived on the edge of sustainability. Racial segregation in access to jobs, housing and services was the external condition setting up the economic game of survival unfavourably for blacks. Thus poor blacks, unlike better-off whites, could not use the resources distributed through a relatively impersonal market and accumulate personal private property to gain their economic ends. They had to play the game by different rules.

Stack, with expectations conditioned by mainstream white society, first realised that there were rules to be discovered when she observed ghetto-dwellers making what seemed absurdly generous gifts and loans to others. It appeared irrational that people who had so little should give it away so enthusiastically. Prized furniture, new clothes, food, ornaments, tools, cars and so on were not defended with the sort of possessiveness typical in her own background. The poor were doing the opposite of what most better-off people would think sensible. They were not maintaining the exclusive access to their possessions, and on the few occasions when they had some surplus, they were not saving this for their own predicted future expenditure – Christmas, possible ill health, children's school requirements. Instead they typically gave it away to others who were facing an immediate crisis. Long-term individual economic prudence seems alien to these poor blacks. But is this evidence of their patho-logical economic irrationality? Are they responsible for perpetuating their own economic failure?

The way to think about the situational logic involved is to ask what you, as a rational individual seeking the survival of yourself and those you care about, would do in similar circumstances. What would you do in a situation where you required money to get what you need but don't have it, because the only income comes from AFDC welfare cheques or wages from the low-paid, seasonal and temporary jobs left open to you by economic racism?

There are several options. You can 'cut your coat according to your cloth' and reduce your costs of living. Right-wing politicians suggest this. But costs of living have already been pared to the bone. Stack describes certain modest expenditures, such as routine use of a laundry, which could be economised on perhaps, although maybe they are practically required by, for example, lack of heating and drying space. Also, whilst Stack does not discuss this, resistance to menial tasks like hand washing clothes might be a reaction against the symbolic degradation inflicted by slavery, or motivated by a desire to ensure that, although poor, one can at least keep up appearances.

However sympathetic we may be, costs of defending status and dignity could, in principle, be saved, and not to do so may seem economically irrational. Such tactics would make little difference though, because the ghetto-dwellers' only major variable cost (besides feeding, clothing and housing themselves) is rearing their children. Short of ceasing to reproduce themselves, the best they could do is to have fewer children. But although costs might be reduced by this, the problem remains, because their poverty is so great that even a single child per adult is not easily supported. Moreover, AFDC payments were a major source of income for the ghetto community, reducing the incentive to limit births. Even the most frugal, disciplined individual, without dependants, will fail to support themselves unaided.

Thus the second major option is to get help from inside the ghetto. What individuals cannot manage independently might be achieved through cooperation by making informal, dyadic contracts. This can potentially be done in a hierarchical or egalitarian way (Stack, 1997: 156). If there are a few well-off individuals with surpluses, they may be willing to act as patrons to the very poor, doing them economic and political favours in return for services, deference, gratitude and moral indebtedness. So one possibility is to subordinate oneself to a patron. White immigrants to the US often did this through local political 'machines' run by city politicians and union elites, an opportunity barred to blacks and anyway largely removed by the 1960s, through reforming legislation. Unfortunately, even the most ambitious ghetto-dwellers find it difficult to accumulate legitimately sufficient surpluses to offer patronage to inferiors. Thus, where this sort of relationship does develop, it typically involves organised criminality. Here the surpluses needed to break out of poverty are only accumulated at very high risk – as shown, for example, in Bourgois' (1995) devastating study of the mid-1980s crack trade in East Harlem.

So without decent incomes from legitimate earning opportunities, without much scope to reduce costs of everyday living and child rearing, without local patrons or low-risk, legal opportunities to accumulate surpluses, strategic options are reduced. If we discount gambling and petty crime, tactics which, however popular, are extremely unreliable for securing long-term advantages, two main life strategies remain. Egalitarian cooperation and individual escape (Stack's 'social mobility'). These are tactics which, unlike cost-cutting, seeking the best paid employment, trying to save, gambling, crime and engaging in patron–client relations, are in contradictory tension with each other. This is exactly what rational choice theory suggests;

long-run egalitarian cooperation depends on punishing defectors, which is what those who attempt to escape poverty by achieving upward social mobility are.

Stack's work shows that ghetto-dwellers prefer egalitarian coopera-tion and that this is a valid, rational choice. Everyone recognises that they need help and that the pressure is most intense when they acquire dependent children. 'You have to have help from everybody and anybody' is the common wisdom. You cannot be too proud or fussy. Since women are the primary child carers, they have the strongest interest in building a network of helpers and becoming experts in keeping these networks going. That means they tend to discipline participants, recruit new members, testing their reliability, and punishing deviants and would-be defectors. Through dyadic network-building, each woman assembles a 'multi-household kin network', sometimes more than a hundred strong (Stack, 1997: 24). Biological relatives and friends are potential members, but their rights to participate have to be proved by deeds, not mere theoretical or legal claims. The idiom of kinship is used to identify individuals who actually deliver, especially fathers (Stack, 1997: 50–3). They must be self-sacrificing when necessary, giving or loaning their goods on demand, and show their commitment to caring for one another and especially for each other's children.

Stack's ethnography illustrates an intensity of domestic life in response to frequent crises, as individuals and households resort to the resources which, at any given moment, may be located in other households containing network members. Households themselves are fluid, with people (especially men and children) moving between them, as personal relationships falter and economic circumstances change. What is largely stable is the functioning 'alliances of individ-uals trading and exchanging goods, resources and the care of child-ren' from which the constantly reconfiguring households are constructed. (Stack, 1997: 28) It is the 'informal circulation of child-ren' between households, which facilitates the distribution and exchange of limited resources.

People with immediately pressing needs follow the resources as they flow intermittently through the households of the ghetto. Network dependence means participants have a strong interest in gathering information about who has what, through visiting and gossip. They must also maintain their good standing, which is contin-ually tested by requests for the giving or loaning of non-essentials, such as clothes. They typically say; 'The poorer you are the more likely you are to pay back' (Stack, 1997: 28). Ensuring one's reliability, as not being a free rider, is paramount. The most honoured service was 'child-keeping', temporary fostering of other's children. The most trusted were those with whom you could safely leave your children. As Stack says, 'Temporary child-keeping is a symbol of mutual trust ... People began to accept my trust and respect for them when I trusted my son with them' (Stack, 1997: 28–9). The closest personal relationships were between women who reciprocated 'child-keeping'. This was the powerful charge that flowed through the strongest dyadic relationships between friends and which made possible Stack's own friendship with her black contemporary, Ruby Banks (Stack, 1997: 11–21).

The final option is individual escape, or defection, whose precondition is self-sufficiency. How can people get enough for themselves, save the costs of contributing to the care of others and deal with crises out of their own private resources without the help of their kin networks? There are potentially two ways. They can get a secure job with a wage sufficient to enable them to buy what they need in the market. This is only a remote possibility and it favours those without dependants or the likelihood of acquiring them, in practice, men. But as Stack says 'those who attempt social mobility must carefully evaluate their job security, even at poverty level, before they risk removing themselves from the collective help of kinsmen' (Stack, 1997: 24). Having broken free of one's network obligations, unemployment will be disastrous unless one can repair the old relationships or make new ones. Help may depend on those one left behind and refused to share with. They must be willing to forgive you. One can easily imagine this position of great weakness will motivate considerable caution about trying to escape.

The other way to seek independence from kin networks is through a stable marriage, that is, a long-term alliance with another individual who is highly trusted and can supply all the necessary resources to supplement one's own in times of crisis. This is a possibility open to women, but requires finding a man with a secure job and a wage large enough to support his wife and provide for the care of any children – substituting AFDC payments and all the help supplied by the kin network. This is not an easy task given black men's weak position in the labour market. Not only must a woman make a careful calculation about the viability of marriage as a method of escape, she must also resist the attempts of the other members of her network to prevent her defection. That networks 'fear the loss of a central, resourceful member' (Stack, 1997: 114) is shown by Stack's friend Ruby, who provides a typical case of social control working against marriage because of the strong conflict between kin-based domestic units and lasting ties between husbands and wives (Stack, 1997: 115).

> Me and Otis could be married, but they all ruined that. Aunt Augusta told Magnolia [Ruby's mother] that he was no good. Magnolia was the fault of it too. They don't want to see me married! Magnolia knows that it be money getting away from her. I couldn't spend the time with her and the kids and be giving her the money that I do now. I'd have my husband to look after ... I couldn't come every time she calls me, like if Calvin [Magnolia's husband] took sick or the kids took sick, or if she took sick. That's all the running I do now ... You think a man would let Aunt Augusta come into the house and take food out of the icebox from his kids? ... They broke me and Otis up. They kept telling me that he didn't want me and that he didn't want the responsibility ... they kept fussing and arguing, so I went and quit him. (Stack, 1997: 114)

Ruby's commitment to Otis was undermined by the tactical negative gossip of senior female kin out to maximise their potential resources including the money and services which could flow to them through their daughters who themselves have children. They inhibit defection by ensuring that anybody considering marriage knows all the risks. When Ruby did eventually pluck up courage to break with the security and stability of her kin group and marry, she immediately left the area in order to prevent them sabotaging her escape attempt (Stack, 1997: 115).

Enough has been said to justify claiming that in this case the poor are not irrational. They think hard about their options and calculate how best to serve their own interests. The favoured method of maintaining 'multi-household kin networks' involves tit for tat reciprocity including forgiving the contrite, failed defectors. Thus when Ruby's marriage failed, she returned to her mother's house 'embarrassed, disappointed and depressed', admitting her mistake and accepting readmission to her network as a potential contributor (Stack, 1997: 126). The rules of the game are learned by children as they 'observe their mothers, fathers, and other men and women in the Flats manage one another. They observe goal-oriented behaviours and try them out on each other, on their fathers when they come around, and on their mother's boyfriends' (Stack, 1997: 120).

Analysing this pattern of social behaviour as the outcome of individuals rationally pursuing their interests clearly helps us to explain why it exists as the preferred option. All the elements are there which RCT predicts on the assumption that individuals are rational self-interested actors. Under conditions of severe deprivation, you would expect individuals energetically to gather information about who has what, to build large networks of reciprocating kin and constantly test their reliability, as well as make calculations about how best to draw on the network without compromising their own reputation. You would expect people to give to others who are in difficulty as a kind of insurance that others will give to them in turn – particularly if they should have the kind of major crisis which cannot be solved with a small saved surplus, but which can be coped with by mobilising a multiplicity of contributions from a large number of network members.

RCT is relevant and useful in this kind of situation. The poor can be shown to be rational actors. But its application depends on first identifying the game being played. The economic situation of the ghetto poor is tightly bounded by external conditions. In America, at a certain point in history, these are capitalism and economic racism. Imagine how different the game might look without racism restricting black access to job opportunities. How different would it have been if there had been more demand for the relatively low-skilled labour which poorly educated blacks could supply? The difference between being rational or irrational pales in significance when set against the difference between being black or white, being skilled or unskilled or being well or poorly educated. However rational ghetto blacks were in the 1960s, they had virtually no chance of breaking out of poverty through their individual efforts to better themselves. Thus RCT, although helpful in understanding how ghetto-dwellers respond to their poverty, does not explain this long-term impoverishment itself.

RCT helps us to explain what people do, as being the consequence of their choices. Choice is important. But RCT thinks of choices as being made only by individuals making rational calculations of the best ways to get what they want. But we must remember that what can be analysed as the outcome of rational choice may actually, in some cases, be the outcome of emotion, habit or accident. Also, people are often cross-pressured by contradictory interests. Economic interests may conflict with status ones, or with interests in pursuing satisfying personal and sexual relations for their own sakes. What is rational for achieving one goal may be irrational for achieving another. One cannot account for the choice between ends in terms of rationality.

But where interests can be taken as given because the game being played can be safely assumed, rational choice analysis can be fruitful. It helps us to see, not just that people make choices, but that they make them on the basis of a hand that has already been dealt them, in technical language, an opportunity structure. This sets up what is possible at what cost, which is what has to be understood by rational actors. However, RCT does not explain how these opportunity structures are set up. Poor blacks routinely make pretty accurate 'opportunity cost' calculations. But explaining these involves resorting to social theoretical concepts such as 'racism', 'capitalism', 'labour markets', 'wage labour', 'social welfare programmes' and so on, which are not properties of individuals, rational or otherwise. They are cultural and social structural concepts which define the game rather than the rationality of the players. Rationality is only one mode of relating to an environment of action. It is not the environment itself. Although the concept of the choosing individual has been shown to be relevant and necessary for social explanation, it is clearly not sufficient on its own, as methodological individualists claim. At the very least it must be supplemented by the concepts of culture and social structure, which is why we give these concepts their own chapters.

Part II

The Concept of Nature

CHAPTER 3

What Does Nature Explain?

The meaning of the word 'nature'

We now start to consider the variety of factors shaping the environment within which individuals act. In the rest of this book, we discuss the forces exerting constraint on human existence which we need to use when explaining social phenomena. We begin by looking at our second concept, 'nature'. This is a complex one, since we can think of it as both something separate from humans but also as something that humans are part of.

In the first case, we can consider nature as a realm of material existence which is self-subsistent, that is, not dependent on human agency. In this sense, it is external to humans, operating according to its own processes or laws. Think of how we talk of an untended garden 'returning to nature' as the plants and weeds begin to go their own way. People can of course act on this 'external' nature – as they did when they first created the garden. They can even breed new types of plant and animals that might never have developed spontaneously, tunnel through mountains or change the course of rivers, but they can only do so within the parameters that nature itself permits. How easy it is to blast through a mountain depends on the geological properties of the rock. Even apparently 'artificial' inventions such as genetically modified crops and cloned sheep depend on the application of human ingenuity to natural processes whose own logic sets some kind of limits to what can be achieved.

On the other hand, humans are also part of nature, one kind of animal among others, which can be said to have their own 'human nature', or their own species characteristics. We will start our discussion by focusing on the nature embodied in humans themselves. Then we will consider how nature, as an environment within which humans conduct their lives, might influence social outcomes.

Humans as part of nature

You will probably have recognised that we have already been considering humans as part of nature in Chapters 1 and 2. There we discussed the implications of thinking of individuals as biological bodies with certain physical properties, or as innately endowed with either or both non-rational drives and natural capacities for reason. We insisted that although biology set the scene, it did not wholly determine how it was played. We also stressed that the theories of the methodological individualist saw key causal powers located within individuals. These key powers were 'already there' prior to any interaction these individuals had with one another. Methodological individualists tended to see individuals as potentially nasty, because they believed that they were self-interested or possessed of drives with a strong potential to generate conflict and disorder. Conversely, they thought of 'society' or the processes of interaction between individuals as, in one way or another, the good or nice solution, keeping this nastiness in check. Thus Freud depicted the whole edifice of civilisation as a device to control human sexual drives. Similarly, rational choice theorists believed people had to curb their short-term, selfish interests if they wanted to keep open the long-term possibilities of advantageous interaction with others.

However, we can also think of humans as part of nature in a non-individualistic way, by putting the *human species* and not the human individual at the centre of our analysis. Methodological individualists do recognise the existence of the human species with characteristics different from those of other species. But they define the characteristics of the species by generalising from the prior properties of human individuals. The alternative sees the properties of individuals as flowing from the properties of the species, an approach brilliantly developed by the young Karl Marx.

Marx and Engels (1964) argued, for example, that humans are characterised by collective productive activity and, while other species are confined to their ecological niches, their nature is to work, both consciously and collectively, to transform the non-human world into things they can use. This view recognises that it is through working together as social animals that humans have been able to make large parts of the globe habitable. Except for short periods and only then with the benefit of knowledge gained from other people, lone individuals cannot produce what they need to survive. *Homo sapiens* does not just adapt to its environment, it deliberately adapts environments to meet its needs. Marx's great insight was that it is part of humanity's nature to transform nature (and in the process develop its own capacities). Certainly some other creatures also modify their habitats. Beavers (as well as civil engineers) can alter the course of rivers when they build their dams. But beavers don't consciously aim for such transformations, or calculate their costs and benefits for those who live downstream. This does not, however, mean that all of humans' environmental transformations are intended. People use their cars to get to work or bring home their shopping, not in order to reduce the ozone layer. But what we really need to underline is that this focusing on the species' productive capacities recognises that before there can be individuals, there have to be forms of social organisation which relate people to one another so that they can cooperate to create what they need.

There is another non-individualistic conceptualisation of the human species which complements Marx's. This focuses not on human beings' essentially collectively productive nature, but on what people have to be able to do before they can cooperate at all. While Marx takes human social interaction for granted, the fundamental importance of the work of George Herbert Mead (1934) is his attempt to explain the prerequisites for cooperation itself, namely the capacity to communicate and interact. This approach to human nature tries to establish the basic linguistic and imaginative requirements of interaction and what the process is by which individuals acquire these skills. It is interested in how collectivities produce individuals able to relate to one another. Relating to others is a complex work of symbolisation and imagination. The approach suggests how the raw material of human organisms (babies for short) are transformed into socially competent people, acquiring the necessary language skills to symbolically represent themselves and others, playing social roles and responding to others' expectations. Basic for cooperation is the ability to imagine how others, in various social positions, are likely to respond to one's behaviour. Social cooperation demands this sort of imaginative anticipation.

These two profound ways of thinking about the essential characteristics of humanity are potentially complementary (Goff, 1980). They both show that there is no contradiction between thinking naturalistically and thinking non-individualistically, once it is recognised that 'being social' is built right into the very foundations of the human species. We cannot become or exist for long as individual human beings unless we are connected with others of our kind. Imagine a baby denied all human contact, whose physical needs were met mechanically. It might not die, but it could not develop into a properly functioning human individual. The ability to communicate, interact with others, represent experience symbolically, anticipate the future and be productive – the basic characteristics of the human species – are all dependent on human sociability.

However, this does not mean that conflict is ruled out. Humans' intrinsic sociability makes cooperation possible, but the models we have been discussing allow plenty of scope for non-harmonious interaction and antagonism between social units. Although we are necessarily interdependent, cooperation is not automatic, as we saw in the last chapter. One major implication of cooperation is social power, which is generally unequally distributed. Indeed, the necessity of production is one very powerful incentive for some sets of people to act together to try to dominate others and force them to cooperate in the productive process on terms unfavourable to themselves. This is a major insight of the political and economic thought of both Marx and Max Weber. Cooperation can involve the threat or use of force. Generally, the dominated and exploited are weak because they have few alternatives open to them and are compelled to cooperate on disadvantageous terms just in order to survive. So, these non-individualistic social theories are not the least bit 'innocent' about the nature of society. They recognise that social organisation involves the exercise of social power and that social reality is therefore not necessarily the solution to the problem of antagonism and conflicts of interest, as individualists suggest. Not just individuals, but society can be a source of nastiness.

So, we can say that when we are trying to explain social phenomena, these kinds of non-individualist understandings of human nature immediately direct us to the social level. However, as we have variously shown in Chapter 2, we cannot account for differences in outcomes entirely in terms of a universal attribute, and this applies whether the attribute is seen as based in the individual or the species. Thus pointing to humans' naturally given and necessary capacity for sociability in general will only get us so far. It is an answer to why we always find people 'collectivised', grouped together, but not to why the boundaries between collectivities lie here rather than there. It helps us to understand why all people cooperate to produce, have language and are able to interact, but does not explain why they organise production in one way or another, or why we find the particular range of languages that we do. However, later chapters will show that the concepts of 'culture', 'action' and 'social structure' can be usefully developed with reference to an understanding of human nature as essentially and primarily social. As we shall see, these three concepts provide powerful resources for helping us get to grips with the problem of what makes collectivities different from one another – the problem of 'difference'.

The natural environment

Now we will move to consider how nature, considered as external to human beings, a part of their environment, is something to take into account when trying to explain events and social patterning. It is easy to think of examples where reference to the natural environment is unavoidable. The town of Pompeii was totally destroyed by the eruption of Vesuvius in 79 AD . The outcomes of many events from battles to harvests have been affected by the weather. Consider the importance of wind direction for the use of poisonous gas during the First World War or the Iraq–Iran conflict, or for naval warfare in the age of sail. The severity of the winter climate defeated both Napoleon's and Hitler's armies when they invaded Russia (in 1812 and 1941). We might also remind ourselves of the constraints and opportunities offered by rivers, mountains and deserts. Mercenaries have often come from mountain regions where poor agricultural opportunities inclined men to look for work elsewhere – think of the British army's recruitment of Nepalese Gurkha troops or the fourteenth-century Italian city states' employment of Swiss pike and crossbow experts (McNeill: 1983: 118). Ancient Egyptian civilisation arose where it did partly because the fertile alluvial soils of the Nile's flood plains provided good opportunities for agriculture and reliable food supply, while the fact that they were surrounded by inhospitable deserts effectively caged the peasantry, making it easy for landlords to exploit and tax them. Exceptional geographical circumstances provided a basis for an exceptional accumulation of power.

This list of examples suggests that there are two broad ways in which the environment can be influential. Firstly, directly, through itself doing something. Secondly, by conditioning human beings themselves to act in certain ways. The erupting volcano, the earthquake, the tidal wave, the major storm, for example, all fall into the first category and can have major social consequences. They can wipe out whole settlements, affect the course of battles, possibly with long-term knock-on consequences. The destruction of Lisbon by an earth-quake on the morning of All Saints' Day 1755 not only massively weakened the Portuguese state, but encouraged a bout of religious theorising about the doctrine of providence (notable contributors were Voltaire and Rousseau) to try to understand how a supposedly just God could allow such a disaster. When we consider a cataclysmic event like Pompeii's destruction, we may even want to argue that environmental factors entirely account for it. Environmental deter-minism seems legitimate in this case. But we should recognise that this is an extreme rather than a routine case. Cataclysmic events are relatively uncommon. And when nature throws them at us, seldom do they entirely determine outcomes. Probably nothing could have saved the inhabitants of Pompeii. But retrospective analyses of natural disasters often show that damage might have been reduced. An earth-quake might have killed fewer people, for example, if officials had enforced building regulations more strictly. A volcano's eruption might have been less devastating if peasants had not had to live on its slopes because large landholders took over their farms in the valley. And once the earthquake has happened or the tidal wave has hit, factors such as the efficiency with which people can be mustered for rescue work will affect the ultimate number of survivors.

If we elaborate the second way the natural environment contrib-utes to producing socially significant events and patterns, that is, through conditioning how humans act, it is necessary to recognise that the strength of conditioning can vary. It hardly needs saying that geographical and biological conditions can heavily influence forms of life. Such conditions can explain the existence of opportunities provided by the availability of raw materials, ease of movement and defensibility. The way the potential resources of the earth are laid out strongly affects where and when particular historical developments happen. We must take seriously the fundamental influence of the environment as an organised collection of constraints and opportun-ities among which humans have made their way since they evolved.

However, when we talk of the variable strength of conditions and their constraining as well as providing opportunities for certain kinds of action, we are also saying that their effect will depend upon what human beings themselves do. Although it is true that the character of the environment creates strong tendencies for humans to act in certain ways (avoiding harsh environments, preferring easy ones perhaps), it is also true that its characteristics, along with biology, only set the scene. It is up to human beings to play it out. In the case of harsh environments, short of cataclysms, negative conditions may be overcome by combinations of human ingenuity, determination, courage and so on. In the alternative case of relatively favourable conditions, which make certain beneficial activities easy, it is always possible that people will fail to take advantage of the opportunities that the environment hands to them.

For example, if we are interested in the origins of agriculture, we have to be interested in how plants and animals which can be eaten and used by human beings are domesticated (Diamond, 1997). Only certain plants can be digested by humans, most cannot. One reason grain cultivation began in the Fertile Crescent (the eastern Mediterranean through Turkey and southeast into Iran), rather than elsewhere was because that region had by far the greatest concentration in the world of large-seeded grass species as potential candidates for domestication. These species developed here because the climate alternates between wet and very dry and plants had to evolve large seeds to survive the dry periods. Because these seeds can be both digested by humans and stored for long periods, cereal farming was more likely to start there.

Similarly, only a few species of animals are suitable for domesticating; those which pay off well are large, relatively docile, fast growing, mammalian herbivores, living in herds, with a dominance hierarchy in non-exclusive territories. Sheep, goats, pigs, cattle, horses (all Eurasian in origin) and dogs are the ones providing a good return on the effort to domesticate them (providing meat, milk, manure, propulsion for ploughs, transport and military assault, hunting assistants and materials such as bone, wool and leather). Their suitability is proved by their adoption all over the world. Whereas, despite their potential as meat, there are no grizzly bear farms and no rhinoceros-mounted cavalry! These species just cannot be domesticated.

The domestication of large-seed grasses and relatively docile animals is an example of people taking advantage of favourable conditions. There was nothing inevitable about the development of farming. But given the human interest in and devotion of effort and thought to securing reliable food, it is not surprising that effort should have first succeeded in a region where the conditions made it relatively easy. The early farmers of the Fertile Crescent simply exploited the naturally available, easily grown, stored and digested grains. They were luckier, we might think, than the inhabitants of the Amazonian basin for whom an available plant was manioc, which, in order to make edible, they first had to perfect the technique of squeezing out

the poisonous prussic acid from its roots. Surely a tribute to their ingenuity, not to say courage, this case shows that people may begin cultivation despite discouraging environmental conditions.

Hence it is reasonable to see chains of causation between climate,
potentially domesticable plants and animals, and farming. And we
can also extend these causal chains further into human social organisation. Thus if we want to know why cities and early forms of
extended power networks (such as the ancient Egyptian kingdoms)
emerged when and where they did, part of the reason is that they
depend on settlement, which in turn depends on the reliable food
production of farming. So the environment (climate, plant and
animal evolution) makes farming possible, which then permits large-
scale sedentary organisation. It can also create the possibility of
destroying nomadic peoples, hunters and gatherers with whom the
farmers and city dwellers come into contact, thus helping us to understand why, throughout history, these earliest forms of life have lost
out to agriculturalists (Brody, 2001). This is because settled societies
with large storable food surpluses can support non-agricultural
specialists in organisational technique (bureaucracy), the control of
information (literacy), military technique (metallurgy and guns) and
so on which make them powerful enemies. They may also have
another devastating, if unintended, 'weapon' up their sleeve in the
immunity they have acquired to the diseases of their domestic
animals, diseases which can be fatal to those conquered by settled
societies (Diamond, 1997).

Before we proceed, it is important to reiterate that we have
discussed environmental effects as creating possibilities, potentialities
and tendencies. Environmental conditions constrain and enable
human action, favouring certain lines of development and disfavour-
ing others. But it is always possible that people may choose not to
take advantage of favourable circumstances or that they may struggle
to overcome unfavourable ones. There is nothing automatic about
responses to the environment.

How much can technical rationality and technology explain?

So far we have argued that the natural environment conditions
action, sometimes very strongly. It therefore always plays a necessary
role in social explanation. Only in the most cataclysmic situations can

the natural environment determine outcomes, when it may be sufficient by itself to explain what happens. But generally we have always
also to consider the human action of responding to environmental
conditions. How is this responsiveness to be understood and what is
its significance for social explanation? If humans themselves have
some choice to influence the impact of the conditions of the natural
environment, then there is an element of unpredictability in the
effects of nature. As Marx made clear, one element of nature, the
human, has the capacity to mediate the other, the environment. This
poses a major problem for social explanation, because it becomes
necessary to analyse the process of mediation. Since mediation
involves human actors making choices and decisions, the issue is how
they make choices about relating to the natural conditions of their
existence. This important question preoccupied Weber, Durkheim and
Parsons in their critiques of individualist and utilitarian forms of
social theory, and their answers, which centre on the importance of
culture, are of enduring significance.

We shall now deal with one very influential answer to this question, 'how do people make choices when responding to the environment?', which has provided the foundation for an important strand of
naturalistic social theory associated with social evolutionism. This
holds that the choices are essentially technical choices and are made
to solve environmental problems as efficiently as possible. Such a
position is closely related to rational choice theory examined in Chapters 1 and 2. It is suggested that technical choices, informed by empirical knowledge and logical reasoning and motivated by a desire to be
efficient, are the ones that really matter when trying to understand
both how people mediate the impact of the environment, and the
organisation of social life. Technical reason and the various technologies are the human response to the problems set by the environment.
Although there is scope for choice in the sphere of technology, the
constraints set by the environment and the criterion of efficiency, on
what can function as an effective solution are seen as pretty tight.

It is important to recognise that, although an element of choice is
allowed, this approach to explaining social life is nevertheless a form
of naturalism. This is because it credits human beings with the powers
to determine outcomes, but only by using their naturally given capacity for technical rationality to develop technical, objectively effective
solutions to the problems set by the rest of nature which forms the
environment. From this perspective, technical rationality is itself an
element within, not outside, nature. Granted the superior technical

power of the human species (which eventually equips itself with the forces of industrialism), it is still nature which calls the shots, setting the agenda for human action. The freedom of choice allowed by technical reason is not an escape from being determined by the two components of nature which this approach acknowledges, namely the natural rationality of humans and the natural environment.

From this perspective, we might suppose that the environment will most clearly spell out the strategies which people need to follow, when nature is at its most extreme – in regions of great cold or heat and drought, for example. In such unforgiving conditions, it might be thought that what counts as an efficient solution to the problems are obvious; for here the dangers of making a technically inappropriate choice will be at their greatest. People will be forced to live in a way that ensures their immediate survival. Their choices ought to be highly predictable. But they are not, as the following chapter's discussion of technical choice in examples of extreme environments will show. We will see that even in these extreme cases, people can live in the same environment, at the same time, in somewhat different ways. Harsh environments powerfully constrain how people act, but they do not appear 'automatically' to compel the use of particular technologies or the development of particular ways of life.

When enthusiasts for explaining social life as shaped primarily by technology try to explain technological variation in similar environments, they typically point to the fact that technology changes over time. Using technical rationality and its criterion of efficiency to invent technologies implies a constant search for ways to improve efficiency. So here we have a sort of 'motor' for historical change; technology is constantly being 'upgraded', and that explains why there is also change in the institutions and culture associated with particular technologies. Given that what counts as an improvement in efficiency is thought of as a matter to be decided by applying objective tests (such as energy and costs savings, for example), the history of technical development can be interpreted as a story of 'progress'. It is held that over time technology will get better and better, and all peoples will eventually converge on the relatively limited number of highly efficient technologies which have emerged. The least effective techniques and organisational forms fall by the wayside, the most effective ones are maintained and developed. The course of change is therefore directional rather than merely random.

The social evolutionists who think of history as a story of technically driven progress are impressed particularly by the development of scientifically based industrialism. Industrial technique appears so much more powerful than others that its claim to superiority seems irresistible. Its status as the cutting edge of human development is based on the promise that it offers the greatest power to deal with whatever the environment might have in store for us. Sometimes making an analogy with Darwinian theories of natural evolution, they believe there is a 'progressive' trend for all societies to 'converge' towards industrialism. This is understood not just as technique, but as a whole set of institutions (for example capitalist markets, nation states, rational law, bureaucracy) and culture (individualism, secularism, egalitarianism and so on).

Explaining technical development and technical choice

We can accept that industrialisation has been a very important and continuing development in history. But explaining why it has happened is not easy. A fundamental problem is that of the coexistence of technologies of different levels of sophistication and the unevenness of the achievement of industrialism. How, for example, are we to account for the fact that societies have moved towards industrialism at different rates?

Attempts to explain this argue *either* that there are variations between different peoples in their capacity for technical reason, *or* that it is due to the different potentials offered by the particular environments to which they are adapting. In the first case, those making slowest progress are seen as less well endowed with technical capacities – an assumption that risks the racist dangers we warned against in Chapter 1. If technical reason is a property of human nature, but some humans are defined as having more or less of it, then we have to find some additional principle of nature to explain this difference. Doctrines about intellectual differences between races try to do that job.

In the second case, some environments are seen as offering more resources for development than others, better raw materials, easier communication routes, for example. Or, it may be argued that some environments offer people more incentive to be inventive because, for example, they provide less easily available food supplies or other harsh conditions that need to be mitigated. We have already provided some examples to show how the different global distribution of

natural resources can certainly help us understand large-scale historical developments and contribute to explaining why particular techniques (for example grain cultivation) first emerged in one place
rather than another. Clearly technical rationality and the potentialities offered by environments are major inputs into the process of technical development. But they are not by themselves sufficient to
explain it. The human mediation of the environment certainly
involves making technical choices, but are these choices informed
only by environmental pressures and technical reason?

Firstly, those who argue that people develop their technologies in
response to the natural environment alone fail to recognise the
impact that the political relations between sets of people can have on
the development and uptake of techniques. Economic and political
competition between the states of Europe helped to hasten industrialisation. Europe's first place, and quick pace, on the road to industrial
development was also influenced by the (largely exploitative)
relations it had with peoples in other parts of the world who made
slower progress. The forced removal of Africans to work on slave plan-
tations in Britain's New World colonies and the suppression of India's
indigenous textile production, for example, both contributed to the
great success of Lancashire cotton manufacture. Moreover, convergence on particular technologies may have as much to do with a
desire to keep up with or deal with competitors as with any original
dissatisfaction with the way existing techniques coped with external
nature. Native North Americans were not necessarily dissatisfied with
their bows and arrows, and did not feel a lack of guns and horses,
until they were invaded by Europeans. When that happened, they
quickly became expert horsemen and equipped themselves with guns
to defend themselves. It was the new element in their social surround-
ings and not the natural environment that produced this change in
their technology. Similarly, nuclear technology was pushed forward in
the context of world war and superpower confrontation. Making technological choices is usually framed by the circumstances of intra-
human competition (Runciman: 1983).

Second, technological change (including 'development') depends
on changes in circumstances including the various 'autocatalytic' or
'feedback' processes which technologies may set in train. Technologies
have positive or negative long-term consequences for what can be
done in the future. Farming was one such autocatalytic process, multiplying food supply, reducing birth intervals, expanding populations
which made everyone more dependent on the success of farming and

so on. But it was also vulnerable to soil exhaustion so was not necessarily sustainable, which is why today the Fertile Crescent is no longer fertile. The wetter Western Europe has been less prone to soil exhaustion but, because it has chosen to expand agricultural productivity using agricultural chemicals and manufactured animal feed, is similarly facing a crisis of sustainability.

The same point can be made about industrialism. It was developed to raise production and place life on a securer footing. But its inherent tendency to exhaust raw materials and pollute makes it itself a threat to sustainable existence. It becomes a problem rather than simply the solution to scarcity. We should not just focus on dramatic cases such as the Chernobyl disaster and think of the downsides of technologies as exceptional. The point is rather that the experience and consequences of past technologies set the scene and present us with choices for future technical development. This fact, that the way people have solved technical problems in the past, with the successes and negative consequences, becomes a condition of how they must now solve them, leads us to recognise that technical choices must use non-technical values to guide which benefits we want and which prices we are prepared to pay.

This point has implications for the meaning of progress. Awareness of the downsides of so-called 'advanced technologies' forces us to ask: 'Are we entirely better adapted to our environment than our predecessors?' Is driving a car using ozone-depleting, non-renewable fossil fuels unequivocally an advance on earlier forms of transport? These kinds of question also suggest that what counts as progress is always relative to some goal. If what we want is quicker, easier movement for us in the present, the car may well be progressive. But if we want to maintain a useable environment for future generations, then maybe it's not. Similarly, there is no value-free answer to whether ways of producing which increase products but reduce leisure are advances or not. Hunter-gatherers in well-endowed environments can find enough to live on with a few hours activity each day. Are they necessarily less well environmentally adapted than farmers or industrial workers, who own more goods but have to work much harder? Problems of the insufficiency of technical criteria on their own, to account for why people react to their environment as they do, also arise when there are different, but equally effective means available to reach the same goal. You may need to paint your house's exterior woodwork to protect it from rot, but does this explain why you chose green rather than shocking pink for the window frames?

Conclusion

We have considered various ways that 'nature' can be held to shape social life. At one extreme, nature is all-powerful, determining our behaviour. Human life is viewed as determined by internal and external forces over which humans can exercise no control. We are at the mercy of our own natures and the environment. This picture was modified, a bit, by the recognition that humans, except in cataclysmic situations, can mediate the impact of the environment by using technology. But, although credited with technical creativity, they were still regarded as essentially responding to environmental pressures. However, even this limited mediating capacity does mean that cast-iron determinism has to be replaced by the idea of environmental conditioning. Conditioning is the concept we need to combine recognition of the force of the environment in shaping human life with recognition of the capacity of humans to intervene to modify the way the environment impacts on them. Allowing for the development of technology is a very limited acknowledgement of the creative cultural powers of human beings. It is the one element of culture which theorists committed to explanation in terms of environmental forces feel able to accept, since it is thought of as the cultural element most directly influenced by such natural forces. Technology is a sort of halfway house between 'nature' and 'culture'; it is culture reduced to the knowledge involved in technical problem-solving which humans naturally undertake.

We have begun to show that explaining social life as being driven by the environment and technical responses to it is far too crude. The relation between environment and technology is obviously an important dimension of human existence, but to explain why people deal with their environmental problems in the ways that they do requires that we refer to more than simply the environment and their technical knowledge. The idea that members of the human species have the capacity to transform nature positively implies that they can impose their will on it to some degree, and that implies that they use more than technical knowledge to assign meaning to their worlds. (This is the lesson of Weber's and Durkheim's critique of utilitarianism.) Humans have much more than the essentially reactive capacity for technical problem-solving claimed by environmental determinists or social evolutionists. In the chapters on culture, we will consider this issue of 'meaning' and what a full-blown concept of culture has to offer to social explanation.

However, to give the idea that social behaviour is driven by the objective forces of the physical environment the best chance to impress us, we should look at cases where the force of the environment seems extremely strong. The next chapter will therefore consider in some detail studies of how the behaviour of people living in very harsh environments is shaped.

CHAPTER 4

Testing the Explanatory Value of Nature

Best cases for testing the sufficiency of environmental determinism

In this chapter we will follow the same tactic as we did in Chapter 2. The limits of the concept of 'individuals' were shown by considering cases of social phenomena which seemed most likely to be explained by it. This easily demonstrated the necessity of using the concept. But the concept was also shown to be insufficient on its own to explain the sort of cases preferred by enthusiasts, thereby establishing its insufficiency in general. In Chapter 2 we called this strategy a 'sufficiency' test. In the case of 'nature', we will focus the discussion on arguments about the influence of the natural environment. There can be no doubting the destructive potential of cataclysmic events. In these cases, at least at the moment of initial impact, the environment approaches being both necessary and sufficient to do all the explanatory work. However, such cases are too easy. Enthusiasts for environmental determinism ought to accept a tougher, although still favourable sufficiency test against cases with some historical depth. Such cases are ones where human beings have been subjected for substantial periods of time to the constraints of severe or extreme, environments. Since patterning takes time, we need non-cataclysmic cases where people have time to respond to the environment. These cases give us the opportunity to see if environments most likely to pattern behaviour actually do so (and are therefore sufficient) and if any other factors are at work.

If we accept, with most environmental determinists, that the effects of the environment are mediated by the technology which human beings develop to cope with it, then the best cases for such determinism are provided by studies of technological development. Is the technology which people use entirely dictated by the nature of the environment, and do they respond to the environment only with technical rationality? Enthusiasts for the powers of the environment and technical reason say 'yes'. They argue that technological choice is tightly constrained by what is technically functional for survival in a given environment. That is the basis for their arguments about the tendency for societies to converge on increasingly efficient technologies. In extreme environments these pressures are at their greatest and technological choice most limited.

Technological determinists suggest that history is a story of progress from primitive to modern, as people discover the most efficient methods for dealing with nature. We can test this theory by making two kinds of experimental comparisons. First, we can compare the technological choices of different peoples relating to the same extreme environment, who the theory would claim to be at the same level of development. Do they have the same technology? If they do not, what else, besides the environment and technical reason, influences their technological choices? Second, we can compare the technological choices of peoples who the theory defines as more and less advanced in terms of their respective technical development when relating to a given extreme environment. Is it the case that the so-called 'advanced' cope best? How is technical competence to be judged? European colonisation provides cases of confrontation between technologies with very different principles and powers, where we can examine the possibility of technological alternatives and what influences technological choice. How do we explain the abandoning of established technologies for new ones, or the persistence of so-called 'primitive' technologies and the failure of the more recent, 'more efficient' technologies to eliminate them? Is history really a story of technological progress?

Before considering actual cases, what do we understand by an 'extreme' environment? We use this term to refer to environments which we would find difficult to inhabit, as typical people used to living in industrialised societies. This kind of understanding informs, for example, the use of the word 'extreme' in the advertising rhetoric of the leisure industry trying to sell excitement and opportunities to 'test oneself' against elemental forces which many feel have been excluded from our normal everyday life. The cases we choose in this chapter are intended to excite this sort of response.

However, this is not to say that these environments are actually easy to live in even by people who have done so successfully for generations without the benefits of industrialism. The dangers are real because these places demand specialist knowledge and techniques and are intolerant of mistakes. Survival requires a level of concentration and attention to detail, which a more forgiving environment does not. But, although environments vary in the degree of difficulty and specialisation they impose, it remains true that the perception of an environment as extreme depends partly on what one is used to. Amazonian visitors to modern cities might be as frightened by the 'extreme' traffic menace, as the inhabitants of those cities would be by peccaries, jaguars, piranhas and even monkeys.

The divergent technological choice of two Amazonian forest peoples

Our first case is the upper Amazon forest environment, the region of the border of Peru and Ecuador between the Maranon and Napo rivers, which flow east into the Amazon basin. This territory has probably been inhabited for thousands of years by many tribal groups. We discuss the technical hunting choices of two tribes, the Achuar, studied by Philippe Descola (1997) and the Huaorani, studied by Laura Rival (1996). Here are two societies whose hunting practices are constrained by the same extreme environment, which will allow us to see the extent of any technological convergence. If there are differences, in order to explain them, we shall have to find factors additional to the constraints of the environment. Moreover, Rival's account of the Huaorani also discusses recent changes in hunting technology, providing an opportunity to see if such change is motivated by considerations of improved efficiency.

First, both people are constrained by the environment to the extent that the forest offers specific edible species living either on the forest floor or in the canopy. Their economy as a whole is diverse and includes growing manioc and gathering fruits, as well as hunting but we will focus only on the latter, concentrating on the techniques for hunting the major prey species. These are herds of peccaries (tusked pigs foraging in rotting vegetation in the swampy conditions of the floor), and various monkeys (spider, howler, but mostly the abundant and highly territorial, woolly). However, birds and monkeys can only be killed with projectile weapons (traps being too difficult to set at great heights). So it is no surprise to be told that Amazonian peoples have developed sophisticated bows and blowpipe technology to fire arrows made deadly by using curare poison. Large and tree-living species can be efficiently taken. The basic fact that the Amazon forest environment contains tree-living prey strongly disposes people to develop these particular hunting technologies. Similar technology has been independently developed by other forest peoples, for example in South-East Asia.

Descola tells of a hunting trip with an Achuar couple, Pinchu and his wife, Santamik. Pinchu uses his blowpipe to kill a woolly monkey and two peccaries from a foraging herd, which they have tracked, aided by his wife's pack of dogs. The Achuar use their indigenous technology for both types of prey but are enthusiasts for the scarce rifles and shotguns which they get by trading, and which have been available in the region for a century. As a note for later, they keep baby peccaries as pets.

Contrast this with the behaviour, until recently, of the Huaorani. Their preferred prey are woolly monkeys killed using blowpipes. They do not use bows and arrows, although the technology is available among their immediate neighbours. Nor do they deliberately track peccaries in the way Pinchu did, and rarely use dogs. They kill peccaries using only spears to defend their settlements from herds which encroach. Many are killed as the herd is driven off and the abundant meat is eaten to excess, making people ill. So here is the problem. Why do these people prefer to hunt woolly monkeys (and other tree-living prey) and confine their use of blowpipes to these, and not hunt peccaries, killing them only with spears when forced to drive off a herd?

Here is a case where clearly the technology chosen has to be effective enough to provide sufficient meat from the available prey. Consider meat supply. By routinely only killing woolly monkeys and not killing peccaries, the Huaorani do not suffer any shortage of meat (200 grams per person per day). By the same token, the Achuar need not routinely kill peccaries. Neither people can be said to be more or less technologically efficient on that count. Next, consider hunting technique. Both use blowpipes to kill monkeys because projectile weapons are necessary. Both could use bows and arrows but these are not more efficient and may be less. Guns are useful but scarce, expensive, noisy and not more efficient at bringing down monkeys and birds. The major difference lies in the refusal by the Huaorani to use blowpipes to kill peccaries. But their use of spears for this purpose is not less efficient; it is just a close-quarters killing technique as opposed to the distanced one of the blowpipe. The Huaorani insist on closing in on the peccaries to spear them, while the Achuar are happy to keep their distance.

It is not possible to explain this kind of technological choice in terms of differences in availability of technical alternatives or in terms of differences in technical rationality. Both peoples are technically competent when responding to environmental pressures. They kill all the meat they need in a sustainable manner (for example by leaving fruit on trees in monkey territories for them to eat). So what else is influencing this difference? Rival suggests that Huaorani preferences about prey, and rules governing the use of weapons, are not dictated by the environment or considerations of technical efficiency. What they do is certainly technically efficient but could be done differently without loss or gain in efficiency. So what explains their strictness about the choice of prey and weapons?

Rival points to a 'striking homology' between the way the Huaorani traditionally treat animals and one another. They live in extreme isolation in upland nomadic enclaves between powerful neighbours. They defend their independence by strongly emphasising their boundary, closing themselves off from outside influences. They refuse to trade with, or marry, outsiders. In this tightly closed social world, cross-cousin marriage is typical and strong, lifelong, brother–sister alliances are encouraged. For people constructing a social world in this way, territorial monkeys are 'sociologically interesting' (Rival, 1996: 150). Woolly monkeys are recognised as individuals and as members of unthreatening groups with which reciprocal relations can be established. Monkeys and Huaorani look after each other. Monkeys are admitted within the Huaorani social order, but peccaries are not. There are no pet peccaries here! As members of parasite-infected, destructive, uncontrolled, anonymous crowds, peccaries represent distrusted outsiders, enemies to be fought off. The Huaorani contrast the corrupting, soft, bland flesh of peccaries with the tough, chewy virtue of monkey meat.

But the closeness of relations within this world, between individual people, and animals and humans, which preserves control and independence against outside threats, itself presents dangers. First, sufficient distance has to be maintained to preserve a necessary minimum of internal differentiation. The most obvious danger is that of incest. Secondly, and more routinely, cooperation is undermined by jealousy between same-sex siblings who compete for the affections of siblings of the other sex. Brothers tend not to get on well with brothers or sisters with sisters.

It is more complex than this, but enough has been said to follow the logic of Huaorani technological choice (Table 4.1). First take the

Table 4.1 Huaorani technical choice

Target	Peccaries = outsiders/enemies	Monkeys = members/insiders
Location	Forest floor (realm of corruption)	Forest canopy (realm of purity)
Value of meat	Low: soft, bland, fatty	High: tough, chewy, muscular
Mode of killing	Occasional, communal and aggressive	Routine, individual, non-aggressive hunting
Weapon (technical choice)	Spears – used by men: technology of exclusion	Blowpipes – used by everyone: technology for inclusion
Mode of relation	Emphatic, physical rejection	Distance kept

relation between peccaries and spears. Peccaries are actually destructive but they also symbolically represent human enemies. Therefore they are killed with the weapons used to wage war, namely hardwood spears used by armies of men in a high state of aggression. The group fights off the herd. That the spear is associated with killing enemies is suggested by the fact that shotguns, although available, are not used to kill human enemies. Enemies have to be ferociously speared to death, close up. In Rival's words, the spear is 'a technology of exclusion' (1996: 157).

Now consider blowpipes and monkeys. This is a 'technology of inclusion' because it is a technology of deliberation and self-control. Blowpipes are products of a long, skilful production process resulting in objects representing beauty, maturity and 'a sense of balance'. All children grow up playing at 'blowing' and both men and women learn the posture and breath control to become competent. Blowpipes are given to kin but not traded and good ones become precious, inherited items. Blowpipe hunting is a quiet, measured process, lacking in forcefulness or aggression (Rival, 1996: 154–5). Its effectiveness depends on judging the right distance, not too close to alarm prey, but not too far (beyond 30–40 metres) to be out of range.

The distance and time which blowpipes introduce in relations between hunter and prey provide a model of how relations between all insiders should be conducted. Using a blowpipe depends on relations of distanced intimacy with the target prey. It is possible for a targeted monkey to 'speak with its eyes' and be spared (Rival, 1996: 150). Among a strongly endogamous, isolated people, where internally generated emotional tensions can become explosive, the habits associated with blow hunting – stopping to judge the distance, being close but not too close – are highly functional for the social order. It is this requirement to consider carefully how to deal with those who are close to you, to inhibit spontaneity, which makes blowpipe technology so potent as a symbol regulating Huaorani social relations. As Rival puts it:

> The blowpipe, which can either bring closer (if too far), or remove (if too close), is a powerful instrument for monitoring social closeness. It puts men in ... control, as defenders of endogamous relationships [threatened by] both incest and open exchange. (1996: 157)

As such, its use cannot simply be a matter of its technical effectiveness. Considerations of effectiveness are not irrelevant, meat is needed and weapons have to kill prey, but such criteria do not help to decide between equally effective technologies. The two examples show that, in a situation of alternatives, technical rationality is insufficient to explain choices even in response to a harsh environment, and we have to find other reasons such as the social relations represented by weapons.

Technical choice and change depends on more than simple functionality. It is no surprise to learn therefore that the Huaorani have recently started using shotguns to kill all kinds of animals as a result of forming relations with trusted outsiders, American missionaries. This is not simply because missionaries bring the guns or that guns are more efficient than blowpipes (which they are not). It is because the traditional weapons no longer have to do their symbolic work. The commitment to fierce separateness has been undermined, opposition to open exchange and the need for careful management of interpersonal relations relaxed. Given a more favourable attitude to outsiders, the rules about prey and weapons have become less strict. Brothers may get on better, brothers and sisters may not need to be so close, or marriage partners chosen from among one's cousins, and the special relationship with woolly monkeys may be abandoned. Relocated in semi-permanent river settlements, more dependent on agriculture, river traffic and manufactured goods, means a new way of life less dependent on the meanings and meat of monkeys. Perhaps some other animal will become as sociologically interesting to represent the newer social choices.

The Dunne-za: aboriginal hunters versus advanced industrialism in British Columbia

We have seen that environmental pressures only partly determine technological choices. Projectile weapons are necessary to hunt in the forest but where there are alternative, equally efficient weapons, which ones are used to kill which kinds of prey is decided by non-technical criteria. The next comparison tests the claim that technical change is a linear development where later technologies which are better able to cope with the environment displace earlier, less efficient ones. If blowpipes give way to shotguns, this ought to be because they are more efficient, but, as we have just seen, the more recent technology of the Huaorani is not more efficient and is adopted as part of a whole package of transformed social relationships, particularly with outsiders. Technological choice clearly has a political dimension.

The political framing of technological choice can be further explored by considering a confrontation between contemporary exponents of the oldest and the newest technologies. Hugh Brody's *Maps and Dreams* (1986) gives a moving account of the confrontation in the subarctic region of British Columbia between the Dunne-za people (long referred to as the Beaver), living in reserves along the Alaska Highway between Fort Nelson and Dawson Creek, and an advancing frontier of oil and natural gas exploration, commercial logging, farming, roads, tourism and sports hunting.

The Dunne-za developed an efficient hunter-gatherer way of life in this region from the end of the last ice age 12,000 years ago. The subarctic is an extreme environment, not just because of the winters, but because it forces hunter-gatherers to be more hunters than gatherers. Hunter-gatherers who live in generalised ecosystems (like the Amazon forest) benefit from substantial opportunities to collect food (the Huaorani eat a lot of fruit, for example). For them hunting is a secondary source of food. Such environments are relatively tolerant of hunting failures. However, the subarctic is a specialised ecosystem with large numbers of a few species and little edible vegetation (mainly summer berries). The Dunne-za are therefore primarily hunters, their traditional diet coming from large, dispersed, land mammals (moose and caribou), supplemented by smaller prey (beaver, rabbits, grouse and fish) (Paine, 1971: 162–3). Brody estimates that the Dunne-za people harvest between 450 and 900 grams of meat per person per day, much more than the Huaorani. The cold and dependence on meat mean that Dunne-za hunting has to be highly energy efficient. Mistakes are costly.

Despite this, until very recently (1970s), the Dunne-za shared the hunter-gatherer tendency to be confident that they can feed themselves. This confidence depends on three principles of practice, movement, open access and flexibility. Expert knowledge of animals and the environment and the development of efficient hunting techniques yield reliable supplies of meat for everyone in a long-term, sustainable way. The taking of prey is limited by the principle of least effort (hunters giving up an area or species long before their predation affects the capacity of the prey to reproduce (Paine, 1971: 159)) and also by restraint, by not killing more than is needed. Where there are only a few species, sustainability depends on being able to move between areas. So the critical issue for the Dunne-za is being able to move freely within their very extensive hunting grounds. Brody gets them to draw the boundaries of their hunting grounds on maps. These show huge areas, including places which may have only been visited once in a lifetime. The whole of these areas are thought of as stores, or 'banks', of food which may be taken when needed. On this basis, hunter-gatherers appear unconcerned about shortage and enthusiastically share food, behaving 'as if they had it made' (Sahlins, 1968: 86).

Central to successful living by hunting for thousands of years is this method of responding to difficulty by flexibly changing species and/or hunting area. Brody (1986: 35–48) tells of hunting trips conducted in a spirit of improvisation and willingness to follow any favourable circumstances which crop up. A 'state of attentive waiting' is typical (Brody, 1986: 43). So although there may be an intention to kill, say, a cow moose (the largest, but relatively uncommon, prey), other smaller animals (rabbits, trout) will be taken on the way, if the opportunity presents itself. Initial searching for tracks is apparently random. Failure to pick up clues to the whereabouts of large prey simply prompts moving to another area. The basic assumptions are that alternative areas are accessible and that the prey they contain has not been taken already.

However, for five centuries, the aboriginal population of North America has confronted the successive frontiers of European colonisation. This has imposed powerful competition for the resources of the land from people operating a different economic system. Europeans cleared forested land for farming and hastened the near extinction of the buffalo whose northern range once extended into Dunne-za territory. The Dunne-za responded to competitive pressure by withdrawing westwards further and further into their 'reserve' hunting grounds, the eastern foothills of the Rocky Mountains. Provided there has been animal-rich territory available to retreat into, the Dunne-za have moved away.

They have always known how to change. Willingness to move is only one of their ways of flexibly responding to difficulties. They have survived by developing an economy and technology based on traditional values and skills, but accommodated to the whites' world of money, markets and the modern state. The fur trade, well established by 1800 by the whites, is now thought of by the Dunne-za as essential to their economy. It partly explains their English name, the Beaver. It reinforces their traditional skills (Brody, 1986: 56–7, 2001). Over centuries, they have adopted guns, horses, metal traps, snare wire, plastic sheeting, pick-up trucks, chainsaws, electricity, store-bought groceries, and now take radios with them when hunting. But none of this has displaced skills such as tracking, making snow shoes and walking long distances in them.

A series of white man's 'frontiers' have whittled away at the land, the animals and the Dunne-za's opportunities to continue moving away. The nineteenth century saw farming and railways extended ever westwards, bringing homesteaders and several gold rushes. The indigenous peoples were confined to living and hunting on reservations. Essentially this amounted to conquest. During the twentieth century the whole region has been rapidly opened up. White farms expanded rapidly between 1900–20, followed by the growth of white trappers during the 1920s and 30s. Prospecting for coal, minerals, oil and gas has gone on for a century or more. Today the whole area of the traditional hunting grounds is riddled with roads, the roughest of which can be travelled by four-wheel drive pickups. The current incursion results from a synergy between the temporary access roads cut deep into the forest for oil and gas prospectors, and the weekend leisure of sports hunting by urban Canadians with pick-ups, high-powered rifles and poor navigation and tracking skills. (Sports hunters kill four times as many moose in two months as the Dunne-za kill for food in a year (Brody, 1986: 231–7).

In the face of these incursions, Dunne-za confidence has faltered. A central figure in Brody's story, Joseph Patsah, an elder, encounters a seismic drilling camp, with its airstrip and a 'hippie' squatters' cabin, in Quarry, his most remote and precious trapping lands, and is overtaken with pessimism (Brody, 1986: 9–13, 181, 224–5). There is no more time, no more room for the white man's intrusion. When asked by a white hunter for advice about where to hunt, he jokes ruefully: 'Deer, moose, chickens, cattle, pigs, everything gone to the west. Pretty soon everything will be gone. All the meat' (Brody, 1986: 271–2).

Confrontation between renewable meat and fossil fuels

Here we have an example of a hunter-gatherer people being destroyed by an industrial society whose emergence was possible, as explained in the last chapter, because of agriculture. Rationally calculating opportunity costs and assessing risks, the Dunne-za people skilfully invest in renewably harvesting the abundant animals. Their energy comes from meat. In a subarctic environment, farming was not an attractive or necessary option. Although the Dunne-za are rational, energy efficient and do no irreparable damage to the land or its animals, their method has limit conditions. The most important for this discussion is maintaining a balance between the rate of killing animals and sufficient territory to allow them to reproduce. The higher the rate, the bigger the territory required. Joseph's pessimism flows from realising that, due to the activity of whites, the rate is going up while the territory is effectively getting smaller.

The incursions of whites show that the sustainability of hunting has depended on a political condition of low inter-societal competition between people of similar, low social power. Europeans could colonise America because they had a huge power advantage, in weapons, organisation and numbers, derived ultimately from a long history of agriculture. Their technology was superior as a technology of conquest. But the ability to dominate and dispossess non-industrial people is only one criterion of technical superiority. Their power techniques were honed in the long history of intense territorial competition within Europe itself. Expansion into the Americas was partly motivated by attempts to gain advantages over rivals, exemplified by the struggle for Canada between France and Britain. As mentioned in the previous chapter, European technical development has been driven substantially by the strategic and military implications of competition between states. That competitiveness created pressure on all parties to expand their resources and continuously improve their effectiveness. The end result is dependence on inanimate power and energy from non-renewable fuels.

The 'energy frontier' in British Columbia is a manifestation of this dynamic. The Alaska Highway was built during the Second World War. The Alaska gas pipeline project is intended to help the USA be self-sufficient in energy. Canadian business and government wants to be made rich by selling fossil fuels to the US. It is therefore unsurprising that the 1978 proposal to lay 400 miles of pipe straight across their lands should have galvanised the Dunne-za into realising that withdrawal is no longer possible. This project was a lightening conductor for the accumulated frustrations of repeated incursions from forestry, farming, hydroelectric flooding, oil and gas drilling, road building and sports hunting.

Here two approaches to the human predicament of anticipating future needs confront one another, shaping maps and dreams. Small bands of aboriginal hunters, in situations of low inter-societal competition, learned to deal with the future by limiting needs and renewable resource harvesting. They are confident that the resources will be there if the land is left untouched. That is what they dream and record on land-use maps. On the other hand, Americans and Europeans face the future anxiously, imagining resources will not be there in the future unless they take steps to accumulate, store and defend them. They try to secure the future by expanding their resource base and establishing exclusive access to it. Their dreams are of self-sufficiency based on economic growth and monopolies. Theirs are the fears and dreams of the elites of settled societies with long histories of agriculture, political apparatuses, stratification systems and high levels of inter-societal competition. Maps are maps of political frontiers and territorial prizes.

However, like all methods, the success of the European way of securing the future has limit conditions, natural, political and economic. Long struggles reduce fields of competitors to those capable of defending their independence. At this point, further efforts at elimination become so costly that cooperation seems more likely to pay. The creation of the European Union following a period of world wars (1914–45) is a clear example. Expansion by colonisation becomes less attractive once the valuable territories have been mopped up. The military contribution to domination is expensive and tends to be replaced by economic and cultural techniques. An example is white fur traders supplying alcohol to force addicted native trappers to visit trading posts to sell their furs. Finally, renewal and growth of natural resources by geographical extension, and intensified extraction, must stop when those resources are exhausted. All technologies have to adjust to the consequences of the way they have been used in the past. Even technologies which have been successful as technologies of conquest become unsustainable and have to change their tune.

The Dunne-za can take some encouragement from the happy coincidence that just as they are experiencing the limit conditions of their way of life, created by land pressure from industrialism, industrialism itself is hitting its own limit conditions. Both are at a threshold of sustainability. Neither Dunne-za 'flexible movement', nor white industrial expansionism, can rely on the 'comforting vastness' of the Canadian wilderness. Just like agriculture (discussed in Chapter 3), industrialism has negative feedback consequences, as it encourages demands which cannot be met without depleting the resource base. Picture the sports hunter's pick-up travelling the access roads of the oil prospectors, burning the petrol they work so hard to extract. Burn more means extract more. Sustainability by resource renewal, which the Dunne-za have done for thousands of years, has become vital for securing the future of industrialism. The possibility exists, therefore, that if whites can see that it is in their interests to conserve resources, limit wants (like sports hunting), reduce demand for non-renewable fuels, slowing the rate of use, and develop the use of renewables, the pressure on Dunne-za lands might relax.

Joseph's sense that soon it will be too late nevertheless acknowledges that there is some time left to turn the forces of environmental destruction. Early in 2001, California's Silicon Valley suffered power failures and responded by importing electricity from British Columbia. Contemporary Canadian energy companies (for example Purcell Energy) naturally view the future demand for natural gas-fired electricity generation as likely to grow over the next 20 years (www.purcellenergy.com, 2001). So the energy frontier is as vibrant as it was when Brody lived with the Dunne-za in the late 1970s. But since then the postmodern sense that industrial energy consumption may have caused irreversible environmental damage, and be ultimately self-defeating, has grown. Time is short for preserving the Dunne-za's hunting environment, but it is becoming clear that it could be ominously short for industrialism too.

Whether industrialism can be made environmentally sustainable will depend on the choices and actions of many peoples. Relations with the environment depend on where people think their interests lie. Like the Dunne-za, we are all involved in making assessments of the costs and benefits of sticking with established technological practices or experimenting with new ones. Articulating the old with the new goes on all the time. The economic argument, which might persuade industrial interests to refrain from the utter destruction of the Dunne-za's lands and way of life, is that the resources of materials and culture are more valuable as potential for the future than squandered on short-term economic growth. Of course, there is a moral argument about the injustice of destroying a people which is persuasive to many, but the economic argument appeals to the self-interest of the powerful and morally unresponsive and is therefore strategically more important. Rather than pursue impossible dreams of exclusiveness and self-sufficiency, the future might be better secured by policies encouraging technological pluralism, the maintaining of alternatives, within relations of inclusiveness and mutual dependency – typically postmodern dreams. There are choices to be made, motives to make them and sufficient time for them to have positive effects. It is because this is so that the natural environment and technology only condition how we live and are not sufficient to explain what we do or how events turn out.

Part III

The Concept of Culture

CHAPTER 5

What Does Culture Explain?

We have now reached a major turning point in this book as we begin to consider the concepts of 'culture', 'action', and 'social structure', which are the primary concerns of anthropologists and sociologists. We are moving to our own turf, so to speak, and can explore the specific contributions of the social scientist to the explanation of human life. Although we do not want to draw too sharp a distinction, it is fair to say that anthropology (particularly in America) has concentrated attention on culture whilst sociology has focused on social structure, and both have had to reckon with action. This chapter shows you why all students of social phenomena, be they anthropologists, sociologists or historians, with their respective emphases, are nevertheless dealing with a common realm defined by the interaction between culture, action and social structure.

The easiest way to begin characterising this realm is to discuss the role of culture in social explanation (Figure 5.1). However, this book aims to show that explaining social life requires all five concepts which we are discussing. So, sociologists, historians and anthropologists need each other's insights, and social scientists need to pay atten-

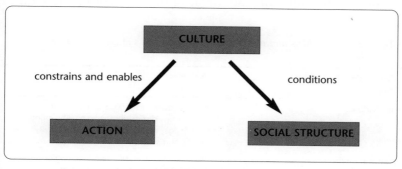

Figure 5.1 What the social sciences contribute to social explanation: culture

tion to natural scientists, biologists and psychologists who tell us a lot about the properties of individuals and nature.

The story so far

Before proceeding we can pause to summarise our progress. We have considered the place of two concepts in social explanation, 'individuals' and 'nature' (Table 5.1). We have explored what is involved in referring to these as causal forces in shaping social regularities and patterns of behaviour. In each case we have argued that the concept refers to a fundamentally important factor in social explanation. On the one hand, individuals, with their bodies, minds, innate dispositions, virtues and unique differences from one another, are always playing their part. Likewise, the natural environment is always at least conditioning social interaction. Individuals and the natural environment are irreducible and have a degree of autonomy, that is, a capacity to exercise an independent influence on social life. Each is consequential, or matters, in social explanation.

On the other hand, we have argued that there are real difficulties in trying to explain social life by referring to these concepts as though they were the only things that matter for social explanation, singly or in combination. They are *necessary* elements in social explanations and must figure in our hypotheses. But they are not *sufficient* elements, that is, they cannot do the job on their own. Thus a very important implication of what we have been saying is that social explanation must always involve showing how the various kinds of causes interact. Moreover, these factors will have varying degrees of importance in different cases. In principle, we ought, to be interested in not just the different kinds of factor influencing what we want to

Table 5.1 Individuals and nature: necessary, but not sufficient for explaining collective phenomena

Relatively autonomous causal forces	Properties
Individuals	Biology, body, instincts, species characteristics, psychology, dispositions, personality, emotions, knowledge, rationality, technical creativity, virtues and so on
Natural environment	Physical, chemical, biological, ecological, geographical, mechanical and so on

explain, but also the relative strength of each factor. But, for now, that is an issue we will put to one side.

So far we have looked at explanatory methods which analyse the interaction between individuals and their environment, by treating people as either determined by forces which they do not control, or as exercising control by using their rationality, empirical knowledge and technical creativity. This latter form of explanation involves a mode of thinking about how actors interpret their situations and give them meaning. But, although it recognises the importance of meaning for human action, its theory of meaning is universal and acultural. It implies that all people interpret the world in the same way, as they make the calculations and manipulate the information demanded by the problems they are trying to solve. It explains differences in what people do as the result of the variable quality of the information available, and their relative success in being rational and avoiding technical errors. But, when trying to explain social behaviour individualistically or naturalistically, we found that it was virtually impossible to explain what people do by simply conceptualising them as rational problem-solvers.

So we can approach the idea of culture by asking if the differences between the ways in which various individuals and collectivities interpret the world are no more than differences between the well informed and ill informed, the rational and the irrational, those who know the truth and the mistaken? Especially in the light of the discussion of technological choice and the idea of progress in the last chapter, the answer would seem to be 'no'. This is because mediating the forces of nature is not simply a matter of technical calculation and coming to the one correct conclusion (Figure 5.2). There are different kinds of knowledge besides technical know-how. Moreover, interpretation involves the use of particular frames of reference and making judgements involves using values. Meaning does not just involve the cold reason of logic but also the hot influence of emotion. Think of the depth of feeling underlying Huaorani technical choices, for example (discussed in Chapter 4).

If one answers 'no' to the question of whether differences in people's interpretation of the world are due only to a differential distribution of irrationality, ignorance and error, it is because one recognises that variations between interpretations can be evidence of the existence of cultures. Every culture makes those who subscribe to it share certain socially important characteristics. Cultures collectivise individuals and in the same process makes them different from

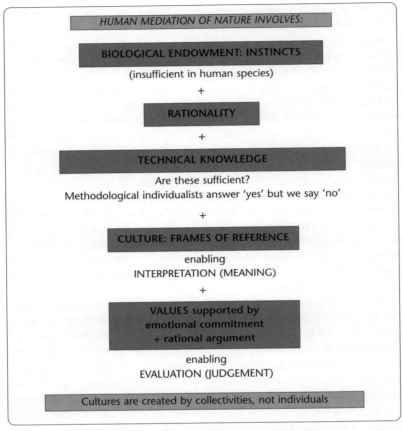

Figure 5.2 What enables humans to mediate the forces of the natural environment?

others, although we must guard against thinking of cultures as separate and isolated entities neatly corresponding to particular 'societies'.

So the first thing to say about a culture is that it puts a population of individuals in the same boat, in some respects. If you want to explain why certain things are done repeatedly by a certain population, for example responding to environmental problems in a certain way, it makes sense to consider if these social regularities are due to the culture they share. We would be foolish not to include in our explanation anything which has collectivising effects. Certainly culture has such effects, although we must always query if it provides the total explanation. Not least we need to ask what generates the cultural features that we decide are causally powerful. We cannot simply take their existence for granted.

What does 'culture' mean?

So far we have talked about cultures in the plural, to bring out their collectivising effects and the creation of differences between populations. But now we must define 'culture' in general. A good guide is *Keywords* by R. Williams (1976). It reminds us that, in ordinary language, the term 'culture' is loaded with evaluative connotations to do with social status. It can be associated with claims to social respectability by persons with a certain education, who believe they possess rare powers of critical judgement about the finer or higher spheres of achievement. In this sense, culture is associated with the arts, refinement, cultivation (reminding us of very early horticultural uses of the term). Or it may be used to claim respectability for subordinated or threatened traditions, communities and practices, in order to improve their position in the competition for resources. Here the term is used to refer to whole ways of life (such as that of the Dunneza or the Huaorani) felt to be at risk. In the contemporary world, being cultured or having a culture is politically important, and we ourselves might want to challenge the snobberies implied in the first usage, or defend the possessors of a culture, in the second sense, from having it incorporated into homogenising modernity. But, for our purposes here, we need a broader concept of culture, one which will help to explain why the term can be used in these evaluative, socially competitive ways. What is at stake in such struggles?

Transmission and learning

The stakes are high because of the way human beings are. They have a few, highly generalised instincts, which are no match for the complex sophistication of the instincts of other species. When we are born, we are utterly dependent on others and the few automatic responses we do have (crying, smiling, grasping, sucking and so on) are designed to get others to take care of us. There then follows an extraordinarily long period of learning, when what is learnt is language and culture. Basic to culture is that it is transmitted non-biologically and has to be learned.

Speaking biologically, the human species has invested in developing its capacity to learn culture rather than in the specialised instincts typical of other species. Culture is made up of the accumulated lessons of past experience, so that we can all benefit from it and do not forever have to reinvent the wheel. Birds instinctively know how to build their nests, but architects can rely on much inter-generationally transmitted knowledge to help them design their buildings. Culture is more than a straight functional alternative for instinct, however, since it offers greater possibilities of flexibly and speedily adapting to changed circumstances. Architects can improvise with new materials if a traditional supply disappears, but the bird that instinctively makes its nest from mud cannot, when faced with a drought, shift quickly to using material quite unlike mud, such as leaves, which could be functional for nest building. Lacking culture, the bird must move to an area where mud is available or fail to nest. Culture, by contrast, offers humans both *history* and an open future. Sociology and anthropology, as disciplines dealing with culture (and social structure), are always involved with problems where the explanation must reveal how the past influences the present and the present the future. In the social sciences, non-biological, historical processes (some but not all of which are cultural) are the equivalent of the evolutionary processes of biology.

Thus, one way of characterising 'culture' is to say that it consists of processes and mechanisms which enable the past to be carried into the present and future. These processes enable people to live in a world with some degree of continuity; they always have some way to begin dealing with whatever they find themselves having to do. A major feature of culture is the use of ways of formulating the lessons from the past in transmittable, teachable and practical form.

At the heart of cultural methods for giving us the past, lies the use of signs to represent experience and the world and the development of rules, general principles, formulae and 'recipes'. That is why language is so highly developed in humans and also why special representational systems such as mathematics are invented. Memory techniques, writing systems, libraries, encyclopedias, information storage and retrieval systems and the Internet are symptomatic of our being culture-dependent. But culture would not work if it were just some enormous shed, electronic or not, filled with the lessons of the past. We need some way of deciding the relevance of these lessons for the present. Given that past and present are not identical, there is a universal cultural problem of matching up the present case to some past cases and generalising from them. Generalisation is valuable but also perilous and much cultural energy has been devoted to trying to improve its reliability. 'When is it safe to generalise?' and 'When ought the rule to be broken?' are culturally generic questions.

Cultural production and elaboration

Implicit in this is that cultures are collective products, produced over long periods of time by large numbers of individuals, most of them now dead (Archer, 1995: 72–3). Culture enables their influence to continue after they have gone. But their influence is *only* influence. Cultural products provide the wherewithal for shaping our activity but they do not actually shape it. Cultural resources have to be applied, they do not apply themselves. Cultural production is the byproduct of this application. It is a process of applying what has been learned to ever-changing conditions and modifying or elaborating it.

When we learn cultural lessons, especially as children, we are given a way of representing the world as a world of a particular kind, classified and organised in a particular way, and which is recommended by those who teach us. It is a preferred version and provides a starting point for our own cultural elaboration as we try to use it to conduct our lives. More than that, our early learning provides some basic, enduring, mental furniture which we will share with others with similar upbringing. As Pierre Bourdieu (1990) insists, it creates deeply ingrained, general dispositions to interpret our later experience in particular ways. People with a common upbringing tend to share not only particular ideas and images, but also styles and methods of thinking and imagining.

It is in this sense that humans are caught up not only in the natural world, but also in the 'second nature' of culture. They have no choice in the matter. Moreover, all this effort put into teaching and learning represents an investment (even if the young do not volunteer for it) in a way of defining and dealing with the world, which may make people rather defensive (or assertive) when confronted with other ways of confronting reality. This claim is reinforced when we remember that among the things we learn are our identities (who we are) and what we really value. Cultural learning brings in train commitment and a deep conditioning of the emotions.

But we must remember that culture cannot exercise its influence without being used and when it is used it has to be applied, interpreted, elaborated and thus changed. Although we do not have any choice about having to use culture to live, culture cannot do our living for us and we cannot but use our creative and discretionary powers. Culture is a bitter-sweet realm of human self-determination.

How culture binds: (a) socialisation

In general, culture cannot be taken as a fixed force which makes us do things. It is not that sort of mechanism. But it can have compulsory effects, particularly on individuals during their primary socialisation and over social phenomena of relatively short duration, where the cultural framework is set and can, for the purposes of analysis, be taken as given. In such circumstance, individuals may certainly be very strongly constrained by it. This is clear if one focuses on the role of culture in the formation of individuals. Obviously, culture contributes greatly in the process of forming individuals, but this truism has provided the basis for some theorists to make a much stronger claim that it is culture which integrates individuals into society. Theorists as different as Talcott Parsons and Louis Althusser have held that social organisation itself is only possible because individuals are socialised to be committed to a culture. This shapes their aspirations, identity and values, patterning their activity into socially productive forms. However, this sort of theory tends to treat culture as a given, emphasising the strength of the mechanisms whereby individuals are hooked up to it, in order to explain its constraining force. These mechanisms tend to reduce the creative and discretionary powers of individuals so that they are imagined to relay culture rather than apply it. On this basis, it is tempting to try to explain why people behave in patterned ways by saying that they are programmed by their socialisation. This is a popular and relevant tactic when trying to explain, for example, the differences between the behaviour of men and women, within a particular society in a particular period. But it does depend on taking the culture as a given and ignoring the scope for acting against type.

How culture binds: (b) the autonomy of culture

The second broad view of how culture binds focuses on the materials and processes of cultural forms and practices themselves. An important feature of culture is that its media, methods, formulations, representations, ideas and images, by virtue of being given cultural form, acquire a large measure of autonomy. That is, they acquire properties of their own which are not the properties of the people who first produced them or, later, try to use them. These things have objective properties, which then feed back to condition the action of those who try to use them. In what follows, we want to focus on these properties because they are fundamental to explanation in terms of culture where we might hypothesise that it is culture which makes people behave in certain ways. Explanation in terms of culture does not consist of only seeing it as a kind of environment, rather like the natural environment, which imposes itself on individuals. Culture consists of practices, which have to be actively pursued by actors who use them for their purposes. So culture should be viewed as providing actors with ways of doing things, as facilitating and enabling action. But although such practices enable, they also constrain.

The logic of cultural systems, practices and objects

In general terms, what we have to consider is the constraining force of the systematic logic of cultural practices, traditions, cultural objects and ideas. By 'logic', we mean any internally generated properties, which both set limits on what can be done and provide opportunities for elaboration of particular kinds. By 'internal', we mean that the various kinds of cultural 'stuff' are made up of elements which fit together in certain ways. Take a very simple example: $2 + 2 = 4$. This describes relations between numbers which are governed by the rules of addition and the meaning of the concepts 'two', 'four', 'addition' and 'equals', as well as the meaning of the symbols '2', '4', '+' and '='. There are right and wrong ways of using these concepts and symbols. What do you make of $4 + 2 = 2$ or $= 4 + 2$ 2? Elementary arithmetic is a cultural system with objective features, which are stated as rules of the practice. So, for example, you can be examined on it and can do it well or badly.

The rules of arithmetic seem pretty universal, although there is a debate about how culturally relative mathematics is; perhaps there are several mathematics, not just one (Bloor, 1976). But even if most cultural systems are relative, not universal, that does not weaken the claim that they have objective internal properties and exercise a relatively autonomous power over action. Take languages for example; each language demands that those who learn and speak it conform to its way of fitting the parts of speech together, its vocabulary and its pronunciation. It has to sound right and, if written, look right. But what counts as correct depends on how the system has been elaborated and what the people who use it reinforce in each other's practice. There is a large element of cultural arbitrariness about this. But despite this arbitrariness, once a way of doing things has become conventionalised and institutionalised, nobody seriously doubts the objective, constraining force of languages, or that there are many different ones.

But all cultural practices are like this; they are many, internally complex, may be mutually incompatible with one another, include a large measure of arbitrariness and are subject to conventionalisation and institutionalisation. Everybody is engaged in cultural practices and all of them have internal properties which constrain the people doing them. It is not just the important-sounding practices of mathematics and languages. For example, think what constrains you when you have a meal or throw a party. You will be using ideas that you have picked up about how these things should be done. You will be aware of certain rules, or general principles, which guide you in the choices you make about, for instance, what times of day are appropriate or what qualifies as appropriate food. Such rules describe a preferred way of doing such things and, given that we do not make up our activity from scratch, these rules constrain us, conditioning what we do. Cultural rules offer templates shaping our action. They simplify life with their ready-made formulae but, at the same time, these formulae have internal complexities which can make life difficult. For example, is it possible to have a party without any form of drink? And if not, can any drink become the basis of a social occasion? The Huaorani drink manioc beer together and the Dunne-za mark autumn with alcoholic binges (but never drink when hunting). Tea party, coffee morning, sherry party, wine and cheese – what about a water party? Perhaps not!

The deeper reaches of culture

The party example suggests that, although cultural practices vary enormously, there may be general properties of parties which unite people across their different conventions and traditions. So if you are going to have a party, you need something for people to share in order to symbolise their participation and interest in one another's well-being. Contributing drink ('Bring a bottle!'), holding a glass with something in it ('Do you need a refill?'), exchanging rounds in the pub, officiating in the distribution of the drink (pouring the tea) and so on, have their equivalents in many cultures, because drink is what it is, and the problems of achieving sociable occasions are what they are.

There seems to be a set of basic conditions which have to be met if you want to throw a party. Similarly, if you want to communicate using any language, or use clay to make pots, or make maps, you cannot do just as you like. What you do will be constrained by the objective possibilities for relating things to each other, available to anybody attempting these or any other kinds of task. To make pots you have to follow the properties of clay – workable while damp, but unworkable when too wet or too dry. Similarly, any language must offer sufficient parts of speech to allow objects and actions to be described and evaluated. Making maps must use some system for projecting three-dimensional space onto a two-dimensional surface. Just as parties do not work well without something doing the function of drink, so potting needs something to control the dampness of clay, language will not work without something doing the work of nouns and verbs, and maps need something to represent gradients, mountains and valleys.

At this level, we find universal cultural problems setting tasks which individual cultures solve in different ways. So there are many languages and traditions of potting and mapping, but each must satisfy the minimum requirements of any functioning language, potting technique or projection scheme. The way in which culture constrains action flows from how the material and symbolic elements of cultural practices fit together: vocabulary and grammar, pots and clay, maps and projection, parties and drink; in each case these are *internally related* elements of cultural practices.

This has several implications for explaining patterns of social behaviour. When trying to explain some bit of behaviour, it is often helpful to be able to relate it to other bits of behaviour by knowing the relevant cultural context. We can go some way by identifying the cultural practices or games being pursued and finding out what their rules are. We can benefit from finding out how people fit different games together. Participants are often consciously aware of how they go about this and can describe it to us. Much anthropology is devoted to identifying these kinds of cultural context and using them to make sense of patterned behaviour. But we also have to consider the nature of the games being played, why the games are the way they are and why people play them in the ways that they do. These questions are about the deeper levels at which practices are organised and the dispositions and orientations of the people operating them. Since these act as the 'spectacles' through which they look at the world, people tend to be less informed and informative about them. They themselves may not 'see' the underlying frameworks which structure how they view the world. Some analysis is required.

Ideas and beliefs, consistency and contradictions, rationalisation

When we turn from considering cultural practices and objects to the other major slice of culture, ideas and beliefs, the same principle, that you cannot do just anything you like, applies. Now we are faced by culture in the form of theories, sets of propositions and arguments. The internal relations involved here are those of logic rather than the requirements of practices such as organising a party. These internal relations are themselves the object of reflection and elaboration. Much culture is devoted to reflecting on and developing culture itself as a semi-autonomous realm.

This cultural reflexiveness and elaboration produces various 'traditions', ways of doing cultural work, of thinking and imagining, centring on particular origins, exemplars, institutions and leaders. For example, ideas and objects may be produced within and ascribed to an entity, such as a school, workshop, imprint, region, or manner, which suggests that they are representative of some tradition of thought and/or practice. Traditions are formed when cultural practices and ideas come to have themselves as their point of reference and leads to the formulation of rules and criteria of conformity. These define what doing it correctly amounts to and what sorts of innovation are acceptable. This tends to happen to any practice which seems to pay off well enough for long enough.

For example, the early centuries of Christianity saw a struggle to come to terms with two contradictory propositions about Jesus: 'He was a man who was once living and was killed' and 'He is God and is alive'. Given that the concepts of 'man' and 'God', 'killed' and 'alive' are mutually exclusive, how can Jesus simultaneously be both man and God, alive and dead? Many argued that if he was a man, he could only be a dead man and not a living God. However, they lost the argument, because at the first Nicene Council in 325 AD, the bishops decreed that Jesus was indeed both, and that what looked like a contradiction was, in fact, the 'divine mystery'. If both propositions were true, logic demanded that they come to this conclusion. The Nicene Creed became the most influential formal statement of Christian belief. The point here is that the bishops were forced into action by the logic of their beliefs about Jesus and the need to resolve finally the scandal of a contradiction, which they did by declaring it a mystery.

In this case, the contradiction was between two sets of concepts. But, equally, people may find inconsistencies between ideas about the world and their experience of it. This gap is fundamental to the process of revising our beliefs about the world. This is not just a matter of improving empirical knowledge through experience. It also applies to our ideas about the extent to which the reality of our lives matches up to our ideals. But, in all cases, formulating beliefs into sets of logically related propositions makes them available for inspection and has a tendency to reveal contradictions or gaps in supporting arguments. It also facilitates separating the quality of beliefs from those who subscribe to them. We can disapprove of the Nazis because of their appalling and murderous racial policies but, perhaps uncomfortably, recognise as sound, on health grounds, the anti-smoking policy they advocated in the 1930s. Questions of truth can be separated from questions of loyalty or identity. We can acknowledge that bad people can have (some) good ideas.

However, the most systematic kind of cultural self-reflection is the process of rationalisation. Rationalisation is what happens when people try to make their ideas more consistent, accurate, relevant and comprehensive. Rationalisation is essentially objective and unending, therefore it tends to push at the limits set by traditions, usually to the dismay of traditionalists. Rationalisation can be moderate or ruthless. Notice how in the example of the early Christianity, the bishops did not question the truth of either of the two contradictory propositions. They applied rational criticism to remove a contradiction between two fundamental beliefs but did not go as far as to criticise these fundamental beliefs themselves. It was precisely because these beliefs were exempt from criticism that there was a contradiction to resolve in the first place. Aspects of their belief were protected from rationalisation by their sacred status.

However, rationalisation does not limit itself automatically. Thus, the practice of formulating ideas and beliefs in propositional form reveals objective properties and exposes them to logical analysis and the tests of consistency and sufficient evidence. Such analysis explores how the elements of belief fit together, and, where the fit is poor, tends to galvanise people into elaboration, revision and research. Similarly, many people have found it useful to separate analytically the question of the moral status of believers, from the question of the truth of their belief. Others have found the precision of measurement invaluable. These are all examples of rationalising techniques for enhancing the effectiveness of culture as a resource. Nothing is necessarily sacrosanct and immune to the reconstructive force of rationalisation.

Whenever we think hypothetically, ask 'what if ...?' questions, speculate about future possibilities, try to imagine how things could be different, playfully juxtapose unusual combinations and invent metaphors and jokes, we are exploring the logic of our repertoire of ideas and representations and, at least informally, rationalising them. This is not to say that all people are embroiled in the finer points of critical methods or that rationalisation is inevitable. It is often resisted. But it is to say that questions of the fit between ideas, other ideas, experience, practice and the social and moral status of the people involved are always there to be coped with in one way or another. There are two major alternatives to rationalisation as ways of deciding about the acceptability of ideas favoured by supporters of traditions; these are tests of collective identity ('this is what *we* believe') and tests of authority ('this is what the parent, leader, priest, expert or teacher says').

Conclusion

The relatively autonomous properties of culture are summarised in Figure 5.3. As we initially suggested, discussing culture reveals something fundamental about the subject matter of the social sciences. We said that along with structure, culture was the product of social and historical processes. It has to be explained by reference to these processes. It does not originate itself but is produced by actors under natural and social structural conditions. Therefore culture is certainly necessary for social explanation but cannot by itself be sufficient (see Figure 5.4). Culture shows us that social reality is historical. As social scientists, we have to get to grips with such historical processes if we are to explain social life. This means that social scientists are always

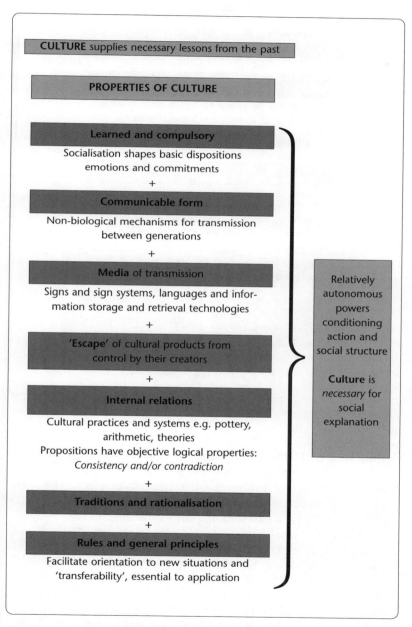

Figure 5.3 Summary: the relative autonomy of culture – how culture works

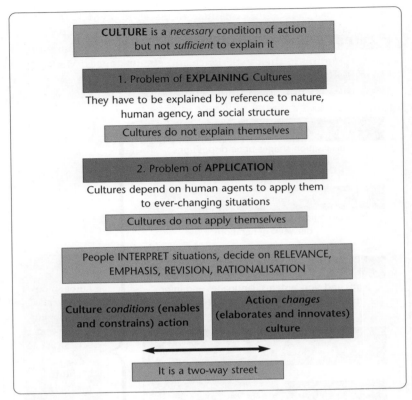

Figure 5.4 Why culture is not sufficient

dealing with problems where the social behaviour to be explained is conditioned by the results, or outcomes, of previous social behaviour. Culture is one set of processes where this takes place. The social sciences are therefore faced by a reality where the object to be explained also plays a part in doing the explaining.

As a rule for social explanation, Emile Durkheim (1982) recommended that we explain the social by reference to the social. This is because social behaviour has effects which condition social behaviour. It feeds back into itself. But this does not mean that our explanations in terms of culture (or social structure) are circular. Circularity is avoided for two reasons. First, the culture that does the conditioning and the cultural practice to be explained are distinguished by a difference of *time*. So the behaviour which does the explaining is not the same behaviour as is being explained. And second, as Margaret Archer (1995) makes clear, the mode in which the past impacts on the present is that of influence, filtered by the creative elaboration of actors responding to their experience and circumstances. Marx (1967: 10) captured this situation by suggesting that although men make history, they do not do so under conditions of their own choosing and they cannot evade the influence of the past.

CHAPTER 6

Testing the Explanatory Value of Culture

Introduction

By now, readers will be familiar with the general form of our discussions of the necessity and insufficiency for social explanation of each of the concepts with which this book deals. We are choosing empirical cases which offer favourable opportunities to show that each concept is necessary, yet cannot do all the explanatory work by itself. It is particularly important to make the latter point in relation to the concepts central to, and most enthusiastically supported by, the social sciences. Indicating the insufficiency of individuals and nature to explain social phenomena involved showing, among other things, that culture is a sort of environment which conditions thought and action. The previous chapter then argued that culture is clearly a very powerful collectivising force with a high level of autonomy. So while one might find it easy to resist methodological individualism and environmental determinism, the temptation to explain everything in terms of culture is seductive.

Certainly there have been many attempts to give culture an ultimate status when explaining social phenomena. It has even been argued, most famously by the German philosopher, Hegel (1956), that human history as a whole has been driven by a logically necessary sequence of ideas. First he claimed that ideas drive the development of ideas, so sophisticated ideas are only thinkable if preceded by earlier, unsophisticated ones. For example, the idea of democracy is said to depend on earlier concepts of tyranny and slavery. Second, he claimed that it is ideas (such as democracy) which enable change in the way people live (the actual development of democracies). In this way, culture is said to be responsible for historical development. Or, as mentioned in the last chapter, culture (usually typified by religion and 'ultimate values') is said (by Talcott Parsons (1951) among others) to explain the existence of social order in society. These theories treat the objective logic of ideas as having compelling force. This logic imposes itself, rather like a force of nature.

Another prominent, if less grand, form of culturalism argues that social relations are best understood as relations between ideas; that is, as Peter Winch (1990) insisted, social relations are actually logical relations. From the truism that people use ideas of social relations in conducting their interactions, the argument moves on to claim that those ideas explain what people do. So social scientists need do no more than find out what people say are the ideas animating their activity. But, as Marx (Marx and Engels, 1964: 64) pointed out, you will not understand something like the complex net of relations typical of a capitalist economy by simply asking a shopkeeper. Social phenomena do not easily reduce to the logic of the ideas in the heads of the people caught up in them. Moreover, if you accept that explanations employing cultural factors have to deal with the central question of how cultural resources are applied, that is, related to cultural and non-cultural circumstances which already exist, then culturalism must be ruled out (see Figure 5.4).

However, although we argue that culture is insufficient, we do not want to understate its importance for social explanation. Indeed, the force of the argument against explaining everything in terms of culture will be increased by showing culture at its most powerful in explanation. We will start with a couple of examples from the field of 'race' relations where ideas which people might *consciously hold* could contribute to explaining one specific phenomenon (and might be thought sufficient). Then we will progress to looking at instances where a range of apparently disparate phenomena can be connected, and partly accounted for, with reference to a complex of beliefs which people may be *unaware they hold* (and are thereby shown to be necessary for explanation).

What can consciously held ideas explain?

Differential ethnic economic success, and differential treatment of mixed-'race' categories

The many recent Asian immigrants to the US have already overtaken substantial numbers of long-established Afro-Americans, on a number of indices of economic success. Why is this the case? Some commentators plausibly suggest cultural causes for the Asians' economic achievements. They value marital stability and extended family obligation, which means that large kin groups can assemble greater amounts of capital for business investment than could individual members on their own. They are prepared to sacrifice their own good for that of their kin group (providing cheap and compliant labour, facilitating successful, family-run enterprises). They value hard work and accept deferred rather than immediate gratification. In contrast, these commentators suggest that Afro-American ghetto culture is the obverse of this, which might seem to explain their economic failure (Waldinger, 1996).

Our second 'race'-related puzzle concerns differences in the treatment of mixed-'race' persons in different parts of the New World. In Latin America, the Caribbean and North America, miscegenation between white European colonisers and their African slaves resulted in a mixed-'race' population. However, in the North American English colonies, persons of mixed 'race', regardless of the relative proportion of black and white in their ancestry, were classed as black. Whereas in the Caribbean and the Spanish and Portuguese colonies of Latin America, those of mixed 'race' were allocated a separate category or categories of their own. (New Orleans, French-held for a time, also had a distinct mulatto category.)

How can we explain this pattern? One possibility is to look at differences in the religious ideas (part of the culture) of the colonists. The Latin Americans were Catholic and committed to the belief that the world was ordered hierarchically. This allowed them to recognise degrees of difference in people they wished to assert were inferior to themselves. In particular they could claim that others were inferior to themselves without having to assert that they were sub-human. In North America, however, the dominant religion was Protestantism, which stressed the equality of all human beings. To be consistent, North American Protestants had to choose between seeing non-whites as equal to themselves (ruled out if they were to be enslaved), or as not humans at all. There was no possibility of seeing them as some degree of lesser, but still human, beings, as Catholics could. Some commentators suggest this was one of the reasons why miscegenation was felt to be so much more of a sin by the North American Protestants than by the Catholic Latin Americans, for whom it had no connotations of bestiality. The extra sinfulness of mixed-'race' sex in the Protestant case may have led to the categorisation of all those of mixed 'race' as black – effectively denying their mixed-'race' status and thus that sinful sexual relations had taken place (Tannenbaum,1946; Diggs, 1953; Harris, 1970; Degler, 1971).

In both these examples, differences between ideas correlate with differences in behaviour and/or other ideas. Correlations suggest causal effects which play a necessary part in our explanations. But although these explanations may seem plausible, they have limits – even if their assumptions about the nature of the ideas in play are right. We have to question their sufficiency. In the first case, we still have to ask what causes the relatively weak commitment of Afro-Americans to marital stability and extended family obligation, deferred gratification and hard work, which such explanations allege. Possibly, the historical experience of forced family separations under slavery weakened the kinship and particularly marital commitments – although we have also seen in Chapter 2 how poor economic circumstances themselves contribute to a looseness of the ties between husbands and wives in the black underclass. Probably the experience of slavery means that working long hours, for white bosses, for low wages is less tolerable to blacks than to newly arrived Asians. Blacks may refuse, as a form of resistance and statement of self-worth, jobs which Asians, with their different history, perceive as a foot on the economic ladder. However, regardless of how they originated, differences in Asians' and Afro-Americans' cultural forms are not the only significant causal factor when accounting for their economic success and failure. We also need to consider differences in levels of racial discrimination against the two categories, the capital some Asian migrants were able to bring with them, their differential geographical distribution between the declining northwest and the economically expanding southwestern states and so on.

The completeness (that is, sufficiency) of an explanation in terms of (religious) beliefs alone is similarly limited in the second case. Firstly, we have already touched on the material fact of the exploitation of black slaves by white colonisers in explaining why whites choose not to see slaves as equal to themselves. However, explanation in terms of religious beliefs alone also fails because mixed-'race' categories are actually recognised in all the Caribbean islands, only some of which are Catholic. If there are cases where Protestants recognise mixed-'race' categories (that is, the correlation between type of religion and type of racial classification is not perfect), then the explanation, although generally promising, needs buttressing by some other kinds of cause.

One powerful material factor might be the impact on power relations of varying white to non-white population ratios in different places. Where whites were in a very small minority, they needed allies from outside their own ranks. These could be found by splitting the non-white population to produce one or more intermediate mixed-'race' categories who whites could, in some circumstances, encourage to ally with them against the (pure) black majority. This was the case in the Caribbean and Latin America, where we do find mixed-'race' categories, irrespective of religious differences. However, in the North American states, whites far outnumbered blacks and had less need to establish alliances with non-whites and overcome their religiously induced propensity to think in terms of black and white alone. This contributes to the absence of mixed-'race' categories we find there (Jordan, 1969).

In general, ideas/belief systems have 'causal powers' and as such explanatory relevance. The specific effects produced by the causal power of any given set of ideas/beliefs will depend on the characteristics of the particular circumstances in which they are mobilised, which will include more than merely 'other ideas and belief systems'. Ideas will have to be linked to non-ideational factors and the interaction between them specified. Where the causal powers of ideas and belief systems are a significant contributor to generating a particular phenomenon, they may well not be the sole causal factors, and hence not sufficient to explain the phenomenon.

Moreover, if we use a set of ideas/belief systems as part of the explanation, we must recognise that these ideas which do the explaining ought themselves to be explained. Otherwise we will simply be taking them as given, which they are not. Furthermore, it is not usually possible to explain ideas *entirely* by reference to other sets of overtly held ideas alone. However, as we will demonstrate next, beliefs that people can consciously articulate may well be linked to underlying systems of thought of which they are *unaware*.

Culture at full power! What can unconscious ideas explain?

We might talk of cultural explanation as at its most powerful when we can use it to make systematic causal links between a range of apparently unconnected spheres of behaviour and thought. To demonstrate culture operating at full power means going below the level at which people consciously make judgements and choices and give reasons for what they do. It involves going deeper than was necessary when explaining why Protestants, given their beliefs in the equality of man, were pushed to see and treat slaves as less than human, since they could not hold them to be both human and inferior. There we used actors' desire for logical consistency to explain their actions. But to demonstrate the conditioning force of culture at its strongest, we need cases where it is necessary to resort to its deeper reaches (which are most resistant to choice) to explain the phenomena (the patterns of thought and behaviour) we want to understand. This is the level of methods, paradigms, habits, biases, dispositions and generative principles, which powerfully pattern the workings of preference, imagination and reasoning. Here, where the very lenses through which people view the world are installed, the autonomy of culture, and hence its necessity for explanation, is at its most impressive.

The cases we need to show culture at its strongest must allow us to demonstrate that there are deep, underlying cultural relations capable of working very generally (although often unrecognised by those who use them) to organise a wide range of behaviour, preferences and beliefs. Useful cases for this 'necessity' testing might be ones where there are contradictions between two or more ideas held by particular people, where what people do contradicts the ideas they hold or where ideas or behaviour seem to be completely arbitrary. Cases of apparent arbitrariness, or contradiction between ideas, or ideas and behaviour, make us ask what might be sustaining the ideas or behaviour in question. We will have provided some examples of culture at full power if we can show that in fact there *is* some other kind of cultural logic operating at a more fundamental, barely conscious level of thought, which holds the contradictions together and explains what seems arbitrary.

Explaining arbitrary ideas and practices: Jewish dietary laws and the prohibition of pork

Everyone knows that Jews forbid themselves to eat pork. Many non-Jews, especially those who routinely eat pork, see no harm in doing so and find it difficult to understand why the Jews find it objectionable. Why do they place so much emphasis on not eating pork? This is the same sort of question we asked (in Chapter 4) about the Huaorani insistence on only using spears to kill peccaries. The anthropologist

Mary Douglas rejects explanations of Jewish dietary laws in terms of the intrinsic characteristics of the pig itself, such as its meat being particularly likely to go off in hot climates. Instead she argues that the prohibition can only be understood in relation to the Jews' fundamental belief that what is anomalous is polluting, and to their subscription to a complex classification of animal species in terms of which the pig (as a cloven-hoofed animal which does not chew the cud) is *category-crossing*. Other category-crossing creatures, such as shellfish (which live in water but lack fins and scales), are also taboo (Douglas, 1970, 1975, 1996).

In fact, uncovering that Judaism places considerable emphasis on classification as such, and that it generally rejects what is anomalous in terms of its classificatory schema (that is, which cross the boundaries of its classificatory boxes) facilitates understanding a wide range of apparently disparate features in the culture. In other words, there is something about the way that orthodox Jewish culture is put together

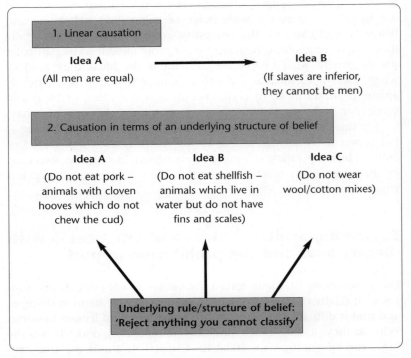

Figure 6.1 Two ways in which ideas cause other ideas

at a very basic level, which has implications for its characteristic beliefs and rules. This example shows that culture is multilayered or stratified; on the surface we find propositions which members of the culture can articulate about, say, what is permitted to be eaten or what one is allowed to wear. But these are generated by a cultural 'method' (a realist might call this a kind of causal mechanism) of which participants may be unaware, which makes a virtue of removing ambiguity. Douglas's analysis points to the possibility that ideas may generate other ideas, not just in terms of linear causation (holding idea A leads to holding idea B), but also in the sense that underlying structures of belief or cultural methods can generate a potential multiplicity of surface forms. The rules 'Do not eat pork' or 'Do not wear clothes containing more than one kind of material' are but particular instances of a more fundamental rule 'Reject anything you cannot classify.' Figure 6.1 summarises the difference between these two types of causation.

Explaining contradictions between belief and behaviour: the case of homophobic acceptance of gays

A study by Cunningham and Parker (1978) found that the heterosexual deck and engine room crew of a passenger ship were deeply hostile to the idea of homosexuality. Nevertheless they tolerated and had positive relations with the openly gay men who they interacted with on the ship. Although generally regarding gays as deviants, they accepted them, subject to very specific conditions. They had to be in certain occupations (waiters or hairdressers, not engine room or deck crew), not be in positions of authority and command (there must be no openly gay officers), conform to the stereotype of gay camp style, take the role of surrogate women (for example as dancing partners) during male-only leisure in the crew's quarters and avoid interaction with crew in the presence of real women or ashore.

Part of the explanation of the apparent contradiction of homophobic crew tolerating members of the category they hated is to be found in the deeper logic underlining the system of rules which they imposed on gays on the ship. At its simplest, the crew thought with a dyadic model of the social world. Things were either one thing or its opposite. Thus social relations of work, power and sex were defined in terms of us and them. Occupations were coded into hard (deck and engine-room work) and soft (waiter, hairdresser, musician). The ship was worked by those who gave orders (officers), and those who obeyed them (crew). Men (who are hard and give orders) were starkly contrasted with women (who are soft and obey orders). So, for the crew, women were at the bottom of their imaginary hierarchy. As for gays, they were dangerous men who do not define themselves as dominating women, and were imagined to want to treat other men as women. They were witches, normally needing to be banned.

Given this method for imagining the social world, but faced with the fact that gay men on the ship could not actually be got rid of or even avoided, this intolerable situation was dealt with by enforcing the symbolic transformation of the gays on the ship into women. This resolved the ambiguity of a third sex, forcing gays to fit into the dyadic scheme as soft and subordinated. Crew actually tolerate women, not gay men. This maintains the consistency of the crew's social world. Just as with Douglas's explanation of Jewish dietary laws, this explanation posits a deeper level of culture constraining belief and action. They are both cases of strong classification and low tolerance of ambiguity which infect every interpretative act, by Jews and crew alike.

However, although these examples do demonstrate the necessity for culture, we still have to ask what causes the factors that we have used in our explanation – in these cases, what causes the disposition to avoid ambiguity? Cultures vary in the extent to which they stress keeping things neatly classified and bounded. Why should Jewish culture classify so strictly? One possibility is to look for interconnections between the realm of ideas and the geopolitical situation faced by the ancient Israelites – something discussed by Weber (1952) in his *Ancient Judaism*. As a people surrounded by other tribes and lacking a clearly defined territory of their own, constantly bullied and displaced and experiencing a high level of insecurity, it is plausible to suggest that the biblical Jews invested heavily in cultural control by claiming a special relationship with God and developing a rigorous classification system. Anxious about geopolitical boundaries they could not fully control, they created and maintained symbolic boundaries which they could. Maintaining symbolic boundaries has remained important throughout their history as a marginalised people. Similarly, compensation for subordination at the bottom of the formal organisational hierarchy of the ship might have led to the ship's crew placing so high and uncompromisable value on what they felt they *did* possess, that is, pure masculine power. Perhaps this stance was also reinforced by their background in the traditional working class, whose social and often geographical segregation from other classes has been similarly seen as fostering a general and deep propensity to classify dichotomously in terms of us and them with no intermediary categories (Lockwood, 1966; Bernstein, 1971; Martin, 1981).

Cultural variety among the British middle classes

Research seeking to characterise durable underlying organising principles of the cultures of such large collectivities as classes, or sections of classes, offers further examples of cultural explanation at its most powerful. Many interesting attempts have been made to characterise fundamental differences between the cultures of the working and the middle class (Bernstein, 1971; Martin, 1981). With the latter's relentless expansion, and stimulated by the parallel growth of postmodern cultural practices and sensibilities, new work has also recently appeared analysing the differences between sections of a British middle class which had often previously been thought to be rather homogeneous. Mike Savage and his fellow authors offer one such account, basing their analysis on data from the 1987–88 British Market Research Bureau (BMRB) survey of spending patterns (Savage et al., 1992).

Savage et al. identify three major types of middle-class culture: the *undistinctive*, the *ascetic* and the *postmodern*. The undistinctive is the British version of the cultural pattern of what Americans have dubbed 'organisation men', such as civil servants and managers, whose lives are governed by the experience of organisational hierarchies (Whyte, 1957). In Britain, managers have tended to be recruited from inside their companies, emphasising loyalty, rather than companies drafting in external recruits on the basis of their cultural assets represented by professional educational qualifications. With the civil servants, their employment advantages tend to be dependent on remaining within and moving up in their organisations which recognise their specific, but not always transferable, skills. These managers show strong preferences for modified versions of traditional country pursuits (kinds of shooting and fishing), membership of squash and golf clubs, and most sorts of drinking, but are averse to all types of high culture (classical concerts, galleries, plays, opera), and avoid camping, holidays in France and keeping fit. The data for civil servants, on the other hand, show that they have no strong disposition for or against any specific form of consumption, although they are 60 per cent more likely to play bowls than the general population (Savage et al., 1992: 110). Otherwise they show a slight disinclination to take foreign holidays, go camping, play tennis or keeping fit, and they avoid squash. High cultural forms, as manifested in biases in consumption, do not seem particularly important to them (Savage et al., 1992: 108, 114). However, despite these differences, there are good grounds for putting managers and civil servants together as 'hierarchists', since both are dependent on their positions within formal organisational hierarchies.

We now turn to look at two categories of the professional middle class. Distinguished from each other in terms of their location in the public and private sector, they both have more independent accreditation than the managers and civil servants. Their cultural biases can be labelled respectively 'ascetic' and 'postmodern' and are summarized with reference to the BMRB data in simplified form in Table 6.1. This shows considerable differences in the cultural biases of the two categories. Professionals in the public sector have strong interests in the consumption of high culture which is largely lacking for their counterparts in the private sector. But probably their opposing styles are most starkly represented by the ascetics' enthusiasm for climbing, rambling and yoga, which do not figure anywhere on the postmodernists' lists, and their rejection of the clubs, champagne and golf which the postmodernists favour. These differences act as social barriers, including some and excluding others. That such barriers exist suggests that relations among the middle classes have a potential for conflict. When interpreting survey data such as these, it is helpful to keep in mind one's own experience of the practical realities of interaction between those with the different tastes and practices referred to. By inspecting the data, can we find any deep cultural principles organising the biases of these two professional categories?

Take the 'ascetics', so-called by Savage et al. because of their commitment to a lifestyle based on mental and bodily health and exercise and modest overall consumption (represented by below-average alcoholic drinking). What do their enthusiasms for the countryside, climbing, hiking, yoga, camping, museums, high culture and self-drive foreign holidays have in common? All involve effort, making use of education and manifesting a certain sort of virtue.

Table 6.1 Cultural biases among professional middle classes in 1990s Britain

Consumption difference from whole population	Professions in *public* sector Education, health & welfare; state employed [ascetic]	Professions in *private* sector Legal & financial services, sales, public relations, advertising, marketing, computing, personnel [postmodern]
250% more likely	Opera	Champagne
20–50% more likely	Climbing, skating, tennis, classical concerts, table tennis, contemporary dance, camping, multi-centre foreign holidays, galleries/exhibitions, rambling/hiking, yoga, museums, holidays in France, multi-centre car touring holidays, skiing holidays	Squash clubs, shooting (clay), skiing holidays, football, pop/rock concerts, golf & golf clubs, cricket, snooker, holidays in Greece, health clubs, Japanese restaurants, jogging/training, port, French restaurants, tennis, jazz concerts, sailing, gym clubs, gin, vodka, game fishing, holidays in America, leisure-centre beach or city foreign holidays, holidays in Italy
20–50% less likely	Gin, health clubs, pop/rock concerts, bowls, traditional English restaurants, snooker, holidays in Spain, malt whisky, golf, port, sea fishing, golf clubs, vodka, coarse fishing, champagne, Japanese restaurants	Sherry and vermouth Note they do not reject much

Source: Adapted from Savage et al. 1992: 108, 114 (Tables 6.2 and 6.4)

Ascetics seem to need to work to demonstrate their competence, sensibility, healthiness and independence. Their resistance to commercialism and insufficiently health-promoting activities, such as snooker and fishing, suggests a commitment to upholding a moral ideal, an idea about what is right. This ideal is held in common with others like themselves. The statistical patterns in consumption indicate the existence of a large group of like-minded individuals prepared to uphold a way of life by the ways in which they use their time and bodies.

It is plausible to suggest that the ascetic pattern is actually formed by a commitment to upholding a collective identity. Can we say anything about the kind of group it is? The rejection of clubs and luxuries, and the enthusiasm for energetic and self-organised activities of a largely non-competitive kind, suggests that ascetics do not acknowledge established social structures and hierarchies, but prefer each individual to equally represent the group. It is a group of moral equals who are not insulated from one another by positions in established structures. They share responsibility equally and can be called 'egalitarians'. Cultural preferences are therefore very important for marking the external boundary of this group. That a boundary is being marked is suggested by the fact that so much is rejected or excluded. Preferences are motivated by the desire to experience and demonstrate moral authority as worthy group representatives and be accepted as legitimate members of the cultural community.

Sometimes described as a desire for authenticity, this means using tests for distinguishing the genuine from the sham (often associated with commercialism) (Bagguley et al., 1990; Urry, 1990). Effort and education and willingness to acquire real experience for oneself (the long walk to the historic site, detailed guidebook in hand) are the defences against inauthenticity or outsiders. Ascetics tend to be suspicious of others, testing their moral quality before allowing them to join in, and are defensive of what they consider matters of principle. They know what to condemn (for example ignorant audiences, snooker, fishing, the golf club, champagne drinking, commercial culture generally). They insist that things be done properly.

The postmoderns, although also individualised, are quite different. As Table 6.1 shows, they condemn virtually nothing, suggesting that they are not committed to upholding a group identity or cultural hierarchies. They are not self-appointed guardians of cultural and moral values and do not seem to be distinguishing between us and other categories. With no boundary to defend, they are in some ways more relaxed than the ascetics. Commercial culture, which has not been academically authorised by education and state institutions such as museums and galleries, is not criticised as inauthentic; in fact they do not use criteria of authenticity at all (Savage et al., 1992: 128–9). All forms of culture can be used for whatever short-term advantage they might bring. Consumption seems to be guided only by individual self-interest, opportunity, pleasure and requirements of flexible networking. Each person is at the centre of his or her instrumental networks. As individualists, they can participate in anything on an experimental basis. Joining clubs as a means of doing things and making contacts carries no moral obligation. Weak commitment and frequently changing preferences are typical. Symptomatic of the apparently contradictory and disorganised character of postmodern cultural consumption is their propensity both to consume rich food and especially alcohol but also to favour sports and exercise – often of a competitive and high-energy kind. They may want to get fit and train themselves, not as a matter of principle, but rather for any benefits this gives them when marketing themselves inside and outside work. (Savage et al., 1992: 115–16) Their basic commitment is to self-promotion rather than any group.

The deep organising principles of each of the types of professional (to uphold an internally, somewhat egalitarian, collective identity, or unbounded, competitive individualism) makes each collection of cultural preferences into a set with a high degree of predictability. Even though survey data paints with the crudest brush strokes, we can recognise the portraits. We begin to see why ascetics and postmodernists place high value on the things they do. We are not surprised that postmodernists seem to cast their net wider than ascetics when it comes to choosing holiday destinations. If we know the deeper principle governing their selections, we can make shrewd guesses about how they are likely to make other kinds of choices. So we might hypothesise that, when gardening, ascetics will tend to take the time to learn about plants and the history of garden design, do the planning and planting themselves and wait for their efforts to mature, whereas postmodernists will tend to go for the quick make-over, following whatever model has caught their eye.

Different attitudes to time and nature are also suggested by this example. We can predict that, for postmodernists, nature is a robust resource available for competitive exploitation, which can be used with only short-term consideration. They are likely to play down talk of environmental crisis. For more anxious ascetics, on the other hand, nature, often conceptualised as the most authentic thing of all, is likely to be viewed as needing long-term conservation for the general good. They will tend to play up talk of environmental crisis. If we bring the non-professional managers and civil servants back into the picture, we might hypothesise, first, that as hierarchists, they are likely to devote their gardening to keeping things tidy and acceptable to their neighbours. Second, they will probably concede that nature is vulnerable to irresponsible action, but believe that the appropriate policies will be forthcoming from the scientists and state authorities. They will not play up or talk down environmental crisis (Douglas, 1970,1982; Thompson et al., 1990: 25–38).

This brief discussion is sufficient to suggest that knowing how to operate the deep organising principles of cultures makes it possible to predict how people using them will respond to all sorts of dilemma. Attitudes to squash can be linked to attitudes to environmental politics, for example. But as with the earlier examples in this chapter, we still need to explain why a whole category of people adopt a particular deep cultural principle in the first place. The beauty of Savage et al.'s discussion is that it clearly links each type of cultural preference to a particular occupational condition, with its associated economic and political interests. Thus, the reason why the culture of the British middle classes has divided towards the end of the twentieth century is that the growth of the service sector of the economy has multiplied types of professional expertise. These now fall into two broad categories, those that rely on state employment and those that do not. Postmodernists explore ways of enhancing their individual market attractiveness in the private sector where competition and instability reigns. Ascetics, having cultural assets which cannot easily be sold on the market, are therefore reliant on state employment, where, until recently at least, job security (if not pay) has been higher and norms of service rather than competition have predominated. They need to maintain the collective legitimacy of their expertise in order to justify taxpayers continuing to fund the public sector. Finally, managers and bureaucrats depend on maintaining and improving their positions in organisations, drawing on their length of service and organisation-specific, non-credentialised knowledge. This contributes to their tendency to despise, rather than invest in intellectualising, high culture (Table 6.2 summarises the argument).

Table 6.2 Occupational interests underpinning the three types of middle-class culture

Occupation and employment	Managers and government bureaucrats	Public sector professionals in education, health and welfare	Private sector professionals in law, finance, marketing, personnel, etc
Major interests	Preserve organisational positions, rewards and opportunities	Preserve legitimacy value of cultural assets against degradation by the market	Exploit market opportunities to convert cultural assets into economic rewards
Cultural type	**Undistinctive**	**Ascetic**	**Postmodern**
'Deep' cultural principle	Each member fulfills their social functions in complex social hierarchies – **hierarchists**	Each individual is committed to maintaining and embodying the social whole – **egalitarians**	Each individual is committed to their self-interest and competitive advantage – **individualists**

Conclusion

We have seen how culture plays its part in social explanations. We have shown that the internal relations of culture are complex and multilayered and that the generative (causal) mechanisms involved may be very powerful; more powerful than we might have first thought and therefore necessary for explanation. The mechanisms at work are often not obvious and can only be brought to light by forms of cultural analysis which may be technically difficult, but, as our examples suggest, such mechanisms both explain and allow powerful predictions to be made, allowing us to test if we have got the mechanism right. So, for example, if our predictions about differences between private and public sector employees' attitudes to environmental risk do not square with the facts, then we would have to rethink the generative mechanism. However, although culture can be shown to have strong constraining effects, the effects are conditioning not determining, just as was the case when we considered the effects of nature. So, despite having underlined the necessity of culture, we have also had to insist that it is insufficient.

In the Introduction we spoke of social theory (a particular kind of cultural product) as offering a set of tools for understanding social life. Now we can suggest that culture, in general, can be thought of as a tool kit which people use all the time and which becomes significant as it is mobilised to sort out particular problems as we live our lives. Some tools operate almost automatically, priming actors to respond to problems in routine ways. But often we lack the perfect tool in the kit, and then we make do by elaborating, modifying and stretching those tools that we can consciously reflect on. Moreover, cultural elements interact with the psychology of individuals, the competitive interests and power of collectivities and groups, and the material and social circumstances of interaction.

It is always important to identify the principles ordering the reasoning and preferences of the people whose behaviour and belief we might want to explain (whether or not they consciously recognise them). Knowing the rules of the game being played and the logic of actors' orientations to the playing is important, just as it was in the case of explaining action in terms of rational choice, as we saw in Chapter 1. Given the frame of some culture and its internal relations, explanation can proceed.

But there are two major limits to cultural explanation, which we will be dealing with in the remaining chapters (see again Figure 5.4). The first, as we have already seen, is the problem of explaining the cultural elements themselves. As in the examples of the Huaorani (in Chapter 4), Jews, the ship's crew and British middle classes, this can involve reference to their social structural location in relation to surrounding societies and position in structures of power. So, the first limit of cultural explanations is this need to supplement them with social structural considerations.

The second limit is that although culture may involve complex and deep generative mechanisms, and have a strong claim to be relatively autonomous from individuals who operate it, as well as from nature and social structure, it nevertheless depends on the agency of human actors for its impact. Even the most enthusiastic culturalist does not imagine that culture can bypass the mediation of human actors, even if only as relays or, as Harold Garfinkel (1967: 68) puts it, 'cultural dopes'. If you do not think that people are dopes, merely using their cultural resources automatically, then you must be interested in understanding what is involved in 'using', 'applying', 'interpreting' and 'creating'. In the next chapter, we will look at the nature of human action, at what is involved in 'doing'. Doing, being practical, is the process in which the constraining legacies of the past, both cultural and structural, are resisted and exploited.

Part IV

The Concept of Action

CHAPTER 7

What Does Action Explain?

Introduction

The discussions of nature and culture and their place in social explanations suggested that they should be thought of as conditions of action. Conditioning is a relatively open concept of constraint which helps to explain regularity, patterning and typicality, but leaves room for the possibility of novelty, innovation and variation from the typical. As used here, 'conditioning' does not mean 'determining'. The force of the relative autonomy of natural and cultural conditions is mediated by how people interact with them. So we have to think about the properties of the action involved in this mediation. This chapter discusses why action is a central concept in social theory and why the way action is related to culture and structure is said to be its fundamental problem. We have already argued that it is necessary to think of these three concepts as a set; it is not really possible to do social explanation without using all three (Figure 7.1). In particular it is not possible to talk about conditioning without talking about what mediates the conditioning, that is, action.

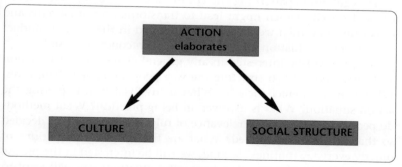

Figure 7.1 What the social sciences contribute to social explanation: action

At the outset, it is important to remember that in the social sciences we are always dealing with problems which are the outcomes of historical processes. These processes may be, and usually are, quite extensive in time. If we are trying to explain some regularity or pattern, which, by definition, must exist for some substantial period of time, and accept that such a phenomenon is the outcome of action constrained by certain conditions (natural, cultural and social structural), then we must be interested in the moment by moment process of action. Social phenomena are the products of what might be thought of as two levels of time; the long durations of patterns and regularities, and the shorter time of the situations of practical action when people actually do whatever is involved in mediating the force of conditions. What people do in the present not only mediates the impact of pre-existing conditions, but contributes to whether or not those conditions continue (are reproduced) or are changed (are transformed). What people do has constitutive effects: action is involved in bringing things into existence and action is required to keep things going. Both the impact and reproduction of enduring conditions depends on how people interact with them in the present.

These processes are clearly central to the historical character of social reality (discussed in Chapter 5). They are fundamental to the way in which, at every moment, social reality feeds back into itself, absorbing the legacy of the past, and at the same time generating the sometimes intended, but generally unintended, outcomes which will become its legacy to the future. We can picture the process as in Figure 7.2.

What are the processes at work in the moment-by-moment advance into the future? Clearly, what goes on in the present of action is very important. If we want to explain cases of repetition leading to social regularities, patterning and continuities, or the opposite, that is, cases of novelty which might lead to transformation of patterns and discontinuities, then we have to be interested in the unique conduct of each action situation and what makes such conduct possible.

First, we will be interested in any general characteristics of action and interaction which structure the way people conduct themselves. What is it to interact socially? What is involved in interpreting the action situation? What is involved in being practical? What methods do people use? How is the relevance of rules and information decided so that they can be applied? What are the necessary conditions of orderly everyday routines? Second, we will be interested in the precise 'micro-histories' of interaction in specific situations. We will want to

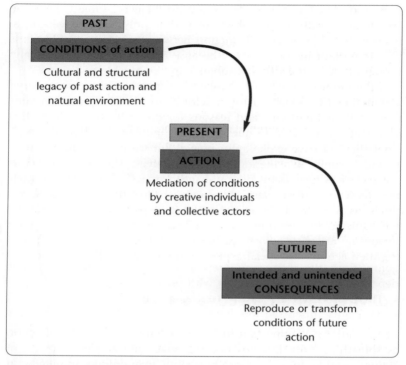

Figure 7.2 The historical process

get close to 'where the action is' (to use Goffman's (1969) phrase), in order to account for both regularities and exceptions.

Action, actors, subjects and objects

Throughout this book we have been using the concept of action because it is impossible to avoid it. But now we must make its meaning clear. We speak of action where conduct is directed by the intentions of a voluntary agent. For there to be action there have to be actors who have motives or purposes. Action is done by actors, those capable of initiating action, rather than simply being forced to behave in some way. Actors can do other than they do and what they do has to be explained, in part, by reference to the *choices* they made. It is this ability to make choices about conduct which qualifies actors to be considered as 'subjects' and not just 'objects'. Subjects have the ability to initiate action which may (but only may) have consequences for objects. The distinction between subjects and objects is very important in social theory because human beings are generally thought to have the status of subjects and be capable of action.

If the problem we want to explain is a specific action or pattern of action done by a specific actor or actors, part of our explanation must refer to their intentions and reasons for doing it. As the subjective agents of the action(s) in question, their motives for choosing to do what they do have explanatory power. But we will still be left with providing some explanation of their motives. The fact that actors make choices for reasons does not mean that their accounts of their reasons for acting are sufficient to understand those actions. Sometimes, as we saw in the last chapter, it helps to know the cultural mechanisms and economic and political interests generating their reasoning. Knowing actors' reasons is only the beginning of explaining their actions and social explanation more generally, not its end.

Individual and collective actors

At this point it is important to limit the tendency to think of action as something only humans do. We ought not to deny powers of action to other animals whose behaviour may only be intelligible if we attribute intentionality to them. Nor ought we to think that action is only done by individuals. Methodological individualists make this mistake and it is tempting to associate powers of action with the properties of each and every human being. But there are two things to consider here. First, simply being human does not mean that one has powers of action. Babies are human, but are the newly born actors *yet*? Adults may also be deemed incompetent to act in particular situations. If you receive a form for jury service, it will ask if you are receiving treatment for mental illness and you may be ineligible to act as a juror if you answer 'yes'. Second, the capacity for action may depend on the formation of organised collectivities which can decide what they want to do and choose a course of action to get what they want. It makes good sense to talk of the intentions and actions of collectivities, provided that one can specify the decision-making roles and positions of power within the organisation or movement, whose occupants contribute to defining how the collectivity will act. It is appropriate to say, for example, that the National Farmers' Union decided to try and change government policy on agricultural subsidies and that the government acted to counter its demand.

Collective action depends on the capability of individuals to act in organised roles, often making decisions as representatives of collectivities. But, conversely, contributing to the action of collectivities enables individuals to do things on a scale and with a significance which would be impossible if they were simply acting on their own. Think what powers to act, and make some impact on the world, depend on your occupying roles within collectivities and organisations. Imagine that you were not a citizen of a state, a member of a family, a bank account holder, signed up to medical and dental practices, affiliated to any specialised clubs or associations. Would your powers of action be massively reduced? In general, the capacity to act depends not just on one's humanity, but on the powers one has by virtue of one's relation to collectivities and institutions. No one would deny that one's position in hierarchies of power affects what one can do. (We will return to these considerations in Chapter 9 when discussing the concept of social structure.)

Social action and interaction

Not all action is social. When one acts on some technical decision, say to remove a punctured bicycle tyre by 'beginning at the valve', one is acting, but not socially. One is just being technically correct (ask your local bike shop). All action is relevant for social explanation. But, as Max Weber's (1968) path-breaking analysis of these concepts has it, action is social when it involves the actor in relating to others and taking them into account in deciding what to do. Orientation to others is crucial, and what flows from it obviously plays a large part in social explanation. Social life and the formation of collective phenomena depend to a large degree on how actors regard and take account of each other. These orientations help to explain how actors interact and any patterns in that interaction.

Interaction between actors can take place wherever there are means of communication and need not be face to face. It can occur between soldiers shouting across no man's land (for interaction in trench warfare, see Ashworth, 1980), between presidents of nuclear superpowers through coded messages and between financial traders using stock market computer networks and so on. However, students of social interaction have tended to concentrate on its face-to-face variety, treating this as in some sense fundamental. (Giddens, 1984: 64–73, who celebrates the seminal work of Goffman, 1959). They have shown that it is a universal dimension of social life, possessing certain relatively autonomous properties, irrespective of cultural differences. This is because only in the physical presence of those with whom we interact can we access the density of fully embodied communicative action. Interaction without the emotional information about sincerity, trustworthiness and tact that we can display and glean from interpreting facial expressions, body language, gestures and tone of voice is generally less morally reliable. The experience of working in cyberspace has arguably revealed the limits of trying to substitute virtual meetings for real ones.

Rules, strategies and practice: what's involved in 'doing'?

What do we do when we act? This is a central question for social theory, since it is here that action's relative autonomy will be revealed. It is not easy to answer because there are really two queries here, one about actors, another about action. Let us start with types of action defined by reference to the actor's state of mind. A useful broad distinction can be made between actions which actors do deliberately, self-conscious action which is carefully considered in advance, and spontaneous action, done without a second thought. Rational choice theory (considered in Chapters 1 and 2) modelled action on the first type. It analysed it as if actors were carefully calculating the advantage of using some particular means to a desired end. But although this sort of rational planning does often happen, we queried whether it was universal. Indeed, there are grounds for thinking that rational deliberation, as a precondition of acting, is the exception rather than the rule.

The reason for this is that rational deliberation takes time and is a bit of a luxury. Most actions are done under the pressure of immediate circumstances. Knowing what to do and making choices has to be based on something other than deliberate rational appraisal. Put slightly differently, only occasionally does action involve following some predetermined plan or ideal rule. Practical social life is not a matter of *first* deciding what to do and *then* putting the plan into operation or conforming to a rule for ideal conduct. Rather than being governed by the logic of rationality and systems of rules, action is better thought of as governed by the 'logic of practice' – Bourdieu's phrase (1990) captures the sense that to be practical we cannot base our action on deliberate rational anticipation. We are too caught up in the ongoing flow of life to sacrifice taking advantage of opportunities for the sake of sticking rigidly to a plan.

Routines, habits, dispositions, practical consciousness

We are entering a realm where social phenomenologists, ethnomethodologists and structuration theorists roam, taking their cue from Alfred Schutz (1967a, 1967b). These theorists have thought a lot about how it is possible for actors to deal with the situations they face, in spite of lacking the time to deliberate and make carefully considered choices. They have pointed first to the process of routinization. Much of our activity falls below the horizon of being consciously decided. We do not even notice (let alone choose) that we are doing something in a particular way. As we grow up, we establish various personal routines (having cornflakes for breakfast, brushing our teeth and putting our clothes on in a particular way each morning). These routines, which we can change if it occurs to us, are geared into the routines of everyday life, such as the working day, the weekend, driving on the left (in the UK and Australia) and so on, which we cannot do much about. But whether we could in principle change things, there are masses of apparently trivial details of our lives which we do not actually choose to do each time we enact them – something we acknowledge when we say that we are on 'automatic pilot'. The suggestion is that this is just as well. Imagine what life would be like if you had to decide about everything you do all the time. Routines and habits are very useful because they free us up to pay attention to relatively few issues which require us to make choices.

A second idea, already encountered in the discussion of culture, is that we can cope with the pressure of circumstances because we learn a general disposition during our upbringing which conditions our expectations and strategies when dealing with any situation. A disposition is a generalising tendency to place a particular sort of interpretation on circumstances, which makes it actionable. We considered examples when discussing the varieties of middle-class culture in the previous chapter and the relation to the environment of the Dunneza in Chapter 4. Acting on the basis of disposition – what we might call a general purpose method for living – results in regularities in our actions and the way we typically deal with problems. Bourdieu (1990), among others, has suggested that there are long-term historical processes in which dispositions are formed for collectivities such as classes. For example, in response to their experience of subordination or domination, members of classes learn about what it is practical to expect, what is achievable and what they can take for granted or presume. Bordieu calls this their 'habitus'. Such dispositions are thus clearly the product of cultural and structural conditioning.

A third idea (from Anthony Giddens (1984), influenced by the philosopher, Wittgenstein) is that the consciousness of people is first and foremost a 'practical consciousness' rather than a theoretically reflective and rationally deliberating one. People know what to do and how to carry on, but they do not need to be able to give reasons for what they are doing. The reasons are below the level of discursive articulation. But the fact that we all know what it is to do things wrongly suggests that our action is being directed by some kind of conscious awareness and knowledge of the relevant rules. Typically it is when we experience mistakes that we find ourselves trying to make explicit the rules we know and live by. We might feel aggrieved, for example, to be offered water to drink at a party, or sense that we should say 'she did' rather than 'she dones her shopping', without immediately being sure why this is the case. The knowledge involved in most action provides a tacit, mutually understood basis for interaction, which does not need to be expressed, except in emergencies or when responding to visiting social scientists such as anthropological field workers. Then, as Bourdieu (1986: 112) puts it, native informants talk to the anthropologist in the way they speak to small children who need to have the obvious explained to them – although children can, of course, ask questions which adults find unexpected and initially hard to answer.

Contingency (accidents) in social life and the uniqueness of circumstances

The above suggestions are intended to help to explain how actors deal with the demands of practical situations where the priority is on 'doing' rather than reflection about what to do. The reason why time is normally too short for reflection, and what makes routines, habits and dispositions so useful, is that we are frequently required to respond to unexpected events and new things which we have not previously experienced. Practice has a certain urgency. The routine stuff can be taken for granted, allowing us to concentrate on the urgent problems that always arise. However hard we try to anticipate and control events, it is normal for these attempts to fail in some way. An Australian army officer, responding to a journalist's question about the 2000 peace-keeping operation in East Timor, offered the old military adage: 'No plan survives first contact.' The really important question is how you cope when plans come unstuck. You do not have to be running a United Nations peace-keeping force to appreciate the importance of this – it is a general condition of life. The answer is that one has to make it up as one goes along, or *improvise*. This involves responding creatively to the opportunities presented by ever-changing situations, being sufficiently flexible about one's goals and what one allows as acceptable means. It involves compromises.

This is where we must return to consider the second question – about action as such (rather than about actors), which was hidden in the question 'what do we do when we act?' Being practical in the face of the unexpected, the new and the uncertain requires that actors do the right kinds of thing. Sustaining interaction in ongoing situations, despite not being sure about what they are doing, demands that appropriate skills are used. Improvisation is not just a matter of actors having the right attitude, but of using the right methods. Viewed in this light, social life is an ongoing process of discovery. The meaning of one's actions changes as we undertake them. This is because we have to reinterpret them in the light of their emerging consequences and changes in the context of action which become apparent. We need to monitor constantly the effects of our actions to stop doing what may be turning out to be negative and to reinforce what seems to be positive for achieving our goals. To keep track of emerging consequences and changes of context is a practical necessity which requires actors to use the appropriate interpretative skills. It is only after the event – retrospectively – that it is possible to even begin to arrive at a conclusion about what some action meant. Actors must know how to manage before such conclusions become possible; although not even the relative stability of hindsight ends the possibility of reinterpretation because the past is interpreted within an ever-hanging context of present action, interests and knowledge.

Following Schutz's lead, Garfinkel (1967) and the ethnomethodologists have tried to specify the techniques of interpretation and action that people use in the face of uncertainty about what is going on. Irrespective of the specific content of one's disposition, which derives from membership of cultural and structural collectivities, actors must also rely on the universal techniques of 'common sense'. This is the practical form of rationality which allows for vagueness and mistakes, tolerates delays, accepts that there are many details and values which do not need to be made explicit and can refer to a background of 'what everybody knows' when making excuses. This is the rationality of doing the best one can in the circumstances, recognising that each circumstance may constrain action in its unique way.

The place of practical action in social explanation

If social life involves action being highly responsive to the unique circumstances in which it is done, we must be interested in how conduct unfolds in these unique situations. It is here that we see, moment by moment, action by action, movement towards the eventual outcomes which we may want to explain. Every moment and act is a potential turning point in the emergence of outcomes, which could, retrospectively, be revealed to be important. *When* and *what* people improvise and create, and *how* they do it, in the face of unique circumstances are important elements in any explanation. And it is true that all actors have to act in this way just to cope with the most humdrum aspects of everyday life.

Unless one is a determinist who refuses to accept that nature, culture and social structure only condition social action, there should be little reason to deny the creativity of actors and the productivity of action situations. Actors are not programmed to follow a text, like the performers in a play. In real life, they adjust and rewrite the 'lines' they may be given, as they go along.

Jazz and total institutions

Certainly there are examples where creative emergence from a unique situation appears very strong. Think of the improvisation of jazz. The music may not be written at all and the musicians have an open mind about what they are going to play. They start and what happens emerges as they play, in a complex, extended process of interaction. The performance is unique, unpredictable and may be literally unrepeatable; if not recorded, something of great musical importance may be lost forever. But even here, the players do not start from scratch. They play around with standard songs, chord sequences or phrases which they all know, and may accept a minimum of musical conventions such as key and time signature for their performance. Actors never entirely escape their cultural heritage – in the case of jazz, African-American culture, slavery, the blues and so on. The freedom of jazz depends on having some relationship with traditions, even if only to contradict them. This dependence on some cultural starting point does not in any way prevent us from allowing that new sounds can be produced in the freedom and spontaneity of performance. The only problem is trying to unpick how the performance happened in the heat of the moment, by, for example, discussing memories and analysing recordings. But however difficult this is, jazz, like any human social enterprise, establishes traditions in which past performances provide the reference points, models and inspiration for current ones. Culture thus constrains and enables action, and traditions are reproduced and, at the same time, developed and changed (Russell, 1972; Sudnow, 1978).

Thus it appears that what people do is not explicable by reference only to the actors and what they do in any given situation. This is true of all situations including those where people appear to act with the greatest possible freedom and spontaneity. Of course, many situations are at the opposite pole, where actors have virtually no room for manoeuvre. Think of what Erving Goffman (1968) called 'total institutions'. Prisons, monasteries, asylums, boarding schools and so on all specialise in intensifying control of action by means of tightly specified rules and powerful sanctions for breaking them. The amazing thing is that although, at the extreme, such harsh regimes can destroy the autonomy of actors, in practice there is usually a lot of effective improvisation and resistance by both staff and inmates. This is because even total institutions are vulnerable to contingencies and have to leave space for people to make it up as they go along from time to time.

Conclusion: conditioning and action

Given so much goes on in the present, it is tempting to treat action situations as providing all we need to understand the phenomena we are interested in. Just look at the detailed process in which they emerged. Who needs history and the past? We have the immediacy of flesh and blood actors in the full flood of ongoing interaction. The jazz session (Russell, 1972: 20–5) the courtroom drama (Atkinson and Drew, 1979), the intimate conversation (Goodwin, 1984) and the recruitment interview (Button, 1987), for example, are all unique, complex events in which who does what matters (a new talent emerges, the innocent go free, a life's partner is chosen, a job is gained, or not). But the present of each action situation cannot be abstracted out of historical time and treated as an autonomous, self-producing entity. Just as individuals cannot be understood without reference to non-individual social concepts (such as roles and statuses), so particular action situations cannot be understood without reference to the wider and more enduring historical contexts of traditions and institutions in which they take place (the conventions and resources put into play by the participants had to come from somewhere).

The creativity of action, the uniqueness of situations and situational emergence are very important but they are not everything. The dynamic of historical change is not reducible to the creativity of actors, although there would be no history without them. It is actors, more or less skilfully, who put the conditions into play and in doing so transform them (Figure 7.3). But they do not make history just as they please.

So far we have considered this relation between conditioning and action by thinking about how culture conditions action, and action produces cultural changes (such as the elaboration of jazz) which become conditions of future action. However, there are two sorts of conditions of action, which are substantially produced by action. Culture is one. The other is social structure. But before considering the similarities and differences between culture and social structure, the next chapter discusses more detailed examples designed to show just how important action is for social explanation, but which also show its limits.

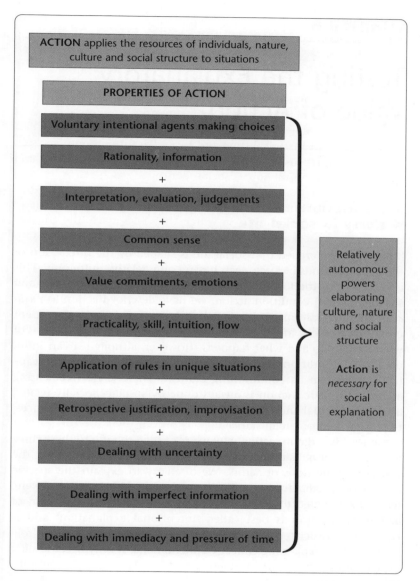

Figure 7.3 Summary: the relative autonomy of action – how action works

CHAPTER 8

Testing the Explanatory Value of Action

Introduction: action, intentionality and activity in social life

So far we have argued that social life is shaped by the interaction of the different kinds of force, each having only relative autonomy. This also applies to the force of action. Whereas nature and culture (and social structure) condition action, we have described action as *mediating* these conditions. This mediation is itself a special ever-present condition of social life. It must therefore figure in our explanations of what people do and what happens. However, although it can influence how conditions affect things, nevertheless it cannot escape being related to its conditioning context. There is no free-floating action, as it were. Action is always done by specific, socially related actors (individual and/or collective), using specific cultural resources, to engage specific circumstances.

Generally, ordinary action explanations tend to refer to these three elements, actors, culture and circumstances, focused around the conscious intentions of actors. We often try to explain the specific actions of specific actors by finding out what their intentions were, what they wanted to achieve by the acts in question. This kind of action explanation is best called 'intentional explanation' and is really to be associated with individualism. It plays only a minor role in the task of explaining collective phenomena, if only because such explanations leave us with the problem of explaining the intentions; they are not final causes.

Although action as a category has human intentionality (that is, behaviour is guided by the actor's sense of purpose) built in to its definition, this is not what makes action a relatively autonomous force shaping social life. The properties of human actors (intentionality, consciousness, capacity for language and so on) are conditions of action but not the properties of action as such. Intentionality may motivate participation in some project or field of action but does not govern what is required to pursue the project. Actors must want things but also go about getting them in appropriate ways. Action is best thought of as a social process of activity, which makes its own demands of actors. They must have certain kinds of knowledge and competence to take part.

Satisfying the demands of action is not just necessary for actors to get what they want. A profound implication of the previous chapter for social explanation is that the existence of collective phenomena, such as cultural practices, depends on them being used and enacted. There is almost unanimous agreement among social theorists about this point. Social reality is stuffed with human beings acting out the conditions of their collectivisation. So, for example, the informal economy of the ghetto (Chapter 2), the cultures of hunter-gatherers (Chapter 4) or the consumption patterns of middle-class professionals (Chapter 6) exist because they are more or less continuously enacted practices; childcare and clothes are exchanged, moose tracked and monkeys killed, and consumer preferences for golf or opera indulged. If those involved stopped being active, using their skills, making their choices and applying their sense of priorities, what we can identify as their respective collective conditions would disappear. This is not to say that action alone is sufficient to keep a way of life in being, only that it is necessary.

When we select our examples of the role of activity in social explanation, we will concentrate on precisely how the social process of action contributes to the production and maintenance of collective phenomena. This means that we will ignore the impact of the unique creativity of the action of specific individuals, because we take it as given that individuals are ordinarily capable of creativity, and that it is routinely necessary to refer to the actions of specific individuals in social explanation.

Best cases for testing the explanatory power of action

The force of action, and the necessity of including it in explanation, is immediately apparent in cases where actors seem to be free agents, able to shape the course of events more or less as they like. We evoked one such example in the previous chapter when discussing jazz improvisation, although we proceeded to show that, even here, the creative capacities of musicians were linked to cultural factors, such as various musical traditions. Similarly, the requirements to take action into account can scarcely be disputed where especially powerful actors, in key decision-making positions, clearly shape the outcomes that occur. But once again, these actors are not entirely autonomous, since their individual or collective power flows from resources attaching to their institutions or gained in a history of competitive struggle. Whilst the directors of major corporations can make or break the economies of whole regions with their decisions about plant locations, they can only do so because of their positions in their firm and their firm's place in the structure of global capitalism. The forcefulness of the action of the powerful is (as we will elaborate in Chapter 9) closely tied to the effects of social structure.

Thus even where action is self-evidently important for explanation, we can show that it is not, on its own, sufficient. But can we also provide cases where it is a necessary component for explanation even though initially this seems unlikely? A necessity test of this sort would be possible where actors may not be especially powerful and appear to be tightly controlled. If we can show that even in such circumstances the action of actors is of fundamental significance for explaining what is going on, then we will have made a strong argument for its necessity. Moreover, if we can also show that their action makes a fundamental contribution to the long-term durability of collective phenomena such as institutions and practices, we will have made a strong case for its importance for understanding social reality in general.

To follow this test strategy, we need studies of the action of people operating within long-lasting and highly disciplined settings. By 'highly disciplined' we mean that actors are required, subject to various sanctions, to account for their actions. Actors must justify themselves, either when challenged, or as a matter of routine. This is typical of contemporary occupational environments with complex divisions of labour, where getting work done depends on coordinating many different tasks and decisions by specialists. The need to incorporate action in any social explanation can be demonstrated by considering how specialised contributors to complex divisions of labour are disciplined and justify themselves. We will therefore discuss, in detail, some examples from different kinds of highly controlled occupational environment.

Practicalities of bureaucratic action: coping with routine crises in a welfare office

We can begin with a classic type of a modern occupational environment, that of bureaucratic administration. Bureaucracy, as Weber made clear, is a technique to make performance predictable and reliable, creating routines by formulating what is expected of actors as precisely as possible in objective, depersonalised rules (Gerth and Mills, 1948). These rules specify what must be done and the reasons for doing it, in order to deal properly with the whole range of cases that the organisation has been set up to cater for. Personal discretion is reduced as much as possible. Actors have tight scripts to follow. The bureaucracy's workers, and the cases it treats, are processed by being fitted into a classification scheme, each instance being defined as an example of a general type which can be processed according to a general formula. The job of the bureaucrat is to apply these formulae of general rules routinely to actual, particular cases. The question is 'what is involved in trying to process real cases to conform to the abstract rules?'

Don Zimmerman (1971) explored this issue in his classic analysis of the conduct of day-to-day business in the Lakeside office of the Californian Bureau of Public Assistance. Typical of state-administered welfare schemes, the office's purpose was to administer the distribution of welfare payments (to the elderly, disabled and sick) according to the legislation, which sets the rules governing whether applicants were entitled to assistance. The workers' basic task was to see that appropriate payments went to qualified applicants and weed out those who did not qualify. The office was supposed to distribute assistance *efficiently*, meeting the legitimate needs of applicants, and *fairly*, within the framework of the law. Given that applicants were often highly stressed, there was a lot of pressure on office workers to be able to justify their decisions as conforming to the legal specification of what ought to be done. So here was a work environment with an abundance of detailed, formal rules of procedure and demands to justify actions by reference to them. There was a strong tension between the theoretical ideal of what ought to happen and the practical reality of what actually did happen.

Zimmerman concentrated on the difficulties faced by receptionists in the intake division, the workers central to managing the practicalities of realising the theoretical ideal laid down in the rules. The division's receptionists did the initial screening of applicants for eligibility to some category of assistance, and then assigned them to intake case-workers for more detailed assessment. At the end of the intake process, eligible applicants were passed on to the approved division for routine administration and periodic reassessment. Situated between a flow of incoming applicants and a number of caseworkers, receptionists were pressured from both sides. Both applicants and caseworkers could be sources of difficulty.

Receptionists were committed to maintaining a smooth, orderly flow of work during the day and ending the day with no half-processed applications. Good order meant, firstly, that cases were processed at a sufficient rate to prevent complaints from applicants, but with sufficient time allowed to investigate each case to ensure that appropriate assistance was given. Speeding up the flow must not be achieved by taking shortcuts and careless work. But, secondly, good order meant that a 'fairness' rule be followed to ensure equality of treatment for applicants and intake caseworkers. The central plank of operationalizing the intake procedure was the rule for allocating cases to caseworkers on a first come, first served basis (Zimmerman, 1971: 227). Each day a table was drawn up listing available caseworkers down one side and numbers for allocated cases across the top. Ideally caseworker A was allocated applicant 1, caseworker B applicant 2 and so on. Only when all the available caseworkers (say, A–F) had cases, should caseworker A be allocated a second applicant. The goal was to distribute the processing equally. If it was, it would be justifiable. Caseworkers would be unable to argue that some are given easier or harder daily caseloads. That was the theory.

In practice, it was impossible to stick literally to this rule, but this did not result in chaos. Nor did it mean that the rule was irrelevant to securing orderly activity, as we shall see. Receptionists secured order in a practical context of varying pressures. Not every day was the same. The number of applicants of different kinds can vary as can caseworker availability. Cases varied in the difficulty they posed for processing – some could be dealt with quickly, others not. Applicants themselves could create scenes, be threatening, confused or have special circum-stances requiring exceptional consideration and so on. Caseworkers had reputations for their strengths and weaknesses when processing particular kinds of case. Some worked faster than others. They had known preferences for certain kinds of cases, just as applicants had preferences for particular caseworkers. It is not difficult to imagine the variety of considerations that receptionists had to keep in mind when allocating applicants to caseworkers. Their practical skill was to do the allocating, keeping the work flowing, keeping queues as short as possible and preventing objections from applicants and caseworkers. Any departure from the ideal had to be justifiable. How was this done?

People must sometimes depart from routines to make the work day 'come out right' (Zimmerman, 1971: 229), as when a third applicant was about to be assigned to caseworker Jones, before she had finished interviewing her first applicant of the day. Keeping to the first come, first served rule, when an early case is taking an unusually long time, will result in a long wait for later assigned cases and create potential trouble. In this case, Jones's third assigned applicant, having waited over an hour, was reallocated to another caseworker. The rule was broken, or rather suspended, but only after discussion and on the decision of a senior receptionist. The unfairness in giving Jones's third case to another caseworker, who had already cleared her own cases, had to be justified by reference to the exceptional nature of Jones's first case. That some cases just do take a long time was understood as a 'fact of life'. Receptionists' interest in achieving the smooth, rapid processing of applicants could be frustrated by intake caseworkers' need to take their time with applicants (Zimmerman, 1971: 231). Similarly, when faced with assigning difficult applicants, it may be wiser to suspend the first come, first served rule in favour of the applicant being dealt with by a particular caseworker who was known to be good at handling such cases. Zimmerman cites an example of two caseworkers, Hall and Kuhn, exchanging applicants because of such considerations (1971: 233–4). Everyone who worked in the intake division knew that there were such exceptional cases, that certain caseworkers handled them best and that suspending the rule of fairness on such grounds was justifiable.

These simple examples show what is involved in the everyday enactment of bureaucratic organisations. The ideals enshrined in the formal procedures do not apply themselves. To be operationalized, bureaucracy needs workers who are competent rule users. They must be positively oriented to being guided by the rules and able to account for their actions in terms of them. But they must also be able to assess the relevance of the rules on a case-by-case basis. Formally organised activity necessarily depends on the creative interpretation of cases and the exercise of judgement about the practical wisdom of suspending rules. This ordinary creative enactment of the organisation depends on two kinds of knowledge. First, workers must understand the general purpose, or spirit, of the organisation, which helps them when deciding whether or not to apply or suspend the rules. Second, they must know about the routine difficulties faced by everyone working in the organisation doing the job. This practical background knowledge includes the typical, if not precisely predictable, snags which threaten the normal flow of business. They must know how to maintain the spirit of the organisation, by operating with ideas of normality (the rules routinely apply) and exceptions (treated as one-offs, which do not compromise the ideal of what ought to happen normally). Exceptions allow the rules to be upheld, but not at the price of impractical, rigid literalism.

To use cultural resources such as bureaucratic rules, actors have to have substantial knowledge about the practical contexts and make judgements about relevance. This is what being reasonable means. Failure to keep the rules can be explained by pointing to features of the practical context that everybody who knew about the job would accept as a reasonable excuse. The very existence of every organisation and culture, once it is set up, depends on this continuous, moment-by- moment, context-specific enactment of rules by its members using their capacity for practical rationality. The creative practical activity of actors energises social forms and keeps them in being.

How haematologists diagnose and treat blood disorders

Our next case involves the occupational world of haematologists, specialists in treating blood disorders such as leukaemias, anaemias or haemophilia. Like the assistance officers, they have to be practical and reasonable, but the very different nature of their work setting affects what it means to 'be practical'. If anything, pressure to be able to justify decisions publicly is greater for medical consultants than for members of the intake division of the Bureau of Public Assistance. Paul Atkinson's *Medical Talk and Medical Work* (1995) gives an insight into the practical activity of supplying haematological expertise in the complex contexts of contemporary hospital environments in the US and Britain. From our non-expert point of view, and as potential patients, we encounter consultant physicians when they deliver authoritative, confident-sounding opinions, which may have major implications for our lives. The individual doctor appears as the expert who carries sole moral responsibility for the opinion. We do not see the interactional process, behind the scenes, where opinions are formed and decisions made, which Atkinson's study reveals.

The work of these experts is shown to involve a great deal of talking. It is not too much to say that specialist medicine such as this would be impossible without talk. Talk is the primary communication medium of ongoing interactional situations in which it is possible for participants, drawing on their knowledge and experience, to express their sense of what is relevant. Talk is quick and responsive to context. So, where one is frequently, routinely and urgently trying to solve complex, often unique problems, such as identifying patients' blood disorders and choosing effective treatments, talk is especially important. Haematologists work by arranging collections of complex and often imprecise data until they feel able to recognise a pattern, which allows them to diagnose the condition and suggest appropriate treatment. They do this in small groups whose members talk all the time. This talk mobilises the available fund of expertise, provides a mechanism for criticism and a basis for moral support. As Atkinson insists, the talk is not *about* the work, it *is* the work.

If one studies the moment-by-moment activity of such work/talk, one is forced to recognise the significance of the microscopic detail of communicative interaction. This is always difficult to convey in print and we do not have the space to reproduce the extended passages of talk discussed by Atkinson. But a few themes can be illustrated to reinforce the general point that without enactment by talking, the institutions of haematology could not deliver their service to the rest of us.

Simultaneous looking and talking

Take looking at slides through a microscope. Slides of a patient's blood are routinely examined during case conferences, and it is striking that the microscope in the seminar room, where patients' cases are discussed, allows for simultaneous viewing by four people. This allows them to discuss one another's ideas about what they are seeing. In a context where little is obvious, suggested identifications of different kinds of cell and their condition are criticised in the search for a consensus. This is particularly important in training students to interpret what they see in the right way, and in teaching them to recognise and describe relative to conventional benchmarks or types. Simultaneous viewing allows senior experts to provide ostensive definitions, defining by pointing and saying 'There' and supplying the technical label. The talk develops students' visual recognition and reporting skills (Atkinson, 1995: 74–89).

Managing uncertainty, authorising opinion, performing seniority

The above example introduces three of Atkinson's interrelated and central themes, dealing with uncertainty, the several ways to authorise opinion and the performative nature of seniority. The reputations of experts depend on providing the best knowledge that there is in their field. This may sometimes tempt them to behave as though they know when they actually do not. But generally, well-founded expertise involves managing rather than denying uncertainty (Atkinson, 1995: 111). Particularly when talking to other experts, knowledge claims must be carefully qualified. The performance of expertise means showing that knowledge contributes powerfully to decisions, but also acknowledging that it has limits.

So typically, case discussion is a formal ritual, beginning with a relatively junior doctor offering a narrative about the patient's condition and history of treatment to a critical audience of students and senior colleagues. The narrative assembles and interprets the available information, including descriptions of personal experience of the patient. These presentations are delivered rapidly and must have sufficient detail, chronology, key events and clinical reasoning, demonstrating sufficiently close attention to the case. It must be interpreted as a history of puzzle-solving, but not overloaded with ill-digested details, supplying information on a 'need to know' basis (Atkinson, 1995: 97–104). Accounts are typically interrupted by requests for additional precision or criticised for their interpretations by senior members of the audience.

Given this, presenters have to be skilled at expressing degrees of certainty and uncertainty and at deploying various authorities for the information in their accounts. Rhetorical skill is required to balance delicate judgements about what weight to place on different parts of the story, depending on context (Atkinson, 1995: 117). Since they are junior, presenters must give the source of their information: other doctors, other specialties, laboratory technicians, journals, textbooks, for example. These sources have to be assigned degrees of trust based on the collective experience of the occupational group. Trust is also involved when it is necessary to tell histories of inadequate investigations, mistaken treatments and treatments which are suspected of making matters worse. A simple example is the tendency of haematologists to disparage the efforts of primary care practitioners to treat blood conditions with additional iron (Atkinson, 1995: 125). Another is the possibility of overdosing patients with drugs such as heparin. Lab reports are known to have margins of error. Data may be mislaid and have to be reconstructed from memory. The following short excerpt displays these features:

> At that point we were concerned that he [the patient] might have heparin-induced thrombocytopenia and /or thrombosis secondary to heparin. So we suggested they discontinue the heparin. I went over things in great detail with Dawson the chief surgical resident, who appeared to remember a lot of the data from the lab sheets and med sheets that were lost. What we thought might be possible is that all the way along heparin has been potentiating his syndrome. If you accept the fact that heparin is bad for him you can sort of go back through his history, and at every step of the way see where the institution of heparin appeared to make him a little bit worse … I'm making up a flow sheet so I can show Dawson and make sure we're not talking ourselves into something that isn't actually true. I'm not completely sure. (Atkinson, 1995: 119)

Here the junior physician is telling a difficult story about incompetent record keeping and decisions that, with hindsight, may have been wrong. Her narration is also about the practical steps taken to recover the situation. She is talking to fellow professionals who all know that mistakes are made and that treatments can make matters worse. Given this understanding, the presenter justifies her actions by appealing to memory, not just anyone's memory, but that of a senior physician, and producing a documentary record, the 'flow sheet', to provide objective substance to the subjective awareness of the problem which had emerged during their talking.

As a senior person, Dawson's memory is thought to be a sufficiently good basis for the reconstruction of the lost records. Seniority is an important resource for authorising opinions. Atkinson calls it the 'voice of experience' (1995: 131). This draws lessons from relatively long and unique personal experience. Most obviously, the diagnostic opinions of certain key consultants are highly respected and routinely cited with confidence. In Atkinson's material, the name of a particular clinical pathologist, Carol Green, was far more frequently mentioned than those of any of her colleagues. Her skill in interpreting biopsies and her careful pronouncements were taken as the best available (Atkinson, 1995: 125–6). This deference was highly functional for the less certain and less experienced. She provided a local, personal leadership.

More ordinarily, senior figures lead by supervising and advising juniors in case conferences. In fact, seniority requires doctors to be able to provide relevant stories from their personal experience to help to shape the interpretation of evidence and decide on treatment. As we have seen, haematology teams must arrive at decisions and over-come interpretative uncertainty. One strong source of authoritative knowledge is the 'voice of science', represented by research journal literature. Citing journal articles routinely supports arguments. But although this may be 'good science', its relevance for actual cases being analysed must be decided. This is where the voice of experience of respected senior figures, speaking from their personal experience, comes in. Juniors support their own suggestions by referring to the published science, but this is articulated with the lessons of practical experience of their immediate seniors. This is often supplied anecdo-tally or as personal maxims, in sharp contrast to the impersonal discourse of scientific medicine generally (Atkinson, 1995: 137–47).

For example, a clinical possibility may be illustrated by a personal reminiscence:

> I remember a case that I saw a couple of years ago that really bears on this point ... Maybe I told you about this girl already but let me tell it again for the benefit of the students ... she was at a party with her family on New Years' Eve and was *well*. The next day didn't feel very good. Everybody was joking ... but she didn't have too much to drink, and she became acutely ill during the day ... and she had a very severe Coombs positive haemolytic anaemia with fifty per cent retics or some-thing like that ... and for some reason we did a bone marrow, I don't know why. It was *very* megaloblastic ... this thing was building up for a few days ... but in *those* few *days* it probably exhausted the folate reserves right there in the *bone* marrow. It's a very early sign of marrow overactivity, or demands on the marrow ... That's what you have here. (Atkinson, 1995: 139–40)

Seniority is also importantly performed, by giving advice. The next excerpt follows a junior doctor reporting that the patient has been treated with 1000 mg of Cytoxan, 30 mg of Adria, and 120 mg of VP16 for a day;

> Senior: I think we should go up on the Adria.
>
> Junior: Right, that's what I thought – keep the Cytoxan where it is? Or do you wanna

Sen: You could probably go up on both

Jun: Twelve hundred?

Sen: Yeah

Jun: And fifty [of Adria]

Sen: Twelve hundred [of Cytoxan] and forty-five [of Adria]

Jun: forty-five

Sen: Hahahh

Jun: Witchcraft. And the VP for only a day?

Sen: You could probably give him two days and see how he does. (Atkinson, 1995: 140–1)

Here, uncertainty about how to fine-tune the treatment is overcome by accepting the senior doctor's advice. The junior doctor's exclamation 'Witchcraft' suggests that they recognise the arbitrariness involved. The decision to go for only 45 mg of Adria, rather than the suggested 50, reflects perhaps the senior's habits of caution, or general disposition to see less experienced doctors as tending to push things too fast. Later in the same discussion, the senior remarks, 'I wouldn't try to push it up. I think you might get into a little trouble', and, 'I'd be dubious about going faster.' This sort of consideration is expressed by another senior doctor to explain his preference for caution: ' I'd probably go with that kind of regimen. And the reason is that I'd like to get a little response before I go in with more multiple drugs, just in terms of her being intravenous' (Atkinson, 1995: 141).

Doctors with a wealth of experience of analysing actual cases perform seniority. Everyone in haematology knows that the standard examples in the textbooks are insufficient as a basis for deciding what to do about actual cases, which present unique problems. Analysis and treatment has to proceed on an investigative basis, constantly checking for emerging negative or positive effects. That treatments have the potential to harm is a constant background worry. That patients have unique histories and conditions means that haematological advice has to be constructed for each on the basis of practical judgement. The whole practice depends on the process of talking to make decisions. This is a collective, interactive process, facilitated by ritualised occasions and deference to the authoritative voices of science and experience.

Conclusion

These studies of the work of a welfare office and a medical specialism show the activity involved in the intense, fine-grained, moment-by-moment realisation of organised practices. There are four major elements, judgements of relevance, talk, justification and practical knowledge. Whatever the content of the formal rules prescribing what ought to happen, these rules have to be judged to be relevant and applicable to the cases currently under consideration. There are always times when to get the work done it is judged better not to follow the rules too literally. Central to making judgements of relevance is talk. Talk is the mechanism of decision-making. This is why the social theorists who specialise in analysing action are drawn to the analysis of conversation. Conversation has proved central to being practical, a fact demonstrated clearly by the haematologists. And finally, the activity of locally producing and reproducing social organisation involves deferring to certain justifying principles or theoretical ideals. Although they provide a moral framework, these principles and rules about what ought to happen cannot make anything actually happen. But they do provide moral resources for representing events and actions as appropriate. However, given that, in the real world, following the rules literally is not possible, justifying stories must also appeal to practical knowledge of experienced people, to excuse, as reasonable in the circumstances, activities which appear to deviate from organisational ideals.

It is therefore true to say that social institutions and practices are, as Harold Garfinkel (1967) and the ethnomethodologists insist, 'skilful accomplishments'. But it is not true to say that to explain social life all we need to do is to focus on episodes when these skills are used. Crucial to our main examples in this chapter is the fact that the activity described takes place within what can be called *establishments*, complex organisations which provide the settings (the places, equipment, roles, powers of office, hierarchies of status, rewards and so on) for the action. Establishments have histories during which they are brought into being and are located in an environment of other institutions and practices which condition what can be done by actors. The easiest way to end this chapter and announce the topic of the next is to point out that nowhere in Zimmerman's account of his welfare office does he make mention of the politics of the taxation which pays for the welfare provision.

Atkinson also suggests the limits (the insufficiency) of analysis restricted to the local work and talk of organisations. First he notes that the activity of his American haematologists is conditioned by their working in a medical marketplace, where everything they do has a published price. Second, he is impressed by the fact that the cultural forms of medicine, the 'ceremonials and liturgies of the clinic', have a remarkable stability, despite rapid changes in medical science, government policies, and bases of financing (Atkinson, 1995: x). These considerations suggest other kinds of process contributing to the constitution of social regularities. After all, medics have a long established and well-developed professional culture and are a powerful occupational group, better able than most to dictate the conditions of work and rewards. This is a matter of the group's location in a structure of relative advantage compared to other occupations and the use of its power to maintain its position. These are matters of social structure which have made regular appearances in our discussion of the insufficiency of individuals, nature, culture and now action. In the following chapter, we can at last give social structure our full attention.

Part V

The Concept of Social Structure

CHAPTER 9

What Does Social Structure Explain?

We now come to our final concept, social structure, which should be as fundamental a part of any social analyst's tool kit as culture and action (Figure 9.1). Although particularly used by sociologists, anybody interested in explaining social life can benefit from learning how to use it. Indeed, we have already found ourselves referring to social structure to fill out the explanation of patterns and regularities, when some of the other concepts have reached their limits.

In the Introduction, for example, we criticised those who believed that patterns of educational success and failure could be explained simply by referring to the properties of individuals, ignoring the fact that they are already located in a class structure of differential access to educational resources. The children in the educational system are not isolated individuals, but start out in life located or positioned within distributional orders. They are distinguished by differences of age, sex, region, class, housing, health, ethnic classification, language and religion, for example. All these are factors we might think conse-

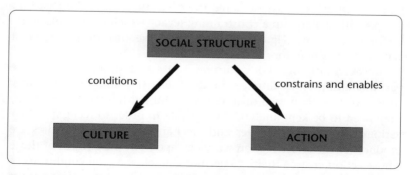

Figure 9.1 What the social sciences contribute to social explanation: social structure

quential for various kinds of educational outcome and worth research-ing. How each child is positioned to engage with the education system affects how they relate to it and vice versa. Children do not choose their position at the start. It is their legacy, for good or ill.

The same point about the effects of structural location was made in Chapter 2 when we saw how the disadvantaged position of ghetto blacks in a racist, capitalist, labour market helped us to understand the economic strategies they pursued. To explain Huaorani technical choices in Chapter 4, it helped to know about their position of extreme social isolation from surrounding peoples. Similarly, in the explanation of patterns of consumption among British middle-class professionals in Chapter 6, we found it useful to see how they were positioned relative to the private and public sectors of the economy. And in Chapter 8, we have just seen that to understand the actions of welfare bureaucrats and medical professionals requires reference to the institutional settings which define positions and assign powers to those who occupy them. Strong tendencies of thought and behaviour are created for those who are located in different positions of this kind.

In all these cases, 'social structure' was used to refer to particular kinds of precondition of action which exert their own sort of constraint. Along with culture, they are part of the environment of action, setting the scene of conditions to which action, at any given moment, responds. For, as explained in Chapters 5 and 7, just like culture, social structures are also produced by action. That is, the social environment which conditions present action is the outcome of past action. In the same way, present action will shape the future by producing outcomes which will condition subsequent action. Social structures share with culture the property of being a medium of this historical process. Both cultures and social structures are outcomes of past activity which have acquired the capacity to carry the past into the present, making up a constraining legacy which conditions activ-ity in the present. Figure 7.2, describing the historical process of action, applies here too.

However, although both cultures and social structures carry the past forward, they are different kinds of relatively autonomous reality which work in their own distinct ways. Thus, although they interact, they need to be kept analytically separate in order to recognise their various distinctive properties and mechanisms. Social structures are products of social interaction which escape from the control of those whose action created them, to become durable material conditions of the action of subsequent agents. Thus, just as with elements of nature, when people think about social structures, it is because these are entities which have specific conditioning properties, whether they like it or not and whatever they may think about such entities. They are not constituted by the logic of the ideas in people's heads. We think about social structures because they can materially affect our powers of action.

Social structure defined: (i) relations between positions

We have already introduced the fundamental idea of social structure, saying that it is a set of interrelated social positions, each one of which is defined and constituted by the relations it has with other positions. It is these relations between positions which have explanatory potential. The idea of a structure can be illuminated by contrasting it with the idea of an aggregate.

A mass of bricks lying randomly on the ground where they have fallen from the back of a lorry are a mere aggregate, with no systematic relation to each other. But if we build them into an arch, they make a structure. Those at the bottom support the bricks above them, while the keystone at the top completes the shape and stops the curve of the arch falling inwards. The way that the bricks are related to each other here has major consequences; the ones at the bottom bear more weight than those at the top; knock out the keystone and large sections of the curve may collapse. People are more like the bricks in the arch than those lying around on the ground. That is, they are systematically related to each other through being located in positions in varieties of social structure, positions which, by virtue of their relation with other positions, have consequential outcomes. People in high positions in social hierarchies, for example, derive relative advantages which are systematically linked to the relative disadvantages of those in lower positions.

Social structural analysis has the job of identifying the many different processes which effectively fix numbers of people into different interrelated positions (placing them into different boats, so to speak) which have consequences for how they typically might act and relate to one another. A structure is a social structure when it is composed of social relations. There are many different kinds of social structure whose conditioning powers interact in complex ways to constitute environments for action. We now have to begin to consider some of

the more important sources of differences of social position ('consequential arrangements') which have the capacity to condition action.

Examples of consequential arrangements: effects of serial ordering, number and scale

We suggested a moment ago that it is helpful to think of the concept
of social structure as referring to all the forms of consequential social
arrangements that constrain us. Notice that this definition suggests
that social structuring involves consideration of the relative autonomy of arrangements as such. We can begin to grasp this sort of
autonomy by first considering some simple examples of unavoidable
positioning which affect social relations.

For example, every child has a position in a birth order which
shapes their relations with their brothers and sisters and parents.
Consider the effects of being an only child, the first-born or later in a
birth order of siblings. Surely these differences of position are consequential? The predicament of only children is often discussed. There
are advantages (usually a 2:1 parent–child ratio) and disadvantages
(relative isolation, being 'spoilt', being cross-pressured to be an ally in
parental conflicts). All positions give their occupants certain powers
but also expose them to liabilities (Sayer, 1992: 105). Now consider
being first-born. Are first-born constrained differently from their
younger brother(s) and/or sister(s)? Does anybody think different
positions in this serial order have no consequences? We doubt it.
There is evidence suggesting that first-borns do better educationally,
but are less confident and adventurous than second and subsequent
siblings. Sulloway (1996: 42–3) found later-born children (Darwin
among them) massively overrepresented in the ranks of scientific
innovators. Although this is a controversial suggestion, it is true that
serial ordering necessarily affects access to resources; in families, only
first-borns are ever going to experience being repositioned from
having all the attention to having only some of it. This is a property
of their position that is independent of the quality of the attention
they receive. It is a strictly objective and structural problem which
insightful parents have to deal with whether they like it or not.

Take a related example. Do you think that the numbers of members
of a group such as a family, and whether they are odd or even, makes
a difference? Doesn't scale affect the resources available for the well-
being of each child? Does the ratio of adult carers to dependent child-

ren matter? Could there be effects for the internal politics of families arising from the possibilities of coalition formation and balances of power of large or small and even or uneven numbers (Caplow, 1968)?

We can extend the discussion of numbers to consider scale effects for examples of much larger organisations such as nation-states. Why are there relatively few small nation-states, in terms of population and territorial extent? Is there something about being small which restricts the likelihood of the emergence and/or persistence of political independence? Does the ability to sustain relations of independence from other states involve questions of access to sufficient resources – raw materials, labour, food supply, trading partners, defensible borders, military alliances, a sufficient degree of internal coordination, transport and so on? Are these things likely to require that the state has a minimum size (Gellner, 1973)?

Conversely, can political and other kinds of organisation become too big for their own good? There are very few large nation-states and generally no more than two superpowers. Maybe there are certain advantages to being small(er). What disadvantages are there to being large, geographically, organisationally, economically, militarily and in terms of population? We do not need to discuss the question of scale effects at length – it is a technically interesting topic – but only to insist that it is an example of a kind of structural constraint. It sets the scene for actors, who have to work around it whether they like it or not.

Social structure defined: (ii) distributions of power and resources

We have emphasised that the way positions are related is a powerful conditioning force in human life. Children are obviously caught up in conditions of life, which they do not control and do not choose. But so are we all; the positioning effects of the past constrain us at every turn, far beyond the point when we have got over our education. The central implication of social structure, we have seen, is that we inhabit a social world, not just of culture, but of relations between positions that is already set up for us. The social world is already arranged and these arrangements are potentially consequential.

We now begin to consider what makes differences of position so consequential, which involves examining the substantive character of social structures. The first consideration is that, as all our examples in this book show, with positions go resources, whether these be the attention parents can give their children, having a room of one's own, opportunities to earn income, having defensible frontiers or the authority conferred on seniority. So this distributional conditioning of the powers of actors is a major reason why the concept of social structure is so important for social explanation.

To appreciate the force of social structures and the part it can play in social explanation, first think of all the important resources one needs in order to act. The list might include money, health, education, housing, information, legal rights, transport, credit, jobs, political representation and so on. Now think how one is constrained by the way in which access to resources is distributed and the social arrangements one has to participate in to have access to any of them. One has to fulfil expectations associated with specific roles (positions) such as employee (to gain wages), student (for access to grants, loans, discounts, cheap fares), next of kin (for possibilities of inheritance), tenant (if you want rented accommodation), citizen (for rights to education, health care, police protection and so on).

Some resources are more abundant and easier to get at than others for someone in a given position. There are, analytically speaking, two interrelated variables here. Improving your resources is not just a matter of increasing their amount, but of altering your relations with some relevant other people. Social structures collectivise people (place them in the same boat) in terms of their access to resources and opportunities for action.

Social structure defined: (iii) kinds of social power and the organisation of practices

In the examples just given, powers were associated with the roles people play as participants in different kinds of practice. Bearing in mind what we said in Chapter 3 about human nature being intrinsically social (since individuals are unable to survive as isolates), location of positions in some sort of organisation is unavoidable. The production of the necessities of existence as well as biological reproduction are only done by engaging in collective practices which involve relations between more or less specialised roles. Collective practices have to be organised and that involves defining the various contributions which participants ought to make to the collective enterprise. These definitions of roles define how those playing them (incumbents) ought to relate to one another and what their respective powers are. Collective practices therefore generate social structures, that is, the sets of interacting role positions which make up the organisation of each practice.

Collective practices, such as producing food, bringing up children or providing health care or justice, for example, involve people in discovering how to do things together, making the best use of the powers that are available to them in the circumstances. This is not just a process of technical development and it has not generally been done in a spirit of equality. Rather, it has involved those with power to dominate trying to force on others forms of practice which they think will be in their, the powerful's, interests. (When considering the destruction of traditional hunting grounds, Chapter 4 asked whose interests were served by the change to industrialism.) The organisation of practices is the result of a combination of constraints. Some are technical, arising from the material nature of what is being done. Others arise from the use of social power. The practices that emerge from this process have to be sufficient to get the job done, but how they are organised will reflect the distribution of power.

The general point is that the social structuring of practices reflects the use of power and has consequences for the distribution of power. Organisations of roles emerge as the consequence of learning and struggles and may be institutionalised, that is, subjected to a process of formal regularisation; jobs are specified, rules are written, expectations are made prescriptive and sanctions are put in place. However, whatever the degree of institutional rationalisation, role performance is never exactly limited by the formal rules, for two different sorts of reason. First, there are those discussed in the previous chapters on action; performing formal roles demands exercising practical judgement. But second, institutional settings of roles provide an environment which role players can work to their own advantage, allowing them scope to create their own structure of positions and relationships which operates informally. We saw, for example, in Chapter 8, how informal exchanges of clients between caseworkers were arranged. This is the realm of discretion, informal privileges, cliques and networks.

Structural problems of organisations

Even though one may be powerful, to build an organisation to undertake some practice or other means having to confront basic objective issues of organisational technique and design. Suppose you want to increase productivity. One method is to analyse the production process and break it down into separate parts. These parts can then be used as a basis for specialisation. This specialisation enables each stage of production to be done efficiently, perhaps with a superior level of skill and increased quality control. However, specialisation cannot yield its benefits unless equal attention is paid to a new problem it creates, which is that of ensuring that each of the now separated departments of the specialised production process remain coordinated – kept working together. In more social theoretical language, *differentiation* creates a problem of *integration*. It is unavoidable and something has to be done to solve it, or the benefits of specialisation will be difficult to achieve. Famously, Durkheim made it his life's work to identify the forces which could maintain social integration in the face of the disintegrating effects of an increasingly specialised division of labour in modern times.

Over the course of human history, people have developed great expertise in the pros and cons of different methods of organisation to define and coordinate roles. Just consider the problem of control faced by the boss of a large company, the head of a large school or the monarch of an absolutist state. They cannot be everywhere at once, directly supervising those they depend on. They will have to use some methods for indirect control. The rulers of the historically early forms of large organisation (for example states and empires) tended to use the threat of force (made credible by intermittent and dramatically staged violence), networks of informers and religious sanctions. But given the opportunity to learn from experience, sophisticated techniques of indirect control have been developed to ensure that role players do what they are supposed to do. One of the most sophisticated (an example was described in Chapter 8), which Max Weber called 'technically superior', is bureaucracy (Weber, 1968: 973).

Advantages and limitations of bureaucracy

Bureaucratic organisation combines various techniques of internal control, such as paying salaries (to stop workers using the organisation's resources for their own ends), appointing people on the basis of their expertise (to ensure that people are competent to perform their roles), regular but not continuous monitoring of their work, formal job definitions (so that there is no doubt about what is expected) and a career structure rewarding exceptional performance (encouraging internal competition and inhibiting workplace alliances). Bureaucracy is an organisational method playing on the internal motivation, self-interest and capacity for self-direction of employees. It is a brilliant political technique of domination which gets bureaucratic workers to discipline themselves, following rules, even emotionally identifying with them, in the absence of close supervision. Rulers who do not use such a technique will have to dominate their own organisations in some other way, perhaps by the actual or threatened use of force (Ivan the Terrible earned his name this way) or by allying with religious authorities promising salvation as a reward for obedience. A state or ruler who has command of bureaucratised administration, and does not have to rely on inherently unreliable military forces or religious authorities, is in a very powerful position to exercise domination over their subjects and competitors.

However, even the sophistication of the bureaucratic method of organisation has its structural problems. First, bureaucracies try to anticipate all the kinds of situation which concern them and to specify rules and regulations for their handling. But, as Chapter 8 pointed out, there are always cases which do not fit the rules or require employees to exercise judgement about which rule to apply. So rules are not enough and the effort to stick too closely to them may result in inefficiency. Indeed, there may be situations where risk-taking and innovation, rather than rule-following, are needed to solve a problem. Thus to encourage conformity by making employees economically secure may be detrimental in some circumstances, if it reduces employees willingness to be risk-embracing innovators.

This is an example of what might be called a 'structural contradiction'. Similarly, bureaucracies are hierarchies, controlled from the top. Those above need to know what is going on below them. But maybe it is in the interests of those at lower levels to control the flow of information upwards so that it does not harm their own career prospects and so on. In any case, usually only those filling a position can really know all the details of what is involved in actually doing it. So those at the top of bureaucratic organisations will always be making decisions based on incomplete information. Bureaucracies are vulnerable to internal differences of interest and shortfalls of knowledge which may get in the way of their effective functioning.

Structural contradictions: the problem of integration

Now we can suggest that there may be more than one kind of contradiction associated with social structures. For example, there are contradictions generated by people's simultaneous location in more than one structure. You are both working class and British, so which way do you jump? Do you support your class interest or your national interest? Will you volunteer to fight the German working class in the First World War trenches? ('Yes' in 1914, but conscription had to be introduced in 1916.) But there can also be contradictions between the elements and practices of a given structure. Put simply, a structural contradiction in this sense exists where an arrangement or way of doing something actually inhibits or stops that something being done. We have just considered the case of bureaucracy. It seeks efficiency by anticipating kinds of cases and expanding the rules to govern practice. But rule dependence stores up the typical crisis faced by bureaucrats which is 'what do we do when the rules don't fit?' So the strength of bureaucracy is also a weakness. That is a contradiction.

Capitalism and its contradictions

Probably the best-known examples of structural contradictions are entailed by capitalism. Capitalism is a form of organisation to produce. It is a way of coordinating labour, materials, technology, decision-making and rewards. Capitalists attempt to secure profits by competing against other producers, driving down the costs of production by keeping wages as low as possible and mechanising the production process wherever they can. However, this form of economic organisation creates several problems for itself. One is the tension between workers' roles as producers and consumers. If workers' wages rise, this threatens profits, but so do wages that are too small to allow workers to buy the products the capitalist is selling. So wages must not be too low, in order to allow profitable consumption. Another is that workers have social costs – health, education and housing needs – which the employer would rather not pay for through wages. So they favour these needs being met by someone else, usually the state. Capitalists therefore have an interest in the welfare state, but the welfare state has to be paid for out of taxation and capitalists do not want to pay high taxes. However, where the threat to the labour supply seems sufficiently serious and the state, for various reasons, is unable or unwilling to act effectively, capitalists may fund these costs, as demonstrated by South African mining companies agreeing in 2002 to pay for the anti-AIDs health education of their workers (and only fund medicine for workers but not their families). A third contradiction is that capitalism historically increases productivity as an outcome of technical developments derived from capitalists' quests for profits. But although this opens up the possibility of producing sufficient to meet general human needs, this potential is not realised, since output can only be produced for those who can pay – poverty and a huge market in luxury goods thus sit side by side.

Coping with structural contradictions

Structural contradictions can be thought of as setting problems for actors to solve. Sometimes the only complete solution is to abandon the structure itself. Total structural change is the strategy of revolutionaries. But it is seldom practical, simply because the past casts too long a shadow and cannot be denied; although some have tried, for example in the killing fields of Cambodia. Utopian social thought tries the experiment of conceptualising perfectly integrated structures without contradictions. But practical social theories tend to acknowledge that perfect integration is not generally possible, although there are instances of smoothly operating organisations. Realistically, social theorists try to specify the points of contradiction and structural tension as issues around which some sort of containment, limitation, careful management and compromise or balance has to be struck. The impression of a smooth running organisation is usually the result of skilful management, a long period of learning about the structural problems, acceptance of necessary compromises, a relatively stable environment of action and good fortune in avoiding accidents.

Thus capitalists cope with the contradictions of capitalism by trying to achieve enough profit (rather than maximise it) and agree to pay some tax while working to keep the state's demands down to a reasonable level. For example, in late 2000, UK car makers threatened to shift their car component orders outside Britain, thereby putting 750,000 jobs at risk, if the government imposed a new energy tax. The chancellor had already cut car manufacturers' national insurance contributions to meet their concern but they felt this was insufficient, given that their industry is energy rather than labour intensive. They used their ability to create job losses, which would cost the welfare state in unemployment benefit, to try to force a change of policy. The government response involved judging the seriousness of the threat and considering whether to reduce the energy tax a bit and/or increase the NI exemption a bit. In the event, they judged that the threat of job losses because of energy tax levels was small and that car makers were influenced primarily by wage levels and labour quality. Motor manufacturers routinely shift their orders for components to get them as cheaply as possible and the energy tax was not likely to be a major factor in making British suppliers uncompetitive.

This sort of situation is generic to social life. Everyone finds themselves having to balance the demands of contradictory structural locations and practices. It is often difficult and generally stressful. One classic case is the experience of people whose roles in the middle of hierarchies mean that they need to satisfy demands from above and below. Should the foreman side with the workers or the management? Does the waitress satisfy the demands of her customers or the people in the kitchen? Is the sergeant one of the men or one of the officers? Is the petit bourgeois shopkeeper a worker or a capitalist? They are structurally required to acknowledge the interests of both positions and are poorly placed to succeed unless they can cultivate special negotiating skills and privileges, for example places (the sergeants' mess, the Rotary Club) where they can unwind away from the constant friction of their public lives.

Structural positions and interests

These examples show that there is a systematic connection between positions in distributional orders, the logic of the kinds of distributional order that they are, and the *interests* of the people in the different positions. Interests are collectively formed by the logic of position and people often act on them. Thus we inhabit a social world characterised by typicality and strong tendencies. To take a very simple example, it is a logical truism that those at the top of any given stratification order cannot go any higher. If they change their position, it can only be for the worse. But although in the logical sense this is a truism, it is nevertheless interesting; it tells us something about the implications of stratification orders. Armed with this understanding, we are better placed to explain why it is that those at the top of stratification systems tend to be against changes which widen the opportunities for upward mobility for those lower down. Their support for such changes can often only be secured by persuading them that they will not lose when those below them gain. This generally involves policies of expansion so that every one can improve their lot, without threatening the differential advantage of those at the top.

Typically, the advantaged seek to conserve their privileges by supporting the status quo, voting Conservative and so on, while the disadvantaged tend to attempt to change the existing state of things by supporting progressive movements and legislation, voting for left-wing parties and so on. Those in the middle who want to improve their situation, but also guard against losing what they already have, tend to be floating voters shifting between left and right. This is a very strong pattern that holds for many social orders, not just the contemporary capitalist liberal democracies such as Britain. But we must remember that the nature of social structuring is to condition, not determine, action and that actors act according to their creative interpretation of the relevance of elements of their cultures. This interaction of the conditioning forces of social structure, culture and action, as well as the distinctiveness of individuals, means that despite strong tendencies creating patterns in behaviour, exceptions are allowed for.

Working-class Tories and socialist aristocrats (for example Tony Benn) are the exceptions to the rule. But they are not unintelligible nor random. They are explained as the outcome of the interaction of contradictory structural pressures, or kinds of experience, strongly held cultural commitments and strength of moral personality which may work against each other. Thus a worker may vote Tory because he or she hopefully anticipates their own individual upward mobility. A less ambitious person from the same class might not have done so. Alternatively, although disadvantaged in class terms, some workers feel advantaged by their membership of a national community and a British way of life, and want to conserve this privilege, more than they want to reduce their class disadvantage. In the case of a socialist aristocrat, the strength of commitment to the political and moral ideals of socialism and democracy mean that he or she must pay a price, by giving up his or her aristocratic privileges. Some people are sufficiently committed to cultural ideals to be willing to accept the sacrifices that their structural location forces them to make. They go against the grain of their structural conditioning. That interests are collectively formed by positions in social structures, that these interests may contradict one another and cross-pressure groups and individuals and that as a result there is a measure of indeterminacy in the way people respond to their structural positions is a fundamental insight of Marx, Weber and Bourdieu, and is a central tenet of realist social theory.

We can sum up the discussion so far by saying that action takes place in an environment of already existing institutions and practices. These have their relatively autonomous properties which condition action. We cannot just do as we like but have to work within the framework of an already arranged social world. What there is to do and what there is to do it with are to a large extent predetermined. These institutions and practices position actors, thereby conditioning their interests, particularly their attitude to change. But positions also create dilemmas for actors because:

- being positioned in several different orders distributing different resources creates conflicts of interest

- the expectations linked to any given role may be contradictory

- there may be contradictions between the expectations of different roles in an actor's role set

- there may be contradictions within and between whole institutions

- there may be contradictions within and between whole institutional spheres.

These are the sorts of relations which figure in the analysis of the integration of social systems and the nature of structural conditioning or constraint

What makes social structures relatively durable and resistant to change?

We can now turn to the question of how action and interaction are implicated in the production, reproduction and transformation of social structures. Various hints of what is involved have already been given. One factor is that practices which work well enough tend to acquire a certain inertia, as people try to extract value from their past investments and avoid the costs of change. Generally, change is forced on people by crisis and the need to remain competitive, as we saw when considering technical choice in Chapter 3.

However, the most important process with implications for the persistence or change of social structures is that of how actors use their structural positions, the legacy of their own and others' actions. But unless we subscribe to individualism, we know that the persistence or transformation of the conditions of action is not simply a matter of the decisions and activity of actors, individually or collectively. Whatever the interests of actors, they have to have the power to influence outcomes if they are to get what they want. And the sad fact is that the power to influence outcomes is unequally distributed. So, if those with the greatest power want to conserve their advantage, they are in the best position to do so. They can use their power to defend their hold on it. They will have sufficient surplus resources to expand them by investing, diversifying, experimenting and consolidating. Typically, the powerful try to control the future by securing legal protections for property, regularising inheritance rights, supervising marriage, investing abroad, securing tax exemptions, cultivating reputations as social benefactors, encouraging deference, influencing political culture and so on. They try to reduce the desire of those below them to oppose them and they take out insurance policies against some future time when their privileges may be successfully attacked – dictators often open Swiss bank accounts. These are all techniques for transmitting positional advantage, and hence social structures, into the future. They are important mechanisms which carry the past, transmitting it into the present to constrain action, equivalent to the transmittable, learnable symbolisation of the mechanisms of culture. Central to the mechanisms of social structure are the media of transmitting differences of power across generations.

Reinforcement, multipliers, thresholds and emergence

This brief discussion of the strategies and mechanisms used by the powerful to defend and increase their advantage provides a simple example of the way in which structure feeds back into its reproduction, reinforcing the hold of a set of conditions of action. Such cycles of reproduction of stratified orders can be very durable. Marx spoke of what he called Asiatic societies as 'vegetating in the teeth of time' (1858) – and we can wonder at the slowness of democratising the British House of Lords. The general point is that where we are faced with explaining the long-term persistence of a distributional and institutional order, we must look at the socially reproductive methods, particularly of the powerful. They are the long-term winners of an extended period of social competition. From an initial episode of securing dominance, the winners (let us say the Norman nobility following the invasion of Britain in 1066) set about dividing up the spoils and consolidating their advantage – their castles can still be seen in Wales, for example. Some of their descendants are only now losing their formal political power, as their residual techniques for defending their position, particularly deference, fail.

The other side of the picture shows the strategies and mechanisms used by those interested in reducing their disadvantages. From a position of relative weakness, the crucial issue is how to assemble sufficient power to counteract the reproductive forces which they are up against. The organising of collective actors is an important *multiplier* of power. All strata organise but it is particularly important in the repertoire of those who, as individuals, are weak. Trade unions, cooperative societies, credit unions, housing associations, new social movements and people power are examples. In each case, the transformation of a structure of disadvantage depends on using techniques to increase power (be it political or economic) sufficient, firstly, to bring about change and, secondly, to institutionalise the new order, that is, place the gains on a reproducible footing. However, although combination can increase the capacities of the individually weak, even collectively they may still be disadvantaged in relation to the individually strong, because it is generally more difficult to sustain a large organisation of individually weak people than a small organisation of individually powerful ones. Small elites of well-coordinated, powerful members are intrinsically better placed to keep themselves ready for action (Piven and Cloward, 1979).

The problem that the disadvantaged face, of putting together sufficient power not only to produce change, but also to sustain any gains and avoid falling back into the previous condition of disadvantage, shows the importance of rising above a *threshold* of power sufficient to permit the emergence of a new configuration of advantage and disadvantage (for 'threshold models', see Granovetter, 1978). Remember in Chapter 2, how Stack's friend, Ruby, failed to accumulate enough resources to cross the threshold required to make her escape from her dependence on kin? Some recent work on black and white access to mortgages, and thus home ownership, in the United States provides us with another example of how low income and discrimination can interrelate in complex ways which make it difficult to escape disadvantaged structural positions intra- or intergenerationally.

A smaller proportion of blacks than whites get mortgages and become home owners. The reasons for this include direct discrimination by mortgage providers (estimated to be 8 per cent of the refused applications), blacks' concentration in neighbourhoods which lenders define as risky, their lower income levels and lesser security of employment. But, in addition, those who do borrow often have to pay more for their loans than whites, for several reasons. Lower incomes and lack of financial help from parents, for example, means that they cannot put down the larger deposits which reduce the interest rates for the remainder of the purchase. They can also only afford smaller loans, which attract higher charges because they are costly to administer. Thus, those who do buy, immediately pay more for less than their white counterparts, which variously reduces their capacity to improve their situation. Paying $4–8,000 more than their white counterparts for a $35,000, 25-year loan, they lose the opportunity of investing this sum profitably, using it to finance their children's education or to help them with house purchase in their turn. They then lose out again because of the far greater capital appreciation of property in all-white than in black or mixed-'race' areas. Thus the disadvantaged and discriminated against pay more for a less worthwhile investment, often failing to acquire the resources which could propel their children out of the disadvantaged situation. Those denied mortgages, of course, make no capital gains from housing at all (Oliver and Shapiro, 1997: 136–70).

The capacity to accumulate sufficient resources to make them intergenerationally transmittable is often a precondition for reconfiguring the long-term balance of power. In fact, humans lived for most of their history in small hunter-gatherer bands which were egalitarian and stateless, because of the difficulty of solving this problem. Although the original hunter-gatherer societies must have been led by dominant individuals on the basis of their physical and intellectual powers, these powers were relatively temporary and could not be stored and transmitted to others, say, their children. There was no way of developing a surplus and getting power above the threshold required to make it inheritable. Power could not be passed down the generations and thus no durable stratification system could develop. This did eventually emerge but under special environmental conditions such as those encouraging the development of agriculture described in Chapter 3 (Mann, 1986: 34–72).

Conclusion

The concept of social structure (summarised in Figure 9.2) implies five fundamental claims:

1. A major feature of social reality is that it consists of interrelated social positions.
2. These organisations of positions have their own properties.
3. These must be distinguished from the properties of the particular individuals who occupy them.
4. These properties include mechanisms which distribute power to actors and make for durable power structures.
5. The action of actors is conditioned, rather than entirely determined, by the positions they occupy.

Social structure is therefore an important source of the predictability of behaviour and contributes to the explanation of typicality in social experience. However, this must be qualified by saying that how these inequalities constrain individuals is a complex matter. It depends on what they are trying to do, on how they work with what they've got and what price they are prepared to pay to act virtuously against the logic of their positional interests. The rich often lose their fortunes out of bad luck or incompetence but also, sometimes, voluntarily give up privileges for moral reasons. Similarly, the poor may get rich by luck and/or effort and talent, and equally make choices about the price they are prepared to pay to get what they want and do what is right. There is room in social theory for unselfish, morally motivated actors who put the good of others above their own, positionally conditioned self-interest. But the fact that virtuous individuals can make a difference in no way undermines the claim that being positioned in a structure of inequality has major constraining effects of a determinate kind on all the occupants of a given position.

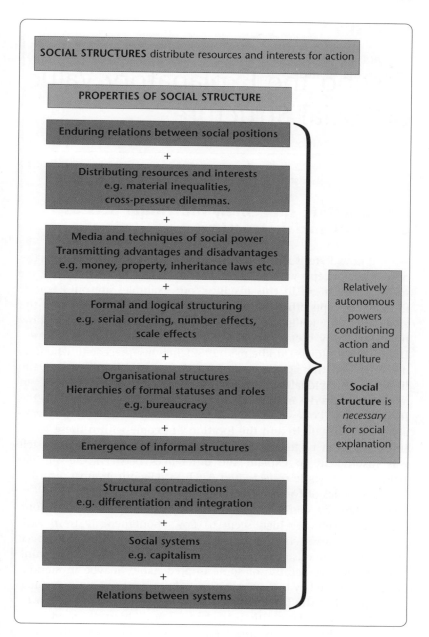

Figure 9.2 Summary: the relative autonomy of social structure – how it works

CHAPTER 10

Testing the Explanatory Value of Social Structure

Introduction: supremely individual acts as effects of social structure

We will now do for social structure what we have already done for the other four concepts we are claiming are necessary, but insufficient, for social explanation. In this instance, our examples are ones where, initially, concepts other than social structure might seem to do all the explaining. But whilst we recognise that they play a role, we show how powerfully social structure is in fact operating in these cases. Doing this follows Durkheim's (1952) famous precedent when he demonstrated the significance of social structure by discussing the limits of individualist and environmentalist explanations of an apparently utterly individual act – suicide. He showed that the tendency to kill oneself varied with the kinds of social structure available to participate in and the location of people within these structures. His chief target was psychological explanation, which he felt was insufficient to explain the differences between the suicidal tendencies of whole collectivities (such as religious groups) recorded in the statistics of comparative suicide rates.

We begin by considering two of many examples of behaviour, belief and feeling, which seem to flow spontaneously from each individual, but which are patterned by the person's location in social structures. A famous example is romantic love. We may like to think that love strikes because of some unpredictable, maybe mysterious attraction evoked by the entirely personal properties of one individual in another. But the fact that the vast majority of us are smitten by individuals in similar positions in class or 'racial' hierarchies, with the same ethnic identities as ourselves, requires us to modify this view. There is cultural and social structural clustering of mate selection.

Indeed, the idea of romantic love itself, and especially belief in its validity for selecting one's future spouse, is not universal or natural, but is particularly characteristic of modern societies where the power of the senior generation to control their children's mate selection is weakened (Parsons, 1954: 187–9).

Tony Ashworth's First World War study provides a further example of social structure's impact on emotions. His work (which parallels Durkheim's *Suicide*) shows that aggression and bravery were not simply individual dispositions, but varied systematically between elite and non-elite battalions, specialist weapon units (for example snipers, machine gunners, hand bombers) and non-specialist ones, and the first phase of local, personal control of violence (before the winter of 1915–16) and the following period of more thoroughly bureaucratised, impersonal command (Ashworth, 1980: 45–6, 77, 82–4). Individuals' behaviour varied with their positions relative to technologies, organisations and command structures (1980: 48–53). Although there might be some variations between the valour of individual soldiers in the same unit in the same situation, the overall differences between units were not to be explained by distinctions in the personal qualities of those who composed them.

However, explanations in terms of any of the key concepts dealt with so far, and not just individualism, are likely to need supplementing by reference to the causal effects of social structure. Below, we continue to illustrate the importance, but then also the insufficiency of social structural explanations, with reference to phenomena where, initially, the claims of nature and then of culture have been argued to be particularly compelling. Both the examples deal with phenomena which are effects of the long-term, global, social structural transformation called 'modernisation', which the social sciences were invented to understand. They are examples of powerful social structural causation, but even here we insist that social structural*ism* is inappropriate.

The origins of modern nationalism and the nation-state

Historical sociology (sometimes called 'macrosociology') tries to explain long-term, widespread change in the patterning of people's behaviour and beliefs. One such development is the emergence and diffusion of the doctrine of nationalism. Nationalism stipulates that the social world should be conceptualised as naturally divided into groups or nations (usually associated with a specific territory) whose members share the same culture and, usually, language. It then argues that each cultural group has an inbuilt desire to be self-governing and enjoy national self-determination. Any inequalities of power and privilege among members of the society should not correspond to differences of cultural identity (for example differences of religion or language). This requires the establishment of special kinds of state – nation-states – to ensure the congruity of political and cultural boundaries. Nation-states promise inclusion (although not necessarily equality) to those who adequately conform to their culture. So the problem is, why should this doctrine and principle of state formation have emerged and become so popular around the world over the past 200 years or so?

Nationalist ideologists themselves have offered one answer by arguing that the human species is naturally divided into the different national groups which they recognise and it is natural for people to reject rule by those culturally different from themselves (Gellner, 1997: 8–9). Nationalists typically see their nations as having great historical depth. However, since nationalist demands for nation-states are comparatively recent, they have to explain why the supposedly primordial desire to avoid rule by cultural outsiders has not always been manifest. Their typical resort to mysterious processes and metaphors, such as 'national awakening' by charismatic leaders, is less than satisfactory. The 'nations are natural and eternal' argument does not explain why national*ism* was switched on and remained on for the last two centuries. We need some other, non-naturalistic factors to explain why the ideas, leadership, emotion and commitment typical of nationalist movements occurred when they did.

Cultural implications of modernity

One of the most influential approaches to this question, Ernest Gellner's *Nations and Nationalism* (1983) and *Nationalism* (1997), suggests that nationalism was produced by macroscopic changes associated with modernisation. This social structural development changed the way people were positioned to pursue their interests during the period in which nationalism emerged. By 1700, Western Europe was organised into intensely competitive states. Extended struggle between fairly evenly matched major states meant that for a long time there was constant pressure to upgrade the techniques of power: 'Each major geopolitical state was itself a virtual network of production, distribution, exchange and consumption ... in a wider regulated interstate space' (Mann, 1986: 514). Production, the organisation of labour, state administration, commerce, transport, agriculture and law, among others, started to break free from traditional techniques. This is the period when industrialisation, bureaucratisation, urbanisation and rationalisation intensified to form, by about 1850, the complex referred to as 'modernisation'. Tried and tested practices and ways of legitimating social arrangements typical of traditional, agrarian societies were challenged by the competitive advantages provided by the new, rationalised, relatively impersonal methods.

Modernisation radically changed the field of action for people conditioned and positioned by thousands of years of experience of agrarian society, where they were organised into a multitude of small communities, identifying with their own local, oral, context-dependent, 'low' cultures. Most people, in societies of this type, interacted within a small area and were, spatially and socially, relatively immobile. The local division of labour and status hierarchy was seen as natural and unchangeable. The few members of ruling elites, whose interaction was not spatially restricted, dominated primarily by military and religious intimidation. They had access to literacy, a basic 'high' cultural technique, permitting symbolic representation and analytical distancing from reality, but used it primarily for intra-elite communication. Such societies did not need the rulers to share the culture of the ruled, so political and cultural boundaries often diverged. Most people did not need the literate high culture of their rulers in order to participate in the local social relations that mattered to them.

Modernising power techniques meant adopting the generalising, analytical approach to all problems encouraged by literacy; attacking ignorance, inconsistency and inefficiency. As we noted when discussing this rationalisation process in Chapter 5, no privileged spheres of meaning were exempt from analysis. In a world understood as universally subject to the laws of science, modernisation broke reality down into bits which might be profitably rearranged into new combinations. Education had to be developed to teach, not the eternal truths held dear by the many local low cultures, but generic techniques for analysing and manipulating reality. This was the new, highly valued knowledge for producing, and participating in, a world of ceaseless change.

Education became standardised, universalised and less specialised, allowing for occupational flexibility during an individual's lifetime. In agrarian societies, specialisation could be very intense; think of the technical brilliance of craft production in agrarian empires. But such specialist achievement was the outcome of generations of workers perfecting their traditions. Modern life, by contrast, requires people to be mobile, spatially, socially and in their imaginations. They must relax their attachments to the tried and tested and search for new improvements. Those well positioned to pursue their interests in modern society are educated into the type of culture which escapes confined local horizons. This culture is high because it overarches the multitude of local cultures.

Modernisation and state education systems

Modernising states promote the dissemination of high culture in order to make their populations competent in the latest power techniques. They need literate, numerate workers, engineers, scientists, officials, the military, teachers, health specialists and so on in order to be competitive with other states. But this interest of state coincides with the desire of many in their population to tap into the benefits of participating in the non-local spheres of interaction which modernisation opens up. Locality and kin are no longer sufficient to provide the generic knowledge needed for effective use of opportunities in the non-local world. Thus many seek formal education and to live in political units big enough to sustain educational establishments which can supply it. Modern states all invest in education systems and are under constant pressure to expand provision (Archer, 1979; Collins, 1979). Access to education is a universal demand of people caught up in modernisation.

Egalitarianism and cultural competition

What are the connections between this process and the growth of nationalism? There are two: egalitarianism and cultural competition. Modernity encourages egalitarianism because modernisation and industrialism constantly change the division of labour in the search for improvement. People try to increase their power by using their generic education to keep up with the latest techniques. However, advantages and rewards from such specialising may be relatively quickly displaced by later, better techniques. This tendency for investments in specialisms to be undermined means that people experience a social world of upward and downward mobility as their fortunes rise and fall. Modern societies have, compared to agrarian societies, relatively open social structures, because mechanisms for accumulating and transmitting social advantages across time are comparatively weak.

This is reflected in their stratification systems and terms for legitimating inequalities. Differences of reward can be great in industrial, class-structured societies but, in relation to preindustrial social orders, they tend to be graduated and not easily used as impermeable barriers to interaction. As suggested in earlier chapters, discontinuities tend to be most likely in the lower reaches, where unqualified labour finds it hard to assemble and transmit resources to lift its children off the bottom. But even such sharp breaks are unintended and not formally prescribed, unlike many of the stratifying divisions in traditional, agrarian societies, where status divides are often strong and interaction between those of different ranks is ritually formalised. Industrial societies tend to encourage flexibility and complexity so that the social properties of individuals become more randomised, difficult to predict and provisional. The working assumption for participants is that although they may have different cultures of origin and be located in classes, they are also strangers, who are in the same modern industrial boat as each other, can operate modern high culture and are all included in the competition for success.

Here is the core of Gellner's theory. He argues that inequalities generated by informal stratification mechanisms of industrial social structures are tolerable for the relatively disadvantaged to the extent that the advantaged are felt to have earned their rewards by their own individual talent and effort, and there are opportunities for the disadvantaged to improve their lot by the same means. Being disadvantaged should not exclude one being considered a legitimate competitor; winners and losers stay in the game. But where the advantaged and the disadvantaged are culturally distinguished, and the persistent disadvantaging of ethnic groups undergoing modernisation supports the suspicion that they are being excluded from the game on cultural grounds, then nationalism will flourish. Gellner describes the experience of the culturally disadvantaged:

> People really become nationalists because they find that in their daily social intercourse, at work and at leisure, their 'ethnic' classification

largely determines how they are treated, whether they encounter sympathy and respect, or contempt, derision or hostility. The root of nationalism is not ideology, but concrete daily experience. (1996: 123)

Given the expectation that the business of modern life be conducted in terms of a unified high culture, a central problem for modernisers is how to transform existing culture(s), the legacy of the agrarian era, into an effective medium of the said high culture. Early modernising states (for example England and France) had already established high levels of cultural and linguistic unity and thus a de facto coincidence of cultural and political boundaries. Their pre-existing cultures could provide the idiom and language of their new education systems. Only at their peripheries did the introduction of a state education system involve overriding local cultures (for example Welsh, Scottish, Breton, Basque). Big cultures became the carriers of the passport to modernity and little cultures declined because they were marginal to modernisation. Their members had to learn the alien tongue or forgo the benefits of participating in modernity.

However, in regions modernising later, and in the context of culturally and linguistically divided states, competition ensued to become the cultures of states big enough to sustain education systems. Where large political units overarched a number of relatively large, culturally distinct populations, suppression was impractical. Here, modernisation involved either the state developing an education system which somehow cultivated high cultural homogeneity, whilst simultaneously giving substantial recognition to the different cultures, or the stimulation of the different cultures to try to establish their own states with their own educational uniformity (for example in the nineteenth-century Hapsburg Empire of Central Europe). To be left as a culture without a state or 'political roof', as Gellner calls it, was avoidable only if the population and potential territory was sufficiently large to resource a sustainable independent state. Generally, cultures big enough to encourage their intellectuals to imagine forming their own state have tried to create one. Little cultures have tended to be squeezed out, or lingered on, suffering the humiliations of cultural exclusion. Gellner (1983: 44–5) suggests that, at best, only about 10 per cent of the world's cultures/languages are supported by a nationalist movement and far fewer actually achieve statehood.

Central to Gellner's theory is the compulsory effect of industrial or modern society whose techniques offer growth and the promise of material improvements. Once this promise is recognised, and the attractions of mobility felt, access to its generic culture matters. The language and idiom of formal education is the gate to this precious high culture. If one already has that language, one is lucky. If one does not, access is more costly. If exclusion from the chance of mobility (because one's culture is not recognised as a medium of high culture by the state's education system) is unacceptable, one has two options; either learn the educational establishment's language and assimilate the dominant form of high culture, or take the nationalist route to try to create a state, so that one's own language can be that of an education system. This route has two ends; to create a state offering mobility chances to its members, and make the agrarian era's cultural legacy into one capable of carrying the burdens of high culture. Successful nationalist movements do not simply revive folk cultures, they remake them into versions of modern culture. Where neither assimilation nor independence is possible, prolonged trouble is probable.

This is Gellner's explanation of nationalism in terms of the social structural development of modernity and industrialism. Basically, the cultural and social structural legacies of the agrarian world must be transformed. Past investments have to be re-evaluated for their usefulness in new conditions. Put simply, does what worked for millennia in the countryside of, say, the agrarian empires of Asia or feudal Europe still work in the industrial cities of modern industrial states? Social structural developments force cultural competition and re-evaluation. So the story nationalists tell about themselves, that nationalist sentiments and the politics of making culture and state coincide are universal and natural, is rejected. As Gellner (1983: 56) puts it: 'Nationalism is not what it seems and above all not what it seems to itself.'

Gellner's is a macroscopic structural analysis placing heavy emphasis on social structure. However, it is not overwhelmingly structural*ist*, because structures are thought of as only conditions of action. Social structures, cultures and action interact. The coming of modernity alters the environment of practices, roles and kinds of power; it alters the potentialities and available opportunities. It forces re-evaluation of past investments and reconfigures interests. But it is actors who move out of the agrarian world, making their choices about how much of the old they want to keep and what sort of investment in the future they want to make. Not everyone sees the nationalists' political solution as the best bet for social justice. Others, for example, have backed internationalism or socialism. They have chosen to play down the significance of cultural differences, seeking to develop new, modern, cultural continuities and political forms which overarch the boundaries of nations. Or they have decided that the unacceptable inequalities are actually produced by class structuring rather than cultural exclusion. Those who are advantaged by class structuring would generally prefer the disadvantaged not to make this interpretation and often use nationalism to deflect criticism of their advantage.

Modernisation and the maintenance of moral reputation: Bangladeshi women in London and Dhaka in the 1980s

We can now turn to our second and different kind of example of what happens when traditional agrarian cultures encounter modernity – Naila Kabeer's *The Power to Choose* (2000), a study of Bangladeshi women garment workers in Dhaka and London. This provides insight into the concrete interactional and experiential realities of the processes which Gellner talks about in a more abstract way when accounting for nationalism. Kabeer investigates a case where modernity has arrived, recently and rapidly. It enables us to see that structural causation has a certain complexity arising from two features. First, people are simultaneously positioned within many social structures and one needs to understand how the conditioning effects of these positions interact. Second, the impact of these combined structural forces is mediated by the action of those caught up in them. Thus, although modernisation radically transforms the opportunity structures open to some women, whether their lives are actually transformed depends on the different strategies used to respond to it. Kabeer shows how its impact on everyday working and domestic life, and the intimacies of personal and family relations, depends on choices.

The paradoxical weakening of purdah in Dhaka and its reinforcement in London

Kabeer studies an emerging contrast between the behaviour of Bangladeshi women in Dhaka and as immigrants in London. Both groups share a religion, Islam, and an agrarian cultural heritage placing strong emphasis on male authority and female subordination, including purdah, the practice of excluding women from the public, non-domestic realm. However, when Kabeer returned to Bangladesh in 1984 after a three-year absence, she saw large numbers of young women going to and from work on the streets of Dhaka. In the short time she had been away something radical had happened; as a matter of everyday routine, women were working in factories, earning their own wages and appearing in public spaces unsupervised by male kin, just as they do in modern Western cities. This contradicted the traditional norms which were in force when she left. Some women, at least, seemed to have rapidly made their escape from the local, agrarian world. How was such a transformation possible so quickly? The problem is compounded by the fact that, in London, Bangladeshi women, far from participating in public life, were virtually invisible. Just where one might expect them to be easily stepping onto the stage of modernity, they behaved as though the traditional norms of purdah constrained them as strongly as ever. They lived more like agrarian village women than modern citizens. What maintained the strength of their traditional culture in London?

So here is the contrast; in Dhaka, where conformity with patriarchy and purdah ought to have been strong, it was weak and in London, where it ought to have been weak, it was strong. Given that both sets of women operate in terms of a common original culture, this culture cannot account for the differences in behaviour. It must be interacting with other causal forces to shape two different decision-making environments. Cultural norms and institutionalised gender hierarchies operate in the context of structure-producing mechanisms which distribute resources to actors playing the roles assigned to them. Patriarchy, male domination, is not merely a principle of political legitimisation. It is system of rule where the cultural norms affirm male dominance and where the mechanisms for distributing material resources favour men as a category. Thus, where we see patriarchy rapidly weakening, it is likely to be the result of changes in the material resourcing of men, rather than a sudden loss of belief in the principles of legitimation. Similarly, where patriarchy is reinforced, we should look at changes in the distribution of resources to find out what is renewing its vigour.

To explain the differences between decision-making environments, we must consider the interaction of all the relevant resource-distributing, interest-forming structures, which can produce the tendencies and typicality we want to understand. These vary in their length of operation, their spatial extension and capacity to influence the lives of large numbers of individuals, cultures and organisations. For convenience we can think of such structures as ranging from the macroscopic, involv-ing large numbers of people, possibly over very long periods, to the microscopic, where positional differences hold for relatively few people for the period that they occupy the positions involved.

How social structures shape decision-making environments: the case of Dhaka

For our purposes we will concentrate on Dhaka. What factors position women to challenge, to 'take on culture' as Kabeer puts it (2000: 136)? At the most macroscopic level, they are part of the late British imper-ial system, participants in a rapidly globalising, capitalist economy and the Islamic world, located in very nearly the poorest country on earth. How these macro-factors link to the relevant decision-making environments of a particular generation of women experiencing rapid change becomes apparent at a more immediate level of structuring. The 1970s was a decade of political and economic crisis in Bangladesh. The 1970 cyclone was followed by a bloody war of inde-pendence from Pakistan (1971), a ruined economy, rising prices, the international oil crisis (1972), massive crop failure (1974–5), the army coup and assassination of Bangladesh's first leader, the secular social-ist Mujib (1976), growing government corruption, unemployment and poverty (estimated to have doubled between the 1960s and the 1980s). All this intensified the long-term crisis in the countryside where population growth reduced landholding size and increased landlessness (which stood at 41 per cent in 1971), making many more people dependent on unreliable wage earning in a stagnating rural economy. The result was reduced participation in agriculture and diversification into trade, services, crafts, transport, construction and, last but not least, migration to less populated regions, abroad, or to cities like Dhaka. In the 1980s, 81 per cent of Dhaka household heads were migrants and only 19 per cent were born in the city (Kabeer, 2000: 58).

This situation marks a shift from a traditional economy of peasant landholding, localised labour markets, kinship, patronage and communal social control, to one of commercialised agriculture, mone-tarisation and impersonal labour relations typical of modernity. Tradi-tional moral certainties gave way to chronic uncertainty. In 1981 real agricultural wages had fallen to 64% of their 1964 level. Better-off farmers economised on labour, invested in mechanisation and commercial gain rather than maintaining their traditional patronage of local labour. They sponsored their sons' education, migration abroad and sought government employment (which grew after independence). But those without land, money, education or elite contacts had no option; they remained dependent on a declining labour market (Kabeer, 2000: 59).

This gives only the broadest sketch of the radical destabilisation of traditional agrarian society in Bangladesh, which radically reduced many men's power to maintain their households from their own efforts as farmers and wage earners. Without land and with only poorly rewarded, irregular, labour market opportunities, they found it increasingly difficult to meet their patriarchal responsibilities (Kabeer, 2000: 136–41). Patriarchy required female obedience in return for male provision. Men were supposed to protect and feed their women (2000: 130–1, 187). But when men's economic power declines so does the value of women and men's normative commitment to them. Women become more of an economic liability – as shown by the growth from the 1960s of 'demand' dowry, which increased what women (and their families) had to pay to get married. Parents with several daughters could be quite impoverished by the effort to marry them. Concurrently, the incidence of divorce, separation and abandonment rose, along with female-headed households (2000: 60–2), and women started to improve their fall-back position by earning and saving (2000: 161–87).

Strategies for reducing patriarchal risk

Women, particularly poor women, became exposed to high patriarchal risk, in that accepting purdah, as the price for male support, became increasingly unreliable. Nonetheless, the female share of employment only rose from 5 to 7 per cent between 1967 and 1987. Most women accepted only home-based work (crop processing, cleaning or crafts) or were prepared to go no more than a few hundred metres to work. Although deeply internalised, purdah's resilience derived from the strength of *shamaj*, the moral economy of the local village, where everyone knows everybody else's business, making deviance difficult to hide. And, as we saw in Chapter 2, maintaining one's moral reputation is particularly important for people reliant on locally based, reciprocal exchanges of resources. Religious authorities used sacred texts to reinforce conformity to traditional norms of gender behaviour. Together with the village elites who exercised patronage in these spheres of reciprocity, they had an interest in maintaining labourers' traditional dependency and deference (Kabeer, 2000: 64).

Poor women's cultural, social and geographical positioning meant that most had to depend on unreliable men or work and risk their own reputations (their purdah) and those of the men nominally responsible for them. The most discrediting work was public, manual labour. One woman forced into such labouring 'worked in the fields at night, by moonlight, or at times when there was the least likelihood of being seen' (Kabeer, 2000: 65). Before substantial numbers of women could reduce patriarchal risk, they therefore needed not only access to reliable employment, but also a means of entering a public realm of work in a way which they felt was not morally discrediting, allowing them some way of keeping purdah – preserving their gender identity and acceptability to their families. Even those drawn to the factories by economic desperation and absence of effective male support wanted to maintain their purdah.

Migration to the city to work in the rapidly multiplying garment factories offered new employment possibilities. Following the 1982 New Economic Policy, when the government offered export incentives to domestic manufacturers, around 250,000 new jobs in large factories, 85 per cent female, were created by 1985 (Kabeer, 2000: 69). This transformation of the opportunity structure for women was the basis for the changes which Kabeer noticed on her return in 1984. Not only did employers prefer to employ women, women preferred to work with other women in a well-organised interior space (2000: 95). The gendered division of labour (cutting, packing and ironing for men, and machining largely for women), spatially segregating the sexes at work and the use of kinship terminology to describe cooperation between the sexes as that of 'brothers and sisters', contributed to framing employment in terms of traditional domestic morality (2000: 96–7). Moreover, migrants coming from many different regions were largely detached from their villages and freed from close observation by critical neighbours. They could be relatively anonymous (2000: 138). This went some way towards satisfying the desire for respectability. Reliable wages lowered patriarchal risk and factory routines and spaces provided a setting which could be interpreted as not compromising purdah (2000, 70–6). However, even women whose male kin accepted the possibility of their working had first to overcome the morally compromising obstacles of actually migrating to and living in the city. While the increase in the number of women factory workers was dramatic, the vast majority of Bangladeshi women remained subject to traditional patriarchal controls in their villages.

Kabeer reveals the ways in which women reinterpreted the conditions of maintaining their moral reputations. Rather than simply abandon patriarchal terms of self-justification, they elaborated traditional beliefs to allow them to take advantage of the new urban opportunities. One major move was to take responsibility for keeping their own purdah. Purdah was 'interiorised' so that appearing in public spaces travelling to work every day was no longer seen as discrediting. As one put it:

> Even if I am wearing a burkah and have to get on a crowded bus, I have to push past men. Wearing a burkah won't change that. The best purdah is the burkah within oneself, the burkah of the mind. (Kabeer, 2000: 91)

Men no longer had to guard it.

Another move was to reject the moral authority of religious officials and the discipline of the community *shamaj*, while insisting on winning the approval of their close male kin and acknowledging their patriarchal status. But only men who might have material patriarchal responsibilities were recognised. As Afifa put it: 'Instead of starving, if a person is working for her living, why should *shamaj* criticise her?' (Kabeer, 2000: 90). Fathers and husbands experiencing their own difficulty in fulfilling their patriarchal obligations, and who had personal knowledge of their daughters and wives, joined in this redefinition of purdah (2000: 87–92). Together they learned about what went on inside the factories (despite traditionalist rumours), what was involved in public travel and possible morally acceptable urban living arrangements (2000: 110–13). Women's moral status rose as their men decided to trust them. As time went by, working in the garment factories became accepted as a new form of women's work and new recruits found it morally easier to participate.

How social structures shape decision-making environments: the case of London's East End

We can now briefly consider the positioning of Bangladeshi women in London, in terms of the structural variables used to explain the Dhaka situation (Table 10.1 below summarises the differences). They

Table 10.1 Interacting social structures resulting in different decision-making environments for Bangladeshi women in Dhaka and London

	Dhaka	London
Macroscopic social structures conditioning opportunities for women Common legacy of British imperialism, Islam, patriarchy and purdah (the norm of female seclusion)		
Type of society	Traditional agrarian Very poor Destabilised; chronic crisis	Modern, urban, industrial Very rich Relatively stable
Type of state	Newly independent No welfare system, unemployment benefit or free education	Old welfare state Economic safety net and free education
Garment industry	New and rapidly expanding factories Export market Factory machining defined as women's work	Old and declining Domestic market Factory work limited and taken by Bangladeshi men Homeworking for women
Patriarchal risk	High	Low
Racism	No	Yes
Less macroscopic social structures conditioning the form of local social control and freedom for women as a category		
Class origin of migrants	Diverse Include the poorest	Relatively well off Landholders
Region of origin	Diverse	One region: Sylhet
Women's migration type	Independent	Sponsored by earlier male migrants
City residence and women's movement in public space	Dispersed Not clustered by region of origin Daily travel to work Visible	Concentrated in ethnic neighbourhoods Little movement outside the home Invisible
Microscopic social structures affecting the fates of individuals		
Marital status and access to male support	Diverse	Most married with access to support
Dependent children	Some	Nearly all
Education and language for employment	Possessed by some	Possessed by very few
Cultural elaboration		
Traditional norm of female seclusion – purdah	Negotiated and interiorised to permit appearance in public	Conformity to traditional domestic confinement

participated in the garment industry only as homeworkers, dependent on being given work by male intermediaries. Their employment was irregular, unregulated and poorly rewarded. It was not strongly distinguished from their other domestic tasks and their earnings tended to be absorbed into the domestic economy. Why should this relatively weak employment position exist?

First, the majority (95 per cent) of Bangladeshi migrants to Britain came from Sylhet, a particularly religious and culturally conservative region (Kabeer, 2000: 195), and from the class of independent, landholding peasants with the resources to pay the fare (2000: 194-6). Migration abroad was an option for better-off men. The traditional community system of social control was continuous between the two counties, marriages and families were spread between them and men regularly returned to Bangladesh. Second, women migrated as the wives of men who had already gained residence rights following the increasingly restrictive Commonwealth Immigration Acts of 1962 and 1968. Men decided relatively late to move their families to Britain rather than maintain the hope of some day being reunited in Bangladesh (2000: 197-8). These factors enabled *shamaj* to continue, facilitated by the migrants' concentration in London's East End, centred on Tower Hamlets, where the face-to-face community had personal networks linking directly back to Sylhet (2000: 267, 270). Third, as wives, the London women tended to be older, have more dependent children and heavier childcare responsibilities than the Dhaka garment workers, whose marital status was more varied. Fourth, Bangladeshi men had already established themselves in the British garment industry so garment work was not defined as female, as was the case in Dhaka (2000: 279-80). The British industry, supplying a volatile domestic market, wanted to maximise employee flexibility – thus expanding homeworking and subcontracting (2000: 207-15). Fifth, homeworking was available and practical for immigrant women lacking education and English. Sixth, men had a variety of employment opportunities, whilst state unemployment benefits meant that even unemployment did not result in economic desperation (quite different to the position of men in the black ghetto discussed in Chapter 2, where state benefits went only to mothers). This financial safety net meant that men's ability to meet their patriarchal obligations and insist on the traditional form of purdah was stronger than in Bangladesh. Patriarchal risk was therefore relatively low, so the pressure on women to earn was correspondingly reduced. Seventh, the welfare state also provided free education, thus removing a major motive for female employment in Bangladesh, where women worked to pay for their children's schooling. Finally, the threat of racist abuse and violence made entering public space beyond the immediate neighbourhood, not merely morally discrediting, but physically dangerous (2000: 270–1).

Taken together, these factors maintained women's dependence on men, confining them to the home. The relative economic reliability of their men buttressed by the British welfare state, together with childcare responsibilities, the absence of female outside employment opportunities, language deficit and British racism all worked to limit women's working to the home (Kabeer, 2000: 278). We see that it is the interaction between the various positioning structures which accounts for differences in the behavioural tendencies of the two groups of women. To show the effect of a particular structure, imagine it was not operating. Imagine the economic activity of East End Bangladeshi women, the changes in gender relations and patterns of residence, if racism was not present. It is probable that women would be less dependent on men, less frightened of public space, more willing to travel to work, better able to renegotiate their contribution to the family economy and more confident of keeping their moral respectability. The community boundary could be relaxed and the opportunities of the modern city taken up. Or imagine the difference made to the power of men if unemployment benefit was not available, as is the case in the black ghetto studied by Stack (where patriarchal risk was very high, creating strong pressure for women to be economically self-reliant). In fact, the combination of racism and the welfare state in London worked powerfully to constrain women to conform to traditional roles.

Conclusion: the necessity of social structure and the interaction of all five concepts

Gellner and Kabeer develop their analyses of the interaction of social structures and cultures in response to naturalist and culturalist arguments which fail to recognise the causal force of social structure. Nationalists claim nationalism is natural and some development theorists suggest that the prospects for change in Bangladesh are poor because of the power of traditional Islamic culture. We saw that both the political ideology of nationalism and conformity to the rules of traditional culture depend on the social structural circumstances. We also learn that although a very general structural concept such as 'modernity', as used by Gellner, is useful, it is important to conduct analysis at a level which reveals the decision-making environments of actors. We can then analyse the complex, uneven, localised, patchy character of the real-life process, which is often obscured by concepts designed to capture the broad sweep of change.

Gellner and Kabeer describe the positioning forces of social structure as distributing powers and liabilities and creating strong tendencies in behaviour and the perception of interests. But these tendencies are only statistical frequencies which measure what large numbers of people do when put in a certain structural position. So, if, as a Bangladeshi woman exposed to increased patriarchal risk because of war, environmental devastation and rural unemployment, a friend tells you about the new factories opening in Dhaka, you are presented with an opportunity. But because you value your relations with your Islamic family and acknowledge the norm of purdah, you are faced with a structural tension between the position you are in and the one you might want to be in – a paid employee in the city. You cannot be domestic/private and economic/public simultaneously. This is a typical structurally induced dilemma. The modern power techniques, such as garment factories in Bangladesh, create a potentiality for social structural change. But actualising it depends on the way actors, such as poor women, respond to such dilemmas. Kabeer shows how some women modified their beliefs and behaviour and set about persuading their families that the apparent contradiction could be removed.

When we face dilemmas such as those faced by these women, the interaction of social structure, culture and action is revealed. Actors always face contradictory demands entailed by their existing social relations and beliefs. They are cross-pressured by their commitments. Because there are contradictions, choices usually carry costs and involve taking risks. The garment factory workers risked their moral reputations and marriage prospects. In fact, they tended to lose only the approval of distant kin, but that was a price worth paying in circumstances of severe economic hardship. They managed to trade the slight loss of moral status for reduced patriarchal risk. Kabeer's interviews show that although social structures and cultures locate actors and define the problems they must deal with, how they do so varies enormously with their determination, knowledge, skill, idealism, courage and ability to strike compromises. The impact of the conditioning forces of social structural location depends on what people are prepared to tolerate or risk losing, the prices they are prepared to pay.

Finally, Kabeer shows how social structural change is a process of redistributing power sufficiently to cross the threshold of sustainability. Once enough women were working in the garment factories, access to the opportunity to become an independent wage earner became routine. Women in Bangladesh became more powerful in a way it could be difficult to reverse. In Britain, although first-generation immigrant women have remained subordinated, their daughters' education in British schools means that the conditions for reproducing their mothers' purdah are much less certain.

Part VI

Conclusion

CHAPTER 11

Get Real: A Perspective on Social Science

We begin our discussion of social science by quickly reviewing our argument so far. We have introduced, as necessary conceptual tools for social explanation, five basic concepts – individuals, nature, culture, action and social structure. We have shown that each has its own relatively autonomous causal power, so explanations must show how they interrelate in particular instances. Our examples have shown that the explanatory power of each concept varies between cases. All five are necessary, but even where a concept is on its most favourable ground, it is never sufficient to carry the whole weight of explanation. We have argued for the importance of these basic concepts by illustrating their strengths and weaknesses as they are put to work. In this chapter we have to shift gear, from demonstrating the usefulness of the concepts, to enlarge on the social theory which informs our choosing them for our tool kit and lies behind our claim that they are all fundamental for scientific, social explanations. This will involve returning to matters briefly considered in the Introduction and becoming a little more abstract, but we hope that what you have read so far will now enable you to follow our argument.

This will lay the foundation for the concluding chapter which discusses the practical implications of social science. The preceding chapters have already revealed how our approach practically contributes to our ability to explain social phenomena, but how are such explanations themselves practical? In what way are they useful?

The social theory behind the choice of concepts

We have justified the tool kit presented in this book by showing that it works. But our initial selection of the concepts comprising the kit was based on our fundamental social theory. Starting from the realist position that social explanations must refer to real mechanisms and processes, it is the job of social theory to say what these are (look again at Figure 0.1). However, realists agree only that it is necessary to discover the properties of the realities responsible for generating phenomena; they do not necessarily agree about what these properties are. Research into the properties of the various realities goes on all the time and we have to be ready to change our ideas about their mechanisms and causal powers. The five concepts have not been chosen on a whim, but because there are good reasons for thinking that each is relatively autonomous. If it should turn out that we are mistaken about this, we would have to revise the list. Although it is unlikely, in principle it is possible that in the future, as the result of scientific advances, what we now take to be realities responsible for causing social life may be rejected and replaced by other causal mechanisms. So, we repeat, realist social theorists agree only that explanation requires reference to causal mechanisms and may disagree about what the relevant, relative autonomies are.

Now we must state what our understanding of 'the social' is, or what, from our own realist perspective, makes phenomena 'social' and justifies why we suggest the list of five concepts as being fundamental. To describe something as 'social' implies that it participates in a certain kind of reality with its own general characteristics. These general characteristics are the components and processes which, at the present state of knowledge, are thought likely to be at work shaping any particular social phenomenon which puzzles us. By selecting our five concepts as the tools for social explanation, and giving them equal potential for social explanation, we have taken a particular position about what, by virtue of their intrinsic natures, has the power to contribute to the constitution of social reality in general. We are saying that social reality is a reality of a particular sort. Other realists may disagree.

The basic constituents of social reality

The grand name for what we are talking about here is 'social ontology' – the theory of the basic constituents of social reality which are capable of sustaining the empirical variety of actual, observable social phenomena (such as those discussed throughout this book). Ontology is a branch of thought, aided by scientific knowledge, which defines the different kinds of reality. The different realities are defined as providing the mechanisms and processes capable of generating the different kinds of existence. Thus, for example, biological reality defines the complex of life-producing processes which are capable of sustaining the empirical variety of organic life forms – plants, animals, bacteria and so on. Similarly, social reality is defined as that which is capable of sustaining social forms – the variety of collectivities – from the moments of fleeting two-person interaction, to the most enduring cultural traditions and organisations of power. Realist social science depends on accepting the idea that there is a class of objects – social forms – which are the products of a set of relatively autonomous generative processes with their own natures. The most fundamental arguments of social theorists are about what kinds of existence-producing constituents and processes must be included in the general theory of social reality, as they try to answer the question 'How does social reality work?' This is the ontological ground on which the classical social theorists, Marx, Weber and Durkheim, thought and why they can all be described as being realists (although Weber's realism, in our sense, is often overlooked).

Social reality has human and non-human components

In this book, our choice of basic social theoretical concepts suggests how we think social reality works. We begin with the most fundamental principle, which is insistence on the objective character of social reality and the rejection of individualism. Although social phenomena are populated by individuals, individuals are not in any sense prior to, or the most fundamental constituents of, social reality. Being socially related is a necessary and unavoidable condition of human existence. There are no unrelated human individuals. Every individual, from birth, participates in ongoing cultures and social structures, which pre-exist them. This being so, social reality at any given point in time must always consist of more than the presently existing individuals and these non-individual elements of social reality are just as important as the individuals. These elements consist of the relatively durable materials and practices, carrying cultures and social structures over time, which must be independent of the lives of any particular individuals.

As suggested in our Introduction, culture and social structure can be regarded as distinct kinds with their own natures, each having its own kinds of causal power and hence relative autonomy. Although distinguishable from one another, both share a common form of time, historical time. This is the time in which the mechanisms of culture and social structure operate, resulting in the persistence and durability of social phenomena. Historical time is distinct from the biographical time of the lives of individuals. Social reality therefore produces necessary conditions of human existence in historical processes rather than biological or biographical ones. The conditions for the existence of individuals include their biology, as well as the prior existence of culture and social structure. But although individuals must organically exist for there to be any social phenomena, their importance is as actors constrained to work with the resources of culture and social structure, which pre-exist them and outlast them in historical time. The conditions of the existence of individuals interact with those for the existence of social phenomena but in order to investigate that interaction, they must be distinguished.

The fundamental mechanism generating variety and change of social forms

Social reality can be thought of as composed of the organic material of human individuals on the one hand, and the inorganic material of relatively autonomous cultures and social structures on the other. Social theory concerns itself with the interaction of these two kinds of material. Because human social forms are conditioned by human biology and natural environment, we must draw on the natural sciences when trying to explain them. However, neither biology nor natural environment explain the sheer range of social forms or why they change. To explain this extraordinary variety and mutability, our theory of social reality must include a powerful generative mechanism to play a fundamental role in social explanation.

That mechanism is supplied by a special kind of feedback process. If we:

■ define the human material component of social reality as capable of action, that is, as actors

■ define the cultural and social structural components as supplying (along with nature) the resources upon which action depends

■ define action as producing culture and social structure (and mediating the impact of nature)

we have the basis for such a process. The human and non-human components making up social reality interact over time. As we said earlier, everyone is born into a preconstituted social world that they did not create. The cultures and social structures which we inherit provide us with some, more or less advantageous, access to resources such as language, meaning systems, values, techniques, raw materials, occupations, roles, statuses, alliances, money, power, dispositions, vested interests and so on. This sort of inheritance gives social reality its objective, constraining force over actors.

However, on this view, social reality is not completely objective but also partly subjective, because human beings are not only objects caught in the coils of a determining process they can do nothing about. Rather, persons are subjects, having self-consciousness, desires, free will, intentionality, imagination and unique personalities. As individuals and as members of collective organisations, they are end-seeking beings, constantly trying to realise their ideals in the face of resistant circumstances. The causal force of cultures and social structures works by distributing resources to actors and would not exist unless there were these actors making use of them in their attempts to realise their desired ends. Cultural and social structural conditioning is not only constraining, it is also enabling (Giddens, 1984; Archer, 1995; Parker, 2000).

Action is conditioned by the resources available to actors, but outcomes are the product of the action which determines how resources are actually used in contingent situations. Action involves actors interpreting action situations, determining the usefulness of their resources and, in the process, innovating, elaborating and changing the conditions of future action. Generally, actors will try to use their resources to perpetuate rewarding situations and eradicate frustrating ones, and, given inequality and differences of values and interests, action will entail conflict and attempts to strengthen positions by allying with others who share common aims. The psychological, natural, cultural, social structural (including the economic and political) conditions of action are liable to be changed as a consequence of action. Cultural systems are changed. Distributions of resources are changed. People themselves are changed. This is the fundamentally historical feedback process of human social existence. Social theory and the social sciences specifically deal with the interaction over time of culture, social structure, individuals and action (albeit in changing natural environments) because these are the fundamental, relatively autonomous forces at work in this kind of reality.

Human beings live in open systems

Thus human action in the present is conditioned by the cultural and social structural outcomes of previous action. Although these outcomes are partly the result of actors trying to get what they want, they are seldom exactly what they intended. The *consequences* of action for culture and social structure are largely *unintended*. The creative initiative of agents trying to get what they want can sometimes, particularly for the powerful, and in the short term, produce intended outcomes. But, more generally and in the longer term, it is unintended outcomes which are produced. These may be welcomed and exploited opportunistically as happy accidents, or alternatively what people may be trying to do may go wrong and be the basis for another round of frustration. For example, medical practices may produce unexpected side effects. Or action, say, to pursue one's religious salvation, may cause totally unanticipated outcomes in some other sphere of life, such as the economy, as Weber suggested in *The Protestant Ethic and the Spirit of Capitalism* (1930). Unintended consequences are effects of the combination of contingency, the logic of particular beliefs and practices and the fact that there are many interests in conflict, all contributing to eventual outcomes which none of them determine by themselves. Thus, intentional action is a necessary part of the process of social production, but that production cannot be entirely explained as the outcome of actors' intentions.

The products of action may acquire emergent, autonomous properties which give them independence from the creative control of the actors who initiated their existence. These properties of what actors produce, which they may not even realise exist, have to be investigated using theoretical ideas about cultural and social structural systems. So humans are subject to the force of cultural and social systems, but these are not automatically self-reproducing; they are not closed systems. Although they can acquire some degree of durability and become strong conditioners of action which cannot be easily changed, they always remain available for transformation by human action, and what is involved in changing them will depend on their objective properties. So social and cultural systems can be said to be 'open', but nevertheless offering differing degrees of resistance to actors who must take their objective character into account, if they want to act effectively.

Given that what goes on in the present is indeterminate, that is, outcomes depend on what people actually do with their resources, subject to contingencies, we cannot know in advance what, in fact, will happen. We cannot be sure in advance if specific arrangements and practices will change or stay the same. We can be fairly certain that there will be some sort of change, in general, but not the specific form it will take. Prediction, on the basis of general laws of change, is not possible in the social sciences. But we can identify strong tendencies at work in the present and make plausible estimates about the configuration of forces at work, which seem most likely to shape outcomes in the immediate or mid-term future. These estimates are inexact, but they are all that can ever be available and are well worth having. Not everything is equally changeable at every moment. The products of past action have durability or a certain momentum to carry on conditioning action. The social condition of humans is one of conditional freedom.

What kind of social science? Explanatory and therefore practical

This statement of our specific view about the nature of social reality underlines the mutual constitution of culture, structure and action and helps to justify our main claim that the five concepts are each necessary but insufficient for social explanation. It implies what kind of social science we support but also what kinds we must reject. Throughout this book we have stressed the need for multi-causal explanation and so cannot avoid opposing social science based on incomplete (or one-sided) ontologies, which overemphasise only part of the picture. Attempts to found social science solely on the objective or subjective properties of only individual actors, or culture or social structure seem too limiting.

Each position reduces the other two. Thus the claim that social reality is no more than human beings, as subjects, engaging in subjectively meaningful voluntary action is the basis of a subjectivist and voluntarist variant of individualism (culture and social structure drop away). The reduction of social reality to being no more than the ideas and symbols of culture is more or less idealist culturalism (individual actors and social structure drop away). Similarly, reduction is involved in the claim that social reality consists only of social structures, the objectivist position of structuralism (culture, subjective meaning and individual actors drop away). Against these approaches, a social science which is capable of recognising that individual actors, cultures and social structures are equally fundamental constituents of social reality promises a more powerful basis for explanation capable of supporting a practical social science.

What is the appropriate sort of explanation for social science? Realism versus empiricism and idealism

The question of how social explanation is possible is crucial. The issues involved are thoroughly discussed in textbooks on the philosophy of social science, so we will be brief (for example Benton and Craib, 2001). In the Introduction we distinguished between three views about explanation which gave primacy to either reality, or experience or language. Realists insist that knowledge and explanation must be governed by the way objective reality actually is, but recognise that experience and language both play a vital role in the construction of knowledge and explanations (see Figure 0.1). That is, they make what really exists the test of explanation, giving primacy to ontological considerations, but fully acknowledge that knowledge involves bringing the powers of experience, observation and evidence as well as logic, theory, reason and language to bear on existence. In the terms of this book, reality, experience and language are all necessary for knowledge, but none alone is sufficient.

By contrast, the alternatives, empiricism and idealism, give primacy to epistemological considerations about the human conditions of knowing. For them, because there is no unmediated access to reality, the mediating elements of either experience or language assume overwhelming importance. Thus empiricists try to build explanations by confining themselves to what can be directly experienced and reliably described. For them, only what can be observed can be said to exist. Their explanations involve describing regular patterns of sequences and coincidences which have statistical reliability and provide the basis for confident predictions about future observations. The empiricist's test of explanatory adequacy is descriptive and predictive reliability. From a realist point of view, empiricists disconnect experience from the reality which generates it on the one hand, and from the language of theory and the contribution of rationality on the other. Experience alone is not sufficient, as empiricists claim.

Idealists, on the other hand, emphasise the dependence of knowledge on the use of language, arguing that there is no going outside the confines of its logic. For them, the fact that knowledge depends on the use of linguistic concepts means that it must be entirely governed by those concepts. There is no way out – they reject the empiricist's tactic by denying that there is any linguistically unmediated experience of the world which could provide an objective basis for description. Language alone is sufficient. On this basis, explanation amounts to no more than being able to offer any number of interpretations in terms of the logic of various conceptual schemes. Explanation is relativised and any hope of accounting for the way the world actually is, is given up. The test of explanatory adequacy is merely consistency with a conceptual scheme.

Thus, idealism gives up on objectivity (collapsing truth into language) and empiricism gives up on reality (collapsing truth into experience). They directly contradict one another and both stand opposed to realism, which makes epistemological considerations secondary to ontological ones. For realists, truth depends on maintaining functional relations between ontology and epistemology and between reality, experience and language.

Everything we have said so far about the ontology or nature of social reality implies that the basic form of explanation in the social sciences must be historical. Social phenomena are emergent outcomes of real processes which take time to occur. They are explained by historical accounts of configurations of the natural, cultural and social structural conditions of the actions of individuals and collectivities – actions which have consequences for the initial configuration's continuity and change. It also follows that social explanation must be concerned with the interaction between the specific objective and constraining properties of the conditions of action and the differential transformative powers of actors.

So we have three fundamental components, historical time, the objectivity of action conditions and the powers of actors. On this basis, explanations are 'retrodictive', which means that they refer backwards in time to the process of the emergence of the thing being explained. Explanations show how the various causal forces interact over a period of time. This is quite different from the view that all we need to explain something is to know how to predict its occurrence.

To be able to predict reliably does not require one to know what is producing the kind of event being predicted. Realism's test of an adequate explanation is much tougher than merely the ability to predict (as empiricists demand) or offer an interpretation in terms of some conceptual scheme (as idealists demand).

What makes this sort of explanation scientific?

In general, an explanation is scientific when it can show relations of material and logical connection between conditions which cause a state of affairs to be the way it is and not otherwise. Scientific explanations expose all the relations between the forces combining to produce the object of explanation to logical and empirical scrutiny. Our preferred kind of social explanation is scientific because it is causal and identifies generative mechanisms which have observable effects. But because these objective forces only condition action, it is not determinist. Action always contributes to why states of social affairs are the way they are. This is why we must reject determinism as a criterion of science for the social sciences. But, by the same token, because action is always conditioned, this type of social explanation is not voluntarist (actors are not free to do just as they like and do not produce only what they intend). It recognises that culture and subjective meaning condition action and that therefore actors' own understandings of what they are doing must play a part in explanation. But because these meanings are conditioned by, and interact with, the other conditions of social life, our preferred form of social explanation is not interpretivist (that is, we do not hold that social phenomena can be explained only in terms of the actors' own understanding of them). Explanation requires social scientists to use their own concepts.

The use of the social scientist's own theoretical concepts, however, does not idealise, subjectivise or relativise social explanation. Concepts are certainly necessary for explanation, but dependence on concepts is not determination by concepts. Thus we reject idealism's claims that there is no objective world existing independently of the concepts used to describe it. Social science, like any science, recognises an objective world existing independently of the scientist. Scientists do not call it into being and cannot just say anything they like about it – subjectivism is rejected. If concepts are to help to make sense of that objective world, they must relate to the experience of that world and not just to other concepts. As we stated earlier, explanation is not governed solely by the internal logic of a particular conceptual discourse. Given this, it cannot be the case that all discourses are equally valuable as instruments for understanding objective social realities. Thus we must also reject relativism, the belief that there are no external, independent standards in terms of which the different concepts can be judged against each other.

The appropriateness of concepts for constructing social explanations is not arbitrary, but is determined by ideas about the basic constituents of the reality being explained (that is, social ontology) and what theoretically guided and interpreted empirical enquiry reveals about social phenomena. Our general theory of social reality helps us to look in the right places, but does not substitute for looking. Often what we discover by looking has implications for the general guidance offered by the theory of social reality. There is constant development of knowledge which results from following the guidance of social ontology, including potentially revising the basic ontological theory of social reality itself, in the light of what one discovers. Adequate social theory must enable us to explain the whole range of phenomena we may be puzzled by. That is one reason why we have introduced our preferred social theory by showing how it underpins the explanation of a wide variety of social phenomena. It must be, and is, empirically robust.

This sort of social science is explanatory, objective, empirical and practical. We think the argument that social knowledge cannot be scientific, because its concept-dependence makes its truths relative to discursive communities and not universal, is mistaken. Similarly, the argument that it cannot offer scientific explanations because it cannot provide firm predictions is not convincing. Concept-dependence does not entail encapsulation within a single, self-referring community, or disconnection from the objective world of experience. The search for the best ways of accounting for experience involves the supporters of various competing discourses interacting critically with each other and with the world of experience outside them (just as we saw the haematologists doing in Chapter 8). Explanation requires revealing the mechanisms which produce the phenomena to be explained. This is not dependent on being able to make reliable predictions. Moreover, the generative mechanisms can (retrospectively) explain why predictions hold when they do and fail when they do.

CHAPTER 12

Being Practical: The Uses and Payoffs of Social Explanation

Why are social explanations useful?

Throughout this book we have shown that the five basic concepts are useful means for constructing social explanations. Now we must consider why social explanations themselves are useful. What sorts of problem do they help to solve and how do they do this? We may resort to social explanation out of idle curiosity. But, generally, social explanation is itself socially caused. It tends to be motivated by an emotionally disturbing experience of the unexpected, contradictory, strange or unjust, which defeats our ordinary social expectations and knowledge. Very often the experience of change of one's positions within cultures and social structures, and/or the cultures and structures themselves, results in the confusion or frustration leading to the need for social explanation. Alternatively, any perceived dissonance between one's ideals about what ought to happen and experience of what actually does happen can motivate resort to systematic social explanation. In such circumstances, our social imagination may fail us, so that we can no longer reliably anticipate how others will act or respond to us. We do not know what positions to adopt, do not know 'where people are coming from' and may feel frustrated, frightened, depressed or angry. This failure of anticipation makes decisions difficult and creates the feeling that we are taking risks.

When we sense these strong emotions in ourselves and others, it is tempting to see them as simply psychological, but in fact they are a sure sign that we are in the presence of powerful social forces, cultural and social structural, which our social imagination does not fully comprehend. Unsurprisingly, a strong appetite for social explanation is stimulated by experience of the confusions of modernisation, upward or downward mobility, migration, recovery from wars, education, technological change, or transformations of generational, class, gender and sexual relations. All of these challenge the social imagination and the ease with which we can take positions and relate effectively to others. Consumption of social theory has increased as the massive and continual transformations of life involved in modernisation have made knowing how to relate chronically uncertain. If we sense that our dilemmas are effects of positioning forces, we will find social explanation relevant.

Social explanation contributes to solving the problems arising in our social experience by identifying their social causes and how these interact with other kinds of causation. In order to solve such problems, we need to know what is really causing them. Rather than rely on various common-sense and everyday sources of ideas about why things are as they are, such as the media, rumour, opinion leaders, politicians and so on, scientific social explanation attempts to provide complex causal narratives which are subject to rigorous logical and empirical scrutiny. Once we have such narratives, our relation with the experience which troubles us is changed. We no longer simply react in a confused and emotional way, but have taken the first step to solving the problem, which is to understand what created it.

Explanatory social science identifies the objective and subjective components of historical mechanisms which generate the social situations we experience as problems. Its causal narratives explain how the consequences of past action continue to condition certain kinds of action in the present, which may be the source of our problematic experience. The conditions of action in the present are shown to have particular kinds of relative autonomy and to have a certain degree of durability or resistance to change. Once we understand what is constraining the action we find problematic in these terms, we are equipped to take the next step towards solving the problem, which is to decide what to do about it.

Understanding does not guarantee that anything can be done about the problem. Sometimes what we learn from the explanation is that the forces shaping action are so strong that it is virtually impossible to alter their impact. In such cases, social scientific explanation can provide only the consolation of understanding. This may free us from being dominated by the reactive emotions which the problem generated in the first place, freeing up energies for more productive activity. Or it can prevent us from investing in trying to change something where the chances of success are slim. Neither of these practical implications of understanding is trivial. They can limit suffering and wasted energy and resources. However, whether one chooses to be content with the consolations of understanding depends on the intensity of desire to change what is causing the problem and the risks one is prepared to take. Some people, knowing that they are unlikely to succeed, nevertheless foolishly and/or heroically go ahead. But generally, by showing us what we are up against, social explanation puts us in a better position to evaluate what we need to do to change things and what the costs are likely to be.

The consolation of understanding: intergenerational relations

Before we explore a bit further how social explanation helps to solve problems, here are two examples of emotionally compelling problems which show that the consolations of understanding offered by social explanation are worth having. The first is the highly emotionally charged experience of adolescence. Why is this so difficult a period for both adolescents and their parents? Where does all the strong feeling come from? Whichever our generational position, understanding why all the anger and resentment is in the air may help us cope with it. It is useful to recognise that, in our society, the institutionalisation of the non-adult status of childhood produces a period of prolonged material and emotional dependency. This is reinforced by extending the period of formal education well past that of physical maturation and restricting the economic opportunities open to the unqualified. This makes entry into full adulthood protracted and difficult.

The young confront contradictory expectations as they struggle to achieve independence from within a position of substantial dependence and make significant decisions about their future on the basis of little or no past experience of making such choices. As they simultaneously play the roles of overgrown child and incompetent adult, they typically wobble between insecurity and overconfidence as they struggle to satisfy what they take to be adult expectations. By turns, they feel elated, triumphant and valuable on the one hand, and depressed, frustrated, rejected, misunderstood and ridiculous on the other. Their overwhelming emotional need is for self-validation or respect. But in a situation where respect has increasingly to be earned by achievements, this is difficult to win. There are complexities of cultural, class and gender positioning which crosscut the generational positioning. The differential investment in educational success, sexual reproduction, violence or music of young females and males from different class backgrounds and cultures has all to be reckoned with. There are also confusions for parents about having to give up roles they may have played for a long time and coming to terms with the increased powers of their children. But enough has been said to make intelligible (and perhaps more tolerable) the frustrations and unhappiness that arise for both parents and children from the conflicts of expectations, the doubts about trust, affection and personal worth as well as the battery of typical behaviour of those involved.

Adolescence is a period of uncertain transition between different statuses and roles. Our second example takes the strong feelings evoked when the structures and cultures in which people are located are themselves in flux. Richard Sennett's *The Corrosion of Character* (1998) documents contemporary feelings of unhappiness among the well-off in the United States and identifies their social structural causes. It shows how the increasing drive for occupational flexibility fragments experience and attachments to locations, occupations, colleagues and, above all, the sense of oneself as morally authoritative. This impacts on the confidence with which people tackle child rearing. Economic short-termism undermines those areas of life, such as bringing up children, which must be done long term. If everything changes all the time, what basis is there for offering guidance to the young? People who are pushed about by disorganised capitalist forces they do not understand can only hone their survival skills to ensure earnings and try to guide their children with unconvincing, nostalgic mantras. As Sennett (1998: 30) says:

> What is missing between the polar opposites of drifting experience and static assertion is a narrative ... they give shape to the forward movement of time, suggest reasons why things happen, show their consequences.

It is social explanation, as we have described it, which can step into the breach and supply such narratives. Understanding that our feelings are caused by social factors and are not simply the result of personal failings or individual psychologies can be helpful in itself.

Social explanation, levers of power and strategies for change

Although sometimes the understanding provided by social explanation offers only consolation, often it provides us with powerful resources for changing conditions which frustrate, or enhancing those which advantage, us. In the social, as in the natural, world, the better we understand how things work, the better our chances are of maintaining them or changing them to be as we want. Social explanations make their contribution to choosing the best means to producing the change that is sought, by identifying the relevant levers of power. Explanatory narratives of the interaction of the various causes of the circumstances we may want to change can be read for what they tell us about opportunities to exert pressure for change in one direction or another. Such opportunities are indicated by, for example, the character and distribution of vested interests arising from culture and social structural positioning, the functional strengths and weaknesses of the various forms of organisation being used by the interested parties, and various contradictions between interests which cross-pressure interested parties. Knowledge of these, respectively allow us to estimate who is likely to support or oppose the change in question (facilitating efficient coalition formation), anticipate structural vulnerability (allowing us to predict moments of weakness in the opposition) and exploit our opponents' dilemmas of having to choose between their interests.

Knowledge derived from social explanation can also help us to decide whether our aims, at any given point, might be best met by doing things bureaucratically or not, or by organising, in this way rather than that, others who support our cause. Will it be better to have a small, tightly structured and controlled set of activists, or go for a broader, looser network of supporters? Will it be useful to build on existing institutional structures or try to create new ones from scratch (Rooney, 1995)? When will reasoned argument be most effective in winning others to one's cause (Flyvbjerg, 1998)?

Strategies must relate available resources to the nature of the resistance being overcome. For example, the ineffectiveness of the London police investigation of Stephen Lawrence's murder in 1993 has motivated an effort to end racist policing practices. But how is justice for all to be achieved? Is it better to try to eliminate the racist feelings of some police officers, as suggested by the Macpherson Report, or simply to insist that they concentrate on treating black people as citizens? Is the psychological purification of police personnel a possible, reliable and preferable method of securing fair policing, when there is the alternative of insisting that they follow the letter of the law? Which is easier to monitor and discipline? Subjective feelings or the following of good rules? The structural and cultural conditions of police recruiting and internal institutional disciplinary practices suggest that the quickest and most reliable results might come from rigorous, non-discriminatory application of the law, rather than attempting the psychological conversion of individual police (Ignatieff, 1999). Racially neutral policing is a desirable and technically possible goal, but we would be wise to choose the quickest and cheapest method for bringing it about. When we deliberately set out to change the social world, we had better know what are realistic goals and how to avoid paying unnecessarily high prices for winning them.

However, although social theory is a practical tool for choosing the best means to get what we want, just as is the case with natural science, it cannot provide us with ultimate moral grounds for action. It is value neutral. Despite this, within the framework of the ultimate values that people adopt – be they self-serving or altruistic or some combination of the two – theoretically informed understanding can help them to specify realistic, achievable goals. Where they do have power to act to implement their preferences, the understanding provided by social scientific explanation can steer them to make better choices. We can illustrate this point with two, representative examples, where lack of attention to the cultural and social structural conditions made possibly well-intentioned people try to implement goals which produced the opposite of what was intended.

Managing conflict between traveller-gypsies and settled society

After a long period of trying to disperse gypsies, the Caravan Sites Act 1968 required British local government to provide fully equipped, authorised caravan sites for nomadic gypsy groups (Okely, 1983: 105–24). To make the sites acceptable to both gypsies and Gorgios (the word used by gypsies for non-gypsies) as alternatives to the increasingly prohibited informal sites (which annoyed some of the settled, Gorgio population), officials often provided expensive amenity buildings containing cookers, kitchen sinks, washbasins, showers, washing machines and lavatories – everything the planners thought was obviously necessary for cleanliness and good living conditions. Unfortunately for the planners, what washing means to people is not obvious. The new facilities were ignored, misused or severely damaged, because gypsies make a very strong distinction between washing food and utensils for eating, and washing everything else – clothes, the body, animals, equipment and so on. They detest the general-purpose sink (which mixes what ought to be kept separate) and buildings where food and eating functions are next to laundry, washrooms and lavatories. Dirt can be visible, but it must be clearly distant from the domestic space. Thus, whilst Gorgios will accept faeces inside their caravans – provided they are hidden away, not visible, in the sump of their chemical toilets, gypsies put their emphasis on distance from, rather than invisibility of, the polluting objects. They will not allow toilets in their caravans, but accept visible faeces, in hedgerows for example, provided they are well away from the domestic interior.

To provide facilities which might stand a better chance of improving the gypsies' situation or at least being acceptable to them, planners needed a crucial lever of power which they did not have at the time. They needed to know that the deep organising principle (see Chapter 6) of traveller-gypsy culture is a very clear separation between inside and outside, which applies to the group, the caravan and the body. What is inside – the group member, the living space, the body's interior – is the pure secret ethnic self, to be protected from corrupting alien forces. The outer body presented to Gorgios produces dirty byproducts (hair, skin, faeces and so on) which must not be accidentally ingested. Hence the highly disciplined separation of cleaning to do with ingestion from all other kinds, and the tendency to use hedges away from sites, rather than lavatories. The symbol of this cultural system is the tea towel which must be washed separately from all the other laundry. The symbol of the alien world is the general-purpose sink which threatens the integrity of gypsy society.

With this understanding, an anthropologist would probably advise planners to concentrate on providing sites for temporary occupancy, not to provide kitchens or general-purpose washing facilities at all (since food preparation ideally goes on inside the caravan), and to locate lavatories right on the outer edge of (or even beyond) sites, as far from caravan interiors and food preparation as possible. Rather than arranged in rows to minimise interaction with neighbours like houses of private families, caravans should be arranged in small circles so members of each group can see each other, and unscreened, so that the occupants have a good view of the approaches. There is no guarantee that this arrangement would work as well as the planners would like, but it is likely to give them more of what they want – sites which are used and not routinely wrecked by their intended occupants. It is simply unrealistic to expect nomadic people to give up travelling, their economy or culture. But, given facilities designed to be consistent with gypsy culture, a possible compromise might be for Gorgios to tolerate what they see as the eyesore of gypsy caravan sites in exchange for the gipsies using acceptably positioned lavatories (Okely, 1983: 77–95).

Post-war slum clearance and the destruction of viable communities

Our second example is also drawn from the planning field, reinforcing the dangers of simply taking one's own cultural standards and social structural position as a universal basis for defining what will make everyone happy. We refer to the notorious example of the negative effects of some of the designs for housing to replace cleared slums. In Britain and the United States following the Second World War, there was strong pressure to reduce what was regarded by many as overcrowding, and renew the dilapidated housing of working-class areas of cities. Developers wanted to use land more efficiently and profitably but also to improve the living conditions of slum dwellers (Fried, 1963; Fried and Gleicher, 1976: 562). By the 1960s, this modernising movement was fully under way, powered by rationalism and utopianism, its typical product being Le Corbusier-inspired estates of mass-produced geometric tower blocks. However, such development often seems to make conditions worse, becoming associated with high rates of vandalism, crime, mental illness, poor health, family instability and so on. This has led to a school of architectural criminology based on Otto Newman's ideas for creating 'defensible space' to control social pathologies (Newman, 1972; Coleman, 1985). Architects and planners have found themselves having to think about the implications of space for social interaction, relationships, power and culture.

The effects of this process of redevelopment have been studied with exemplary thoroughness among the Italian working class of Boston's West End (Fried, 1963; Gans, 1972; Fried and Gleicher, 1976). By comparing how things were before the change with how they are following it, these studies allow us to judge its effects. Utopian redevelopers would not have been surprised by the failure of their projects to provide a better life had they paid attention to what was good about the life of the original slums. Slums were not just overcrowded and dilapidated properties, but settings for intense interaction, complex social organisation and satisfying lives. Boston's West End working class was dependent on participating in large numbers of local interlocking networks. For them, home meant not just their residence, but the locality from which they drew their opportunities, information, security and identity. Access to the immediate vicinity outside the dwelling was crucial. Localism involved a territorial approach to space. The West End was possessed, not as private property, but as actively occupied public space. No wonder their response to being moved and the destruction of this space was grief, a considerable price paid by those who should have benefited from renewal.

Urban redevelopers of the 1960s tended to plan on the basis of their own, typically middle-class, orientation to space and home. For them, home stops at the boundary of their private residence, public space is not possessed by anybody in particular and networks are spatially dispersed, so consequently their use of space is selective rather than territorial. Middle-class people tend to lead spatially extensive lives. Lacking the working-class sense of dependence on locally concentrated social resources, they did not see that along with the buildings, they were demolishing whole social worlds, homes made of more than simply private residences. Living in a tower block might seem tolerable to mobile people with spatially extensive networks who were not dependent on the locality. But, to be successful and compatible with the conditions of interaction, social structures and cultural characteristic of the territorial use of local space, the new housing needed to, but did not, provide suitable areas for public occupation beyond the walls of residences. Without this functional space, working-class people experience being rehoused as being cut off, reducing any pleasure in nice new kitchens, bathrooms or central heating.

In particular, what was needed was the kind of space which facilitates effective informal social control, familiarity with neighbours, informal observation of comings and goings and children's play, reduced anonymity and which encourages increased local commitment and interest in maintaining the condition of buildings. The lesson of the failures of 1960's modernist utopian renewal is that planning levels of residential density, and the emphasis to be placed on privacy, needs to relate to residents' mobility and dependency on local networks. Relatively immobile, poor, working-class people needed easy access to their neighbours and appropriate public space, more than they needed privacy. They needed housing with a form which allowed them to reinvest in close interpersonal ties, encouraging them to take responsibility for each other again, as they did in the slums.

A final word

Thus, our final position is a firm but modest one. We think that everyone would benefit from understanding the nature of social reality and being able to use the basic concepts of social theory to explain its various manifestations. However, we should not overestimate the powers of social theory. Like any other discipline, social science has intrinsic limitations due to the character of its subject matter, as discussed in the previous chapter. There are also always limitations flowing from the shortcomings of its present practitioners and the discipline's own state of development. At any given point in time, there will always be areas open to dispute. This should suggest a certain caution. We might be wise generally to avoid imagining that we have final explanations of why things are the way they are or final solutions as to how things should be for all time. There are two very general safeguards against making the destructive mistakes exemplified by the utopian planners. One is always to consult those in whose interests we may be trying to act. We cannot presume to know what people want or what is acceptable to them, although research and theory may enable us to make useful predictions. The other is to be as well informed as possible, but also not to be too ambitious in each step we take. We should ensure the possibility of feedback and monitoring the effects of changes we make, and should be willing to change our line of attack in the light of events and new knowledge. Given this modesty, what social theory has to offer is powerful and useful. If we understand what social theory does and does not promise, we can make the most of it in a clear-eyed way and without too much disappointment.

Do it Yourself: Using the Tool Kit to Develop Your Own Hypotheses

The proof of the pudding is in the eating. Throughout this book we have shown that our five basic concepts are necessary for social explanation, and in so doing have drawn on the explanations of a wide range of phenomena offered by a variety of social scientists. These examples have not, however, shown the precise way in which these theorists have arrived at their explanations. Although we argue that our five basic concepts are necessary cultural resources for explanation, they do not apply themselves automatically. They need to be applied and elaborated by actors (theorists) in the context of the particular problem they are trying to solve. We have looked at the product of these social scientists' sociological imaginations, rather than reveal the details of the actual process of being theoretically imaginative. So how do they (and how can you) do it?

There is no precise formula. But the following suggestions as to how, from a realist perspective, you might begin to hypothesise the causes of the particular phenomenon mentioned below provides an example which we hope will help, and further substantiate our claim that the five concepts provide a basic tool kit which can be used by anyone seeking to explain puzzling social phenomena. In constructing it, we drew on ideas that students had come up with when they had been asked to hypothesise causes of the following situation reported in the press in late 1999:

> Internet use at this time was age-related, with 60 per cent of 18–24-year-olds participating, as compared with 53 per cent of 25–34-year-olds and only 8 per cent of over 65s.

Suggestions as to how to start hypothesising reasons for this pattern

The starting point is that we are considering a description of differences of cultural action (Internet use) by individuals, categorised by age (a natural biological condition) and hence structurally positioned in age sets, relative to one another and the historical phenomenon of the Internet. So we see that the report itself involves interaction between the five concepts. But we must also take care to consider what the statistical pattern is recording. The report does not discuss the *extent* of participation (maybe some of the over 65s spent all day on the Web, and some 34-year-olds log on only occasionally). But it does generally suggest that Internet use increases by age category. We can also remind ourselves that such age sets are distinguished from each other, not only by how old their members are, but by their particular historical experiences. For example, the Internet was not invented when those who are middle-aged or older today were teenagers. But today's teenagers will have lived with the Web more or less all their lives.

Aware of the above, we now need to think about

1. The relations between the properties of *individuals* and *human nature* and use of something like the Internet (why should physical age make a difference?).

2. The properties of the Internet as a *cultural artefact* which defines the sorts of capacity that users have to have to use it (are these capacities related to age?).

3. The properties of actually using the Internet, its contingencies and spheres of discretion, the *action* involved (do these impinge differently on age sets?).

4. The properties of the *social structuring* of age sets, which might distribute relevant interests and resources, constraining and enabling individual actors as members of their age sets in their use of the Internet (is use related to the distribution of relevant interests and resources?).

If you are dealing with this 'puzzle' of differential Internet use, this is the stage at which you might begin writing down all the ideas you can think of, relating to the above queries. It would be useful to put down everything that occurs to you, however obvious or tentative it might feel. In general, you will have to think about the differences between the conditions of life of the young, the middle-aged and older in the late 1990s and how these conditions might affect Internet use. You might begin by considering your own Internet use (or lack of it). What factors affect this and how might those factors apply to age groups other than your own? Perhaps you think that you use the Web because you got hooked on it at school and because it is free for you at university. Maybe you wonder if what is on the Web would be of interest to your grandparents and so on.

With your list of possibilities in front of you, you can now usefully engage in a little 'theoretical abstraction' of concepts to help to focus on what is critical for explaining the phenomenon to hand. That is, you can look for (or devise) concepts subsidiary to the five basic ones, which are immediately applicable to this particular explanatory problem. So, for example, thinking about your list, you might recognise that it suggests that Internet use varies in relation to these three variables: *ease of access, competence and interest.* These are factors conditioned by nature, culture and social structure and mediated by differences between individuals. Using these concepts, you can now systematise and build on your original ideas. For example, you might develop your thinking along the following lines.

Possibilities of access

What are the conditions governing access to the hard and software? You have to buy or rent it (and therefore have the ability to pay) or you get access in some other way. You may hypothesise that possibilities of access are age-related, in that:

- income, particularly disposable income, varies with lifecycle stage

- age affects possibilities of the two main types of free access, through the education system or employment (some young people may also have access through equipment owned by their parents).

All the above relate to *social structural positioning*. However, the *actions* of some key actors in powerful positions have also been important; for example education ministers' decisions to get all universities online and encourage IT in schools, the latter having been supported by other actors as diverse as Tesco and the BBC. (What if ministers had pushed for cheap PCs for the over 65s and Tesco produced computer vouchers for pensioners instead of schools? Why didn't they?)

Possibilities of acquiring competence

What are the conditions governing how people learn to use the Internet and how do these relate to age? You might hypothesise that possibilities connect to opportunities and abilities, more specifically:

- education and work both provide major opportunities to learn and are differently available by age (a *social structural* factor)

- abilities to learn new skills may be age-related. This may be largely due to the *natural biological processes* of aging, but you might suspect that *culturally given* ideas about these natural processes ('you can't teach an old dog new tricks' and so on) may affect how people perceive their abilities and act in relation to them.

Interest in acquiring access and use

What are the conditions for having an interest in gaining access and learning how to use the Internet, and how is this related to age? Here, for example, you might hypothesise that:

- General interest in innovative technologies may vary with age, but also what is perceived as innovative may differ by age cohort. Youth *culture* may particularly value innovation (partly for *social structural* reasons – youth have positions to gain, not to defend). However, because young people today have grown up with it, email and the Web may not seem so novel to them as to the current older generation.

- Interests may be generated by having goals that can be furthered by Internet use. Success in the educational and occupational *structures* may be dependent on it – factors which will provide motivation for the young and middle-aged but not the older generation.

- Interest will also depend on what being online itself offers. It offers a particular (*cultural*) content. If this content is itself age-related, this will affect the interest of different age categories in using the Net. Relatedly, you might consider whether Internet use, whatever its content, connects to a desire, which might be age-related, to participate in the outside world. But you would need to be careful to consider what Internet use *means* to people – for some it may be a retreat from, rather than a way of focusing on, the outside world.

■ Finally, the character of Internet *interaction* might be significant. That it is low cost in terms of time and the securing of co-presence (is not face to face) may be more attractive to some age categories than others.

Ease of access, competence and interest are variables which can be high or low, and potentially vary independently. We would expect highest users to have a combination of easy access, substantial competence and high interest. Lowest users should be low on all dimensions, medium users could either be moderately placed on each dimension, or exhibit some combination of high on some but low on others.

Put this understanding together with the hypotheses about how age can be related to access, competence and interest and the beginnings of a plausible explanation of the original puzzling pattern has been arrived at. It can be summarised economically, but allows for causal complexity. Nor does it prevent us accounting for instances which go against the general pattern (the 70-year-old Web fanatic, the non-using teenager) in terms of differences between *individuals*. This 'theory of Internet use' (implicit in these hypotheses about Internet use) can also be related to scholarly literature about this phenomenon and is potentially testable.

Conclusion

The development and changing patterns of use of the new technology is a fascinating research topic. The above is not intended as a definitive analysis, but it does show how the five concepts alert us to look in the appropriate places for relevant information which might explain the pattern of age-related use at that time. Culture and social structure set the scene, differentially distributing resources and commitments to certain interests. These are interpreted strategically and creatively taken up (or not) by actors in the immediate contexts of their own circumstances, subject to the constraints of their personalities and biologically conditioned capacities, some of which generally deteriorate with age.

But this generalisation should not be taken as a prediction about the future pattern of use. When today's 18–24-year-olds are retiring, they will almost certainly be using the Internet, assuming that it still exists in a form they recognise, and that they have upgraded their skills in step with the changes in the technology and rules of use during their working lives. And doubtless they will live in world in which the technological preferences and competences of the young will be different from their own. There is unlikely to be technological convergence between generations. This is a matter of history and generations rather than one of biological aging and the natural deterioration of capacities.

Glossary

Action, actors, intention, intentionality Action is behaviour informed by the actor's intentions. Actors initiate and steer what they do in relation to their intentions. Intentions are the purposes, ('goals' or 'ends') which actors want to achieve by their actions. Because actors can initiate and direct their own behaviour relative to their intentions, they are subjects not just objects. (See **Social action; Subjectivity**)

Agency Agency is the capacity to make a difference to outcomes, intentionally and/or unintentionally. Collectivities and non-human animals can be agents. Actors may be morally responsible agents of their actions when they understand their likely consequences, and could have done other than they did. (See **Action; Practice; Realist social theory; Structure; Structuration theory**)

Agrarian empires Ancient large-scale political units, where the accumulation and centralisation of power to capital cities is based on domination over extended regions of agricultural production, usually through effective administration of agricultural supervision, taxation, irrigation and grain storage, backed by force. Peasant food producers are therefore subordinated to the central administration. Examples are the ancient Egyptian kingdoms, the Assyrian Empire of Mesopotamia and so on.

Althusser, Louis 1918–1990 A structuralist Marxist with strong functionalist tendencies, who attacked the traditional primacy which Marxism gives to economic relations, giving equal weight to political and ideological relations. (See **Functionalism**)

Archer, Margaret S. 1943– A leading contributor to the realist tendency in contemporary social theory. Her 'morphogenetic' approach to social analysis, which opposes the 'structuration' approach of Anthony Giddens, gives priority to describing how the cultural and social structural conditions of action are transformed by action over time. Past action and actors (producing objective conditions for action in the present) must be distinguished from present action and actors. Subjectivity and objectivity are distinguishable, balanced and interdependent contributors to the historical process ('morphogenesis') of social life. (See Further Reading; **Structuration theory**)

Aristotle (See **Dialectics**)

Autocatalytic processes A technical term referring to a kind of feedback process, where among the outcomes of systems are conditions for the transformation of the system itself; for example agricultural processes which lead to soil exhaustion, which then threatens agricultural viability.

Bourdieu, Pierre 1930–2002 Bridging sociology and anthropology, basing himself firmly in empirical research, Bourdieu built a synthesis of classical social theory to help to explain his findings (a bit like Merton). He explores the logic of practical action and the way social power is exercised culturally through 'symbolic violence'. His most famous concept is 'habitus', meaning the historically emergent, deeply engrained, general orientation or disposition which guides the practice of members of different social strata. (See **Classical social theory; Merton; Practice; Social power; Social status; Stratification**)

Capitalism Capitalism is a way of organising economic activity. Marx emphasised the relations of production, that is, the way labour and decision-making is organised, separating workers from ownership of the means of production (by moving them off the land into towns) and making them dependent on earning wages from capitalist employers who owned the largely industrial means of production. This relation between the two classes of labour and capital was one of conflicting economic and political interests. Weber agreed with much of Marx's analysis but emphasised the importance of the universalising of market relations and the rationalising of all spheres of action by monetary calculation. Both thought capitalism had dire effects for morality and the meaningfulness of human life. (See **Class; Classical social theory**)

Causation, generative mechanism, causal process Causation is the general process which results in states of affairs in the world. What exists, individuals, events and changes, are all subject to causation. Causes are mechanisms capable of producing (generating) individuals, events and so on. These mechanisms produce their effects over time in complex combinations. Causal analysis tries to identify the relevant mechanisms and how they interact over time. (See **Natural kinds; Realism; Winch**)

Class Class systems are one type of stratification system. In class systems people are collectivised into classes, that is, objective positions of relative economic and political advantage constituted by mechanisms which distribute important material and cultural resources for action. Classes differ according to their relative material advantages and the opportunities and methods open to them to maintain or improve their access to resources. Class positions of individuals tend to be shaped by what can be inherited, that is, property, wealth, income-earning occupations and education, and are heavily influenced by the state's legal protection of private property, inheritance and tax law and educational policies. A defining characteristic of class systems is that the real processes generating the boundaries between classes are indicated empirically by statistical regularities; they are informal and not formally, legally or culturally compulsory. Thus mobility ('openness') is permitted and even encouraged, but, nevertheless, the regularities of inherited advantage and disadvantage endure over generations, ensuring a predominance of immobility across generations. However, class societies vary in the relative extent of their 'openness' or 'closure'. (See **Stratification**)

Classical social theory; Durkheim, Marx, Weber Something is described as 'classical' when it has enduring historical value. The classical world of ancient Greece and Roman provided a model of eternal values and examples of architecture, literature, law, culture, organisation, military expertise and so on for Renaissance Europe. Similarly, the nineteenth-century classical social theorists provide a wealth of ideas and problems which continue to be at the centre of our efforts to understand modern social life. (See Bibliography for Introduction and Chapters 3, 5 and 10; Further Reading; **Durkheim; Marx; Weber**)

Collectivity, collectivism A collectivity is a population with some shared characteristics. A social collectivity is a population with shared characteristics, such as language or structural position, which make a difference to the way they relate to themselves and others. Collectivism is the position in social and political theory which gives most value to the interests of social wholes such as groups. It is opposed to individualism, which gives priority to individuals. (See **Individuals**)

Conditioning, determination Things are conditioned when they are partially shaped by conditions of existence. So persons are conditioned by their upbringing. But being conditioned does not mean being determined, that is, entirely shaped by conditions. Thus the way a person turns out will be the result of their response to their upbringing as well as other factors, such as historical events which did not originate with themselves, their families or education. (See **Relative autonomy**)

Constraint and enablement Giddens' 'structuration' theory popularised these terms when examining how culture and social structure condition action. He said that this conditioning involves a negative element, constraint, and a positive element, enablement. To act, actors must use enabling resources, but they are also constrained by the limits which resources impose on what they can do. (See **Conditioning; Structuration theory**)

Context To interpret the subjective meaning which actors give their action and situations, we must locate these within a wider social and historical context. This requires a skilful widening and deepening of the background context which may include highly influential factors which help us to make better sense of what is happening. But context has no fixed boundary; there are no rules for getting it right in some final sense.

Contingency This refers to the unpredictable and unsystematic conditions of existence which we must allow for but cannot define in advance. For example, when sailing, the wind may suddenly and unexpectedly alter, forcing a rapid change of sail and direction. Social life is always coping with contingencies equivalent to a sudden change in the wind. (See **Structural contradiction**)

Cross-pressures   The actions of an actor are motivated by many different interests which generally arise from their positions in various social structures. These interests often conflict and require the actor to give priority to one, or some, over others and take the consequencies. (See **Dilemmas; Interests; Role(s)**)

Culture, symbols, signs, meaning(s), language   Culture is the humanly invented realm of producing artefacts and meaningful interpretations of experience and their symbolic representation. Central to this invention is complex symbolic manipulation embodied in natural language. Language consists of complex signs which perform the symbolic function of standing for meanings other than themselves. This capacity is fundamental to the human imagination and ability to anticipate experience by thinking about representations of it, a source of enormous power, enabling humans to tap the experience of past generations, which is denied to non-humans.

Decision-making environment   Actors make decisions in environments comprising various kinds of constraints and enablements, natural, cultural and social structural. To the extent that these environments are relatively stable, it becomes possible to predict what the typical issues are about which choices have to be made, and which choices are likely to be made by which kinds of actors. We illustrate how this worked for Bangladeshi women in Chapter 10. (See **Opportunity costs**)

Determination   (See **Conditioning**)

Deviance, moral economy, moral reputation   Social life depends to some degree on a 'moral economy' of definitions of ideals of appropriate behaviour in specific contexts. These define what ought to happen. Positive and negative sanctions, respectively, reward conformity and discipline non-conformity or deviance. Deviance is defined relative to the upholding of particular ideals of behaviour and belief by certain people, and is always felt by them as a threat to predictability and good order. Deviant actors may acquire reputations for being unreliable, morally suspicious and untrustworthy. They may start careers during which their early transgressions start to 'spoil ' their moral reputation. Eventually, deviants may learn to think of themselves as deviant, and adopt the positive self-identities offered by 'alternative' lifestyles.

Dialectics and Aristotle   Dialectical thought construes the world as consisting of natural kinds of existants, all in a continuous process of 'becoming' as they move towards realising their potential. The model is Aristotle's ideas about human beings' potential during the course of their lives, to achieve higher and higher levels of wisdom and virtue. Central to this tradition are ideas about the potentialities of different kinds of existence, and the temporality of becoming. Marx (building on Hegel) is probably Aristotle's most important representative in modern times, analysing the conditions for the historical realisation of the potentiality of the human species to become self-determining, or fully subjective, beings. (See **Marx**)

Differentiation   Differentiation refers to the process and result of division of an entity into subsidiary parts, each with its own qualities. The most famous social example of differentiation is the development of the division of labour, whereby production is broken down into a large number of specialised roles. Institutions internally differentiate a range of offices and functions. Another example is when status systems become increasingly differentiated by introducing finer and finer distinctions between status positions. Differentiation need not entail structural contradiction. (See **Division of labour; Integration; Structural contradiction**)

Dilemmas   Dilemmas are situations where actors have to reconcile contradictory interests and demands. Situations vary in the contradictions presented to actors in different roles and positions. (See **Cross-pressures; Role(s); Situational logics**)

Dispositions, personality   Dispositions are general tendencies of persons and collectivities to relate and behave towards social experience in patterned, predictable ways. Dispositions are partly generated through participation in historically produced cultures which transmit ways of relating to life on the basis of specific historical experience. This historical conditioning of persons makes their personalities similar, but does not override the fact that, as distinct persons, each has a unique personality. Personality embodies collectively influenced dispositions, but each person is a unique source of elaboration on their social and cultural conditioning. (See **Personal identity**)

Division of labour   The division of labour refers to the organisation of complementary production roles. The complexity and contingencies of production suggest some element of specialisation will be helpful and throughout human history there has been some sort of division of labour. However, industrialisation involves intensifying the division of labour into more and more specialised functions, to reap benefits of speed, consistency and quality, but which incur costs of what Marx called 'alienation'. That is, work which does not contribute to the human potentiality for creativity and freedom. (See **Differentiation; Industrialism**)

Durkheim, Emile 1858–1917   French classical social theorist who argued that social reality was distinct from psychological reality and needed its own science, sociology. He opposed individualism in social theory, arguing that the high value we place on individual life and freedom depends on particular social structural conditions. His study of suicide suggested that being constrained and enabled (socially regulated and integrated) by social relations was necessary to inhibit any individual tendency to self-destruction. Society was the source of meaning, giving point to individuals' existence. His later work showed religion to be a complex practice for maintaining social solidarity. His sociology of knowledge argued that ideas and logical relations derived from the experience of living in groups, and has been associated with Wittgenstein's theory of meaning. (See Bibliography for Chapters 5 and 10; **Classical social theory; Division of labour; Integration**)

Elites   Elites are relatively small numbers of people at the top of hierarchies. They are usually organised to some degree to promote their common interests. Where membership of elites overlaps, this creates opportunities to reinforce privileges and advantages. Elites often try to monopolise resources and restrict entry to their ranks (by imposing difficult educational, cultural or monetary tests), maintaining the scarcity of their valued services and privileges. (See **Class; Social status**)

Environment, environmental determinism   (See **Nature**)

Emergence   (See **History**)

Empiricism   The epistemological theory that knowledge is possible because humans are sensory beings in direct physical contact with the world which provides 'sense data'. The empirical world provides sensory information which we can faithfully record. Knowledge is essentially descriptive and non-theoretical. The problem with this theory is that it cannot say how the language used for descriptions is to be chosen, for example what terms should we use to describe colours of objects? Description is not automatic; cultural and socially relative judgements of appropriateness are involved. This is why Wittgenstein insisted that knowledge could not be merely a matter of experience, as empiricism claims. (See **Idealism; Realism; Wittgenstein**)

Enablement   (See **Constraint and enablement**)

Epistemology   Epistemology is the theory of knowledge, that is, how we know things. What are the general conditions of knowledge? How is knowledge of the various kinds of reality possible? These are epistemological questions. (See **Empiricism; Idealism; Realism; Ontology**)

Ethnography   Ethnography is the practice of describing cultures. It is the basic practice of social anthropology, a social science developed by people who wanted to understand societies other than their own. Ethnographies are vitally important for the social sciences in general, and sociologists also produce them for their own societies. Ethnographies usually provide the first steps towards adequate social explanation by giving information about the interaction of environment, culture and social structure.

Ethnomethodology   Harold Garfinkel invented the term 'ethnomethodology'. It analyses the methods that actors use to interpret their experience and establish meaning and truth sufficiently plausible, for the time being, to provide a basis for continuing to act. Ethnomethodology emphasises the dependence of meaning on immediate concrete contexts of interaction. Meaning is essentially provisional and constantly reinterpreted. People use 'ethnomethods' to maintain a continuous sense that they inhabit an intelligible and actionable reality. For ethnomethodologists, techniques for inhibiting doubt and uncertainty are central to the rationality of common sense. Meaning is a 'practical accomplishment' dependent on actors' interpretive skill and shared background understandings of what the practical demands of types of situation are. That social phenomena involve the continuous use of these skills, strongly influenced Giddens' 'structuration' theory and relates to Wittgenstein's theory of meaning as being dependent on actors' judgements. (See **Schutz; Structuration theory; Winch; Wittgenstein**)

Explanation and understanding   We explain something by showing why it had, necessarily, to be the way it is. This requires an account of the interaction of all the causes contributing to producing the thing being explained. Science aims for explanation. In a general sense, understanding is enhanced by explanations. However, 'understanding' is also used in a more restricted way to refer to the interpretation of symbolic expressions, cultural objects, texts and uses of language, using appropriate cultural rules, so that they can be understood relative to some point of view, usually those of the originator and the interpreter. Because human action is informed by symbolic expressions, particularly of intentions, the social scientist must achieve an understanding of what actors are doing in the actors' own terms, as a necessary step towards explaining what they are doing.

External relations   (See **Internal and external relations**)

Foucault, Michel 1926–84   A good starting point for investigating Foucault is Sheridan's book: *Michel Foucault; The Will to Truth* (Sheridan, 1990).

Functionalism   Functional explanations explain why any social phenomenon is the way it is, by showing what its functions or effects are. In some cases, once in existence, the effects of something (for example an education system) can feed back to ensure its continued existence (for example those who have benefited from it support it). But functional explanations cannot explain how that something comes into existence in the first place. Functionalism has difficulty explaining historically produced phenomena. Parsons' abstract functionalist systems theory implies that the functional needs of social systems produce the institutions and practices required to meet those needs. (See **Althusser; Parsons**)

Garfinkel, Harold 1929–   (See **Ethnomethodology**)

Gender, sex   Biologically, human individuals are sexed beings, most of whom can function as either male or female in the process of natural reproduction. Individuals and cultures respond to and mediate this natural fact of life. They vary greatly in how they interpret the implications of sexed bodies and sexual reproduction for social relations. In particular, sex sets the problem of defining implications for the social identities of individuals and the sexual categories of male and female. Gender identities are the social identities attached to sexual categories, defining such things as rights and duties, appropriate modes of behaviour, roles and social status. The social implications of sex centre on differences of social power between the sexual categories and the distribution of responsibility for bringing up children. (See **Culture; Hierarchy; Individuals; Social identity; Social power; Social status; Stratification**)

Generative mechanism   (See **Causation**)

Giddens, Anthony 1938–   A good introduction to Giddens' ideas is I. Craib's *Anthony Giddens* (Craib, 1992). (See **Structuration**)

Goffman, Erving 1922–82   Goffman is the most important contributor to the school of symbolic interactionism and theorist of what he called the 'interaction order'. The latter consists of universal principles governing the process of interpersonal interaction, especially where the persons are physically present and 'face work' is possible. Goffman explores what is required for successful interaction to occur. He shows face-to-face interaction is the basis of trust because it makes it difficult to hide insincerity, morally compromising information and so on. Goffman studies practical morality and the serious moral business of exercising tact to allow saving face where claims are compromised. (See **Symbolic interactionism**)

Habermas, Jürgen 1929–   A good introduction to Habermas's ideas is W. Outhwaite's *Habermas* (Outhwaite, 1994).

Habitus   (see **Bourdieu**)

Hierarchy   A dimension of social structure, hierarchy is the ranked social positions within some sphere of action. Most institutions are organised into hierarchies. These positions define kinds and amounts of social power, privilege and discretion. (See **Elites; Social power; Social status**)

History, emergence, time   History is the product of the social process involving the interaction of the conditions of action with the creative input from action itself, producing largely unintended outcomes. Emergence refers to the way that, in this process, outcomes 'emerge' over time, sometimes rapidly, sometimes more slowly. Social causation takes time to work itself out.

Idealism   Idealism, as an *epistemological* position, holds that knowledge depends on the logical and meaningful relations between ideas. The world, existing independently of what is thought, is regarded as inaccessible. Idealism is the opposite of empiricism. Idealism in *social theory* holds that social phenomena are explained by reference to subjective meanings, that is, the ideas which actors hold and refer to to organise their action and social arrangements. Idealist social theory tends to place all the explanatory weight on culture and systems of meaning. (See **Empiricism; Epistemology; Realism**)

Individuals, persons, individualism   'Individual' is a logical term referring to one of a class of entities. All such classes, say, cats, farms, volcanoes or bicycles, are composed of individuals. The class, 'humanity', is made up of individual humans. This kind of individual has the species characteristics of humanity including the potentiality to become a person, which almost all born as humans thankfully do become. In social theory, individualism treats human individuals as the necessary and sufficient condition for explaining social phenomena. In political and moral theory, individualism defines the individual as the source of the good, and the well-being of individuals as the highest value against which to test political arrangements and moral principles. (See **Rational choice theory; Utilitarianism**)

Industrialism   Industrialism uses inanimate sources of power (for example water, steam, hydrocarbons, nuclear, 'renewables') to vastly extend the speed and volume of production. Mechanisation, urbanisation, rationalisation and modernisation are all entailed by the shift from traditional ways of production to industrial ones. (See **Division of labour; Integration**)

Institution   An institution is an organised way of doing certain things, the outcome of a process of institutionalisation, whereby preferred ways of doing things are progressively reinforced, making them relatively reliable. This process usually involves conflict and the exercise of social power (as in the institutionalisation of parliamentary government in the UK which involved a civil war). Institutions may be defined formally by constitutional rules, hierarchies, career paths, job descriptions and so on, but they may be entirely informal, such as the conventions of good manners (for example forming an orderly queue).

Integration   Integration refers to the modes of relation between differentiated elements of structures. Being 'well integrated' implies relations of compatibility and absence of contradictions. In social theory, 'social integration' refers to the qualities of relation between interacting individuals and groups, and 'system integration' to relations between the non-human components of social systems. (See **Differentiation; Division of labour; Structural contradiction**)

Intentionality   (See **Action**)

Interests   In social theory, interests do not refer to just anything which particular individuals might be interested in (say, fishing or football). They refer to relatively enduring orientations to social relations conditioned by structural positioning and cultural commitments. Interests are essentially collective phenomena and form a background against which individuals make their own choices about whose side they are on in competition between interests. (See **Bourdieu; Cross-pressures**)

Internal and external relations   Internal relations are relations between the elements making up differentiated, complex wholes. For example, institutions, cultural practices, works of art and arithmetic calculations all have their 'internal relations' which define the nature of what they are. Such relations can be distinguished analytically from 'external relations' with elements which lie outside the entity defined by its internal relations. Winch promoted the phrase 'internal relations' to insist that the logical relations 'internal' to the use of language were immune to the influence of 'external', non-logical, causal relations with non-linguistic reality.

Macrosociology and microsociology   A useful, if imprecise, distinction between the study of large-scale and long-lasting social phenomena and the study of small-scale and relatively short-lived ones. Social theorists now focus on how these two 'levels' interrelate, such that it becomes possible to recognise that in some situations small-scale interaction (for example between powerful heads of state) can have major consequences for long-lasting phenomena, and that macroscopic phenomena (such as language and law) are important conditions of small- scale and momentary phenomena.

Mann, Michael 1942– A major contemporary social theorist whose *The Sources of Social Power* (Vols 1 and 2) (Mann, 1986), continues in Marx and Weber's footsteps, and should be compared with the similar contemporary work of Runciman. (See Bibliography for Chapter 9; **Agrarian empires; Archer; Marx; Nation-state and nationalism; Runciman; Social power; Weber**)

Marx, Karl 1818–83 Social theorists must distinguish Marx from Marxism. Marx's work was a genuine revolution in thinking about social reality because he broke decisively with empiricism, idealism and individualism, defining the human species as collectively producing the conditions of its existence by transforming nature and, in the process, transforming itself. Marx insisted that human existence was a historical one, in which people elaborated on the legacies of past generations, producing new ways of organising themselves, new culture and new nature. Some of Marx can be hard to read, but the effort is rewarding. *The Eleven Theses on Feuerbach* (Marx and Engels, 1964), less than two pages long, is a landmark of social theory and has greatly influenced this book. (See Bibliography for Chapter 3)

Mead, George Herbert 1863–1931 Mead invented a dialectical theory of human social development which showed how mature and self-controlled persons, possessing genuine subjectivity, were the product of a long, natural and objective process of social interaction. He showed how newborn babies start out as objects but, by acquiring language in a context of social relations, learn to take an objective perspective on themselves and imagine how they are understood by others. He suggested that to be self-defining subjects with personal identities, we must 'become objects to ourselves', thereby achieving relative autonomy from our social identities as defined by others. We thus have both personal identities and social identities. Like Durkheim, Mead shows how subjective individuals are emergent products of objective social processes. Mead is much more important for social theory than one might gather from symbolic interactionism which claims him as its founding father. (See **Dialectics; Durkheim; Personal identity and social identity; Relative autonomy; Symbolic interactionism**)

Mediation The power of actors to alter, modify or shape the way in which natural, cultural and social structural conditions impinge on them. (See **Conditioning; Constraint and enablement; Relative autonomy;**)

Merton, Robert, 1910–2003 An advocate of 'middle-level' sociological theory, insisting that there is two-way traffic between the development of theory and empirical studies. His famous work *Social Theory and Social Structure* (Merton,

1982) contains important contributions to the sociology of deviance, bureaucracy, reference groups, intellectuals, influentials, mass communications and
especially science. (See **Reference group theory**)

Microsociology   (See **Macrosociology and microsociology**)

Modernity, modernisation, modernism   Modernity is the general condition of
social life where change and improvement is actively sought. Modernisation,
which some see as universal and inevitable, is the historical process of displac-
ing premodernity where life is lived according to examples from the past and
the wisdom of the old, and traditional cultural authorities. It usually involves a
confrontation with traditional forms of religion. Modernism refers to a cultural
attitude of preferring the modern in any sphere of activity, although it
has been prominent in the self-reflection of art and architecture. It is odd
that modernism in art (late nineteenth century) appeared long after modernisation began (no later than the mid-eighteenth century). (See **Postmodernity;
Universalism**)

Moral economy   (See **Deviance**)

Nation-State and nationalism   The nation-state is a type of political organisation where the state monopolises the use of force and law-making within a
territory in which the population is imagined to subscribe to a common cultural identity, usually involving speaking a common language and sometimes
sharing important cultural commitments such as religion. These common cultural identities are used as a basis of constructing the political identity of citizens. Nationalism is the doctrine that each culture should be self-governing
and have its own state. This has been a popular idea during the course of modernisation, which tended to uproot traditional forms of political organisation.
(See **Modernity**)

Natural kinds   Natural kinds are realities deemed to have, by virtue of their
basic natures, irreducibly distinct properties and mechanisms exercising causal
powers. They have natural necessity, that is:

> the necessity implicit in the concept of the thing's real essence, i.e. those prop-
> erties or powers, which are most basic in an explanatory sense, without which it
> would not be the kind of thing it is, i.e. which constitute its identity or fix it in
> its kind. (Bhaskar, in Archer et al., 1998: 68)

Knowledge of natural kinds is formulated in real definitions which are 'fallible
attempts to capture in words the real essence of things which have already
been identified' (1998: 86). A natural kind acts in the way it must because of its
intrinsic nature, it follows or is driven by its potentialites or 'natural tendencies'. (See **Realist social theory**)

Nature, environment, environmental determinism   'Nature' refers to realms
of self-subsistence which have their own processes and potentialities and are
not dependent on human mediation. Nature is that which has its own nature

or intrinsic mode of being, and this includes humanity. Nature may be mediated by human action and culture but does not originate with these. The natural environment is the setting for action constituted by all the various, naturally produced conditions. Environmental determinism argues that these natural conditions of action are sufficient to explain what people do. (See **Conditioning; Naturalism; Relative autonomy**)

Naturalism   Any approach to social science which argues that all kinds of nature must be explained in terms which are compatible with one another. Traditionally, the term has been used to refer to the idea that nature is a 'unity' and that to be a proper science, social science should adopt the methods of the natural sciences. This has been the position of 'positivism', the doctrine that the only worthwhile knowledge is scientific knowledge. Realism is naturalist, but not in the traditional sense, because it regards 'nature' as consisting of the different natural kinds, each requiring its own appropriate mode of scientific investigation. Crucially, realism accepts that social reality is partly constituted by the meaningful action of human subjects, a natural kind which cannot be studied using the methods developed solely for studying the rest of nature. (See **Natural kinds**)

Necessary and sufficient conditions   Conditions are necessary where they *must* obtain if the conditioned entity is to exist. Oxygen is a necessary condition of human life. But it is not sufficient because human life requires a lot more than just oxygen. Only where all the conditions for the existence of an entity are operating are they sufficient. (See **Natural kinds; Relative autonomy**)

Objectivism   In social theory, objectivism directly contradicts subjectivism, holding that only properties of and relations between objects are relevant for explaining social phenomena. (See **Subject/subjectivity**)

Ontology   Ontology theorises the basic conditions of existence and what can possibly exist. It is a precondition for theorising about the possibility of knowledge which is the province of epistemology. In part, knowledge depends on the properties of knowers and the objects of knowledge, which are ontological questions. (See **Epistemology**)

Opportunity costs and opportunity structure   'Opportunity costs' is a phrase from economics referring to what is involved in making rational choices between alternatives. Each option is an opportunity to make some gain but has some cost attached to it. Rational choice theory uses this concept and it is useful when analysing choice-making in situations where we know about the field of alternatives which actors are considering when choosing. Opportunity structures are configurations of opportunities (with their associated costs and benefits) open to given actors in given positions and situations. They can be described as predicaments. (See **Decision-making environment; Rational choice theory**)

Parsons, Talcott 1902–79   His *Structure of Social Action* (1968 first published 1937) introduced classical social theory to the US, arguing that it is not possible to explain voluntary action without reference to cultural values. He went on to develop a highly complex abstract theory of the way social systems function, in which action virtually disappears. Giddens' structuration theory was designed to replace Marxist and Parsonian 'functionalism'. (See **Althusser; Classical social theory; Functionalism; Giddens; Structuration theory)**

Persons   (See **Dispositions; Individuals; Personal identity)**

Personal identity and social identity   Personal identity is the way in which persons understand the meaning of their own positions in the world. It involves a constantly developing narrative, reflecting about their past and their intentions for their future. It is a private construction and interpretation of their experience. It makes reference to, but is not defined by, that person's social identities. A persons' social identity is the way they are defined by others for the purpose of social interaction. These definitions are primarily positional, referring to roles, statuses and social types. Social identities, unlike personal identities, are not private and unique to each person. (See **Archer; Individuals)**

Postmodernity and postmodernism   Postmodernity is the general social condition of having been modern but struggling to find alternative orientations and arrangements to those developed to aggressively seek change and improvement. The symptoms are the developing structural contradictions of industrialism and nation-state politics, and the emergence of postmodern*ism*. Postmodernism is the cultural reflection on the situation of postmodernity, which tends to favour abandoning modernity, modernism and associated universalism, in favour of relativism. (See **Modernity; Universalism)**

Practice, practices   Practice (in general) is what all humans do when they individually or collectively apply their imaginations, equipped with their cultural and structural legacies, to try to realise their various interests. Practices are particular distinct ways of doing things which have their own relative autonomy; thus what is involved in making pots or wine or motorcycles are distinct practices and this making is distinct from the practices involved in selling pots, wine or motorcycles.

Production, means and relations of   (See **Capitalism)**

Rational choice theory (RCT)   RCT tries to explain the actions of individuals and the emergence of collective phenomena as being the outcome of the rational calculation of opportunity costs by individuals equipped only with natural self-interest and rationality. Social phenomena depend on the pre-social properties of individuals. This theory is individualist and rationalist. (See **Individuals; Opportunity costs; Reason; Utilitarianism)**

Reason, rationality, rationalisation   Rationality is humans' capacity to use powers of reasoning. Reason concerns itself with the objective, empirical and logical properties of the world and the truth of theoretical representations of it. Reason is concerned with defining what has to be accepted about the world and our situations, whether we like it or not. In this sense, it is dispassionate. But reason is not disconnected from the emotions, since strong feelings may be justified or not, depending on an objective, rational assessment. Rationalisation is the general process of using reason to criticise practices and theories objectively, to make them more efficient at achieving desired goals.

Realism   As an ontology, realism holds that objective realities exist independently of the experiences they offer us and what we can say about them. Because experience only give us surface evidence of the workings of reality, it is necessary to theorise what reality consists of. So, as an epistemology, realism holds that knowledge depends on theoretical discovery of the properties of reality, by asking what would have to be the case to produce what we experience. Theoretical reasoning and empirical evidence interact in the knowledge process. (See **Empiricism; Idealism; Natural kinds**)

Realist social theory   Realist social theory tries to specify the complex objective and subjective properties of social reality which are responsible for social experience and are therefore necessary to explain it. Realism does not equate social reality with social phenomena which can be experienced, or with what participants say about their experience. It holds that only if social reality is viewed as a complex interaction between the relative autonomies of the natural kinds, such as individuals, nature, culture, action and social structure, can it have the necessary causal powers to produce the variety of empirical social phenomena which we experience. (See **Archer; Dialectics and Aristotle; Empiricism; Idealism; Individuals; Marx; Natural kinds; Realism; Relative autonomy; Structuralism; Weber**)

Reference group theory   Developed by Merton to exploit the insight that people's attitudes to their social experience vary depending on who they compare themselves with. It is an example of 'middle-range' theorising, building on the theoretical stimulus of the data in *The American Soldier* (Stouffer et al., 1949). (See **Merton**)

Relativism   (See **Postmodernism; Universalism**)

Reasons as causes   (See **Winch**)

Relative autonomy   Realist social theory suggests that the different kinds of cause are autonomous to the extent that they have their own distinct causal powers and must therefore always be reckoned with; but the autonomy of each is relative to (limited by) the autonomy of the others. Each relatively autonomous kind of cause only contributes by conditioning outcomes, and is therefore necessary but not sufficient to explain outcomes. Determination of specific outcomes is the product of a combination of relatively autonomous causes. Each kind of causation 'mediates' the force of the others. (See **Conditioning**)

Role(s), role sets, expectations   Social roles are positions entailing prescriptive expectations and rules defining how incumbents should behave. These ideals are backed by sanctions. A person occupies a set of roles and must cope with the pressures to satisfy various expectations, which may be contradictory, making choices about which sanctions they can avoid or tolerate. (See **Dilemmas**)

Rules   (See **Winch; Wittgenstein; Ethnomethodology**)

Runciman, Walter G. 1934–   Runciman leads the revival of neo-evolutionary social theory. His *A Treatise on Social Theory* (1983, 1989) is a major contribution to theoretical historical sociology. Like Mann's work, it advocates a general theory of historical development of human social organisation in the tradition of Marx and Weber.

Schutz, Alfred 1899–1959   Schutz developed 'social phenomenology' to analyse the subjective experience of, and kind of common-sense knowledge and rationality we use to conduct ourselves in, everyday life. (See **Ethnomethodology**)

Sex   (See **Gender**)

Signs, symbols   (See **Culture**)

Situational logic   The analysis of the relation between the objective properties of the circumstances of action, the powers available to actors and what they hope to achieve in those circumstances. Situations may favour or disfavour the attaining of particular goals and present actors with more or less costly options. Generally, situations require us to be opportunists when presented with favourable circumstances, make compromises to get a measure of what we want against oppositions and choose what must be defended at any cost without compromise.

Social action   Action is social when the actor intentionally takes account of the consequences of their action for other people. Weber provided the most important analysis of the concepts necessary to think about social action.

Social identity   (See **Gender; Personal identity and social identity**)

Social power, its media and techniques   Social power is the capacity to get others to act as you want them to. It involves controlling other people which requires appropriate resources and techniques. These include actual and threatened violence and other forms of intimidation, bargaining, bribery, credit, rewarding by offering symbols of social status and so on. Such techniques use resources such as money, physical force, legal rights and cultural authority. These provide the wherewithall of domination. There are three interrelated bases of social power; cultural (the capacity to define the meaning and value of situations), economic (the capacity to control the production and distribution of material resources) and political (the capacity to determine decision-making and have available effective use of physical force). (See **Bourdieu; Mann; Marx; Runciman; Weber**)

Social status   Social status attaches to persons and collectivities on the basis of some principle of evaluation by others. Weber uses the phrase 'social esteem'. High social status can be used to dominate others, secure privileges for children and accumulate material resources. For example, the high social status of some religious orders idealising poverty, such as the Franciscans in the thirteenth century, enabled them to accumulate vast wealth and Papal patronage. (See **Bourdieu; Hierarchy; Roles; Stratification**)

Strategies, strategic action   Strategies are preferred methods for orchestrating action and situations to achieve goals at acceptable costs. They involve interpreting the opportunity costs entailed by situational logics. (See **Action; Opportunity costs; Rational choice theory; Situational logic**)

Stratification   The process generating inequalities of various kinds. The results are structures of 'strata' or 'rungs' on ladders of relative advantage and disadvantage. Stratification happens at micro- and macro-levels of structuring and may be short-lived or endure over generations. Once inequalities appear, differences of interests are created and become a focus for social competition. (See **Agrarian empires; Class; Elites; Hierarchy; Industrialism; Social power; Social status**)

Structural contradiction, logical contradiction   Marx introduced the notion of structural contradiction to help to understand how major social change happened. He suggested that, over time, systems for producing tended to feed back negatively, undermining the conditions necessary for the system's continuity. This idea that human social arrangements, which start out functioning well, can come to undermine or contradict themselves is of fundamental importance for social explanation. A logical contradiction is where propositions or arguments use incompatible elements; formally they assert 'a' and 'not a'. Both cannot be true. (See **Autocatalytic processes; Internal and external relations**)

Structure, social structure, structuralism   A structure is an organisation of components. A social structure is an organisation of social positions with consequences for social interaction. There are many ways in which interaction is socially structured. A given person is located in a number of social structures which condition their interests and actions, sometimes in contradictory ways. Structuralism is the doctrine that the properties of structures are most important in explanation. French structuralism, associated with Lévi-Strauss, holds that the organisation of language and the structural properties of cultural practices and texts are most important. (See **Interests; Relative autonomy; Realist social theory; Structural contradiction; Structuration theory**)

Structuration theory   Giddens adopted the term 'structuration' to refer to the process of structurally conditioned action feeding back to produce those structural conditions. He argued that the relation between 'structure and action' was one of 'duality'. That is, they were not analytically separable because structures only existed when they were 'instantiated', that is, used by actors. His favoured example is language. When not being used, structures have only a 'virtual' existence. This position is opposed by realist social theory, particularly by Archer, who argues that structures have a real existence and causal force, whether or not they are used by actors. (See **Archer; Constraint and enablement; Giddens; Realist social theory**)

Subject/subjectivity, subjectivism   Subjectivity involves having a unique point of view, a self-identity, from which to be self-reflective about the meaning and consequences of one's own life and actions. A subject is a being which can, in Mead's words 'be an object to itself'. Subjects' intentions can guide their actions as opposed to the non-intentional behaviour of objects. Subjectivism in social theory holds that the subjectivity of actors holds the key to explaining social life. (See **Action; Mead; Objectivism**)

Sufficient conditions   (See **Necessary and sufficient conditions**)

Symbolic interactionism   A school of sociology concentrating on the immediacy of interpersonal interaction and the negotiation of meaning. It celebrates the creativity of actors in the ongoing work of performing their roles and social identities. It contributes to microsociology, but has difficulty linking this to social phenomena and processes which endure for long periods of time. Its social theoretical focus is on individuals, action and culture, at the expense of social structure. (See **Ethnomethodology; Garfinkel; Goffman; Mead**)

Tendencies, typical(ity) statistical probabilities or likelihood   The evidence for the existence of the mechanisms of social reality takes the form of descriptions of the general properties shared by populations of individuals. Social characteristics are more or less statistically measurable tendencies that members of populations share some characteristic, creating what can be said to be typical of that population. Shared characteristics may be more or less common among a population. Because individuals are unique and mediate the influence of social causes conditioning them, not every individual will exhibit typical characteristics. There will be exceptions. The social conditioning of relatively autonomous individuals allows for both shared social characteristics (social facts) and individual exceptions who act against type. (See **Class; Durkheim; Weber**)

Understanding   (See **Explanation**)

Universalism   This holds that it is possible to identify truths in our knowledge of the world and moral principles and virtues to guide our social conduct and administration of justice, which are valid for everyone, irrespective of their personal feelings, cultural differences or historical context. Universalism opposes relativism, which argues that such truths are relative to and dependent on such differences, and therefore that there are as many truths as there are points of view. Universalism holds open the possibility of deliberately transcending what it regards as the contingencies and restrictions of cultures, by the use of reason to assess evidence and logic of arguments. Universalism is implicit in rationalisation and the realist approach to social science. (See **Modernity; Postmodernity**)

Utilitarianism   The school of moral and political philosophy which argued that empirical information about what made the majority of individuals happy should be used to test the moral justifiability of acts. This 'principle of utility' was individualist and empiricist. John Stuart Mill (1806–73) offered the most sophisticated version of utilitarianism. His niceness meant that he failed to acknowledge that sometimes what makes most people happy (say, persecuting minorities) may be evil. Talcott Parsons criticised the whole mode of thought from the perspective of classical social theory. (See **Opportunity costs; Parsons; Rational choice theory; Situational logic**)

Virtues   Virtues are the various general positive moral dispositions, which can attach to actions and actors. Examples are courage, generosity, care for others, honesty, sense of justice. Some virtues may be argued to be universal, but others (for example obedience to elders) may be culturally specific. Social theory has room for the human potentiality to acquire both types of virtues. (See **Dialectics and Aristotle**)

Weber, Max 1864–1920   To realists, Weber is the greatest social theorist, giving equal weight to individuals, action, culture and social structure in social explanation. Each has its own irreducible mode of influencing historical outcomes and they all interact over time. Weber comes closest to specifying the general nature of the historical process, and provides impressive examples of the complex causal narratives required to explain social phenomena. No social scientist can afford not to read Weber.

Winch, Peter (1926–97) Reasons as causes   Winch's *The Idea of a Social Science* (1990) used an interpretation of Wittgenstein's recognition that meaning depends on 'agreement in judgements', to argue that causal explanation was completely inappropriate for understanding social reality. Unfortunately, he only argued against the empiricist concept of cause represented by what David Hume called 'constant conjunction' (Hume, 1888: 139). Since relations between social meanings were logical and thus internal relations, they could not be causal relations which were necessarily 'external' and contingent. This is true, but realists argue that causal social science is possible because causes are internally related, generative mechanisms (rather than externally related, empirical phenomena) and this notion of cause can incorporate the logical relations among reasons which Winch held to be irreconcilable with causal relations. For realists reasons can be causes, for Winch they cannot. (See **Explanation and understanding**; **Wittgenstein**)

Wittgenstein, Ludwig 1889–1951   Wittgenstein's philosophy of meaning profoundly influenced social theory. He argued against the claims of empiricism (that the meaning of words is defined by direct experience of the things they refer to) and idealism (that the meaning of words is defined by their relations with what individuals privately think). He argued that the only way language could be made to refer to the world was for a community of people to define the rules governing how to use words correctly and to correct one another's mistakes and teach children the rules. Meaning becomes dependent on public social interaction. Rules do not apply themselves. Instead, creative actors collectively interpreting their unique situations have to judge the relevance of rules. This insight is the basis for ethnomethodology and is important for Giddens' 'structuration' theory. Wittgenstein drew attention to the irreducibility of human beings making judgements; there is no substitute for the necessity of social humanity. (See **Garfinkel**; **Rules**; **Structuration theory**)

Bibliography

Introduction

Davis, D.B. 1966, *The Problem of Slavery in Western Culture* (Ithaca, NY: Cornell University Press)

Lewis, B. 1990, *Race and Slavery in the Middle East* (New York: Oxford University Press)

Merton, R.K. 1982, *Social Theory and Social Structure* (USA: Macmillan)

Moore, B. 1967, *Social Origins of Dictatorship and Democracy* (London: Allen Lane)

Patterson, O. 1982, *Slavery and Social Death: A Comparative Study* (Cambridge, MA: Harvard University Press)

Pipes, D. 1981, *Slave Soldiers and Islam: The Genesis of a Military System* (New Haven, CT: Yale University Press)

Runciman, W.G. 1966, *Relative Deprivation and Social Justice* (London: Routledge)

Sennett, R. 1990, *The Conscience of the Eye* (London: Faber)

Skocpol, T. 1979, *States and Social Revolutions* (Cambridge: CUP)

Stanworth, H. n. d., *Protestantism, Environment Conservation and Urban Renewal: The Swedish Case* (Research Paper, SSSID, Swansea)

United Nations, 1991, *Contemporary Forms of Slavery: World Campaign for Human Rights*, Fact sheet 14. (New York: UN Centre for Human Rights)

Watson, J.L. (ed.) 1980, *Asian and African Systems of Slavery* (Oxford: Blackwell)

Weber, M. 1930, *The Protestant Ethic and the Spirit of Capitalism* (London: Allen & Unwin)

Westermann, W.L. 1955, *The Slave Systems of Greek and Roman Antiquity* (Philadelphia: American Philosophical Society)

Chapter 1 What Do Individuals Explain?

Baert, P. 1998, *Social Theory in the Twentieth Century* (Cambridge: Polity)

Barth, F. 1959, *Political Leadership among the Swat Pathans* (London: Athlone)

Chapter 2 Testing the Explanatory Value of Individuals

Bourgois, P. 1995, *In Search of Respect* (Cambridge: CUP)

Stack, C. 1997, (2nd edn), *All Our Kin* (New York: Basic Books)

Chapter 3 What Does Nature Explain?

Brody, H. 2001, *The Other Side of Eden* (London: Faber)
Diamond, J. 1997, *Guns, Germs and Steel: A Short History of Everybody for the Last 13000 Years* (London: J. Cape)
Goff, T. 1980, *Marx and Mead* (London: RKP)
Le Roy Ladurie, E. 1972, *Times of Feast, Times of Famine* (London: Allen & Unwin)
McNeill, W.H. 1983, *The Pursuit of Power* (Oxford: Blackwell)
Marx, K. and Engels, F. 1964, *The German Ideology* (London: Lawrence & Wishart)
Mead, G.H. 1934, *Mind, Self and Society* (Chicago: University of Chicago Press)
Runciman, W.G. 1983, 1989, *A Treatise on Social Theory*, Vols 1 and 2 (Cambridge: CUP)

Chapter 4 Testing the Explanatory Value of Nature

Brody, H. 1986, *Maps and Dreams* (London: Faber)
Brody, H. 2001, *The Other Side of Eden* (London: Faber)
Descola, P. 1997, *The Spears of Twilight: Life and Death in the Amazon Jungle* (London: Flamingo)
Paine, R. 1971, 'Animals as capital: comparisons among northern nomadic herders and hunters', *Anthropological Quarterly*, **44**: 157–72
Rival, L. 1996, 'Blowpipes and spears: the social significance of Huaorani technological choices', in Descola, P. and Palsson, G. (eds) *Nature and Society; Anthropological Perspectives* (London: Routledge)
Sahlins, M. 1968, 'Notes on the original affluent society', in Lee, R.B. and DeVore, I. (eds) *Man the Hunter* (Chicago: Aldine)

Chapter 5 What Does Culture Explain?

Archer, M. 1995, *Realist Social Theory* (Cambridge: CUP)
Bloor, D. 1976, *Knowledge and Social Imagery* (London: RKP)
Bourdieu, P. 1990, *In Other Words* (Cambridge: Polity)
Durkheim, E. 1982 (trans.), *The Rules of Sociological Method* (Basingstoke: Macmillan – now Palgrave Macmillan)
Marx, K. 1967, *The Eighteenth Brumaire of Louis Bonaparte* (Moscow: Progressive Publishers)
Williams, R. 1976, *Keywords* (London: Fontana)

Chapter 6 Testing the Explanatory Value of Culture

Bagguley, P., Mark-Lawson, J., Shapiro, D., Urry, J., Walby, S. and Warde, A. 1990, *Restructuring: Place, Class and Gender* (London: Sage)
Bernstein, B. 1971, *Class, Codes and Control* (London: RKP)
Cunningham, P.G. and Parker, J. 1978, 'Two selves, two sexes: deference and the interpretation of a homosexual presence', *Sociology and Social Research*, 63(1): 90–111

Degler, C.N. 1971, *Neither Black nor White* (New York: Macmillan)

Diggs, I. 1953, 'Color in Colonial Spanish America', *Journal of Negro History*, **38**: 403–27

Douglas, M. 1970, *Purity and Danger* (Harmondsworth: Pelican)

Douglas, M. 1975, *Implicit Meanings* (London: RKP)

Douglas, M. 1982, *In the Active Voice* (London: RKP)

Douglas, M. 1996 (rev. edn), *Natural Symbols* (London: Routledge)

Garfinkel, H. 1967, *Studies in Ethnomethodology* (Englewood Cliffs, NJ: Prentice Hall)

Harris, M. 1970, 'Referential ambiguity in the calculus of Brazilian racial identity', in Whitten, N.E. and Szwed, J.F. (eds) *Afro-American Anthropology* (New York: Free Press)

Hegel, G.W.F. 1956 (trans. J. Sibree), *The Philosophy of History* (New York: Dover)

Jordan, W.D. 1969, 'American chiaroscuro: the status and definition of mulattos in the British Colonies', in Foner, L. and Genovese, E. (eds) *Slavery in the New World* (Englewood Cliffs, NJ: Prentice Hall)

Lockwood, D. 1966, 'Some sources of variation in working class images of society', *Sociological Review*, **14**(3): 249–67

Martin, B. 1981, *A Sociology of Contemporary Cultural Change* (Oxford: Blackwell)

Marx, K. and Engels, F. 1964, *The German Ideology* (London: Lawrence & Wishart)

Parsons, T. 1951, *The Social System* (New York: Free Press)

Savage, M., Barlow, J., Dickens, P. and Fielding, T. 1992, *Property, Bureaucracy and Culture* (London: Routledge)

Tannenbaum, F. 1946, *Slave and Citizen: The Negro in the Americas* (New York: Vintage)

Thompson, M., Ellis, R. and Wildavsky, A. 1990, *Cultural Theory* (Boulder, CO: Westview Press)

Urry, J. 1990, *The Tourist Gaze* (London: Sage)

Waldinger, R.D. 1996, *Still the Promised City? African-Americans and the New Immigrants in Post-industrial New York* (Cambridge, MA: Harvard University Press)

Weber, M. 1952, *Ancient Judaism* (New York: Free Press)

Winch, P. 1990 (2nd edn), *The Idea of a Social Science* (London: Routledge)

Whyte, W.S. 1957, *The Organisation Man* (New York: Touchstone)

Chapter 7 What Does Action Explain?

Ashworth, T. 1980, *Trench Warfare 1914–18: The Live and Let Live System* (Basingstoke: Macmillan – now Palgrave Macmillan)

Atkinson, J.M. and Drew, P. 1979, *Order in Court: The Organisation of Verbal Interaction in Judicial Settings* (London: Macmillan – now Palgrave Macmillan)

Bourdieu, P. 1986, 'From rules to strategies', *Cultural Anthropology*, **1**: 110–20

Bourdieu, P. 1990, *The Logic of Practice* (Cambridge: Polity)

Button, G. 1987, 'Answers as interactional products: two sequential practices used in interviews', *Social Psychological Quarterly*, **50**: 160–71

Garfinkel, H. 1967, *Studies in Ethnomethodology* (Engelwood Cliffs, NJ: Prentice Hall)

Giddens, A. 1984, *The Constitution of Society* (Cambridge: Polity)

Goffman, E. 1959, *The Presentation of Self in Everyday Life* (New York: Doubleday Anchor)

Goffman, E. 1968, *Asylums* (Harmondsworth: Penguin)

Goffman, E. 1969, *Where the Action Is: Three Studies* (London: Allen Lane)

Goodwin, C. 1984, 'Notes on story structure and the organisation of participation', in Atkinson, J.M. and Heritage, J. (eds) *Structures of Social Action: Studies in Conversation Analysis* (Cambridge: CUP)

Russell, R. 1972, *Bird Lives!* (London: Quartet Books)

Schutz, A. 1967a, *Collected Papers* (The Hague: Marinus Nijhoff)

Schutz, A. 1967b (trans. Walsh, G. and Leheert, F.), *The Phenomenology of the Social World* (Evanston, IL: Northwestern University Press)

Sudnow, D. 1978, *Ways of the Hand* (Cambridge, MA: Harvard University Press)

Weber, M. 1968 (eds Roth, G. and Wittich, C.), *Economy and Society* (New York: Bedminster Press)

Chapter 8 Testing the Explanatory Value of Action

Atkinson, P. 1995, *Medical Talk and Medical Work* (London: Sage)

Gerth, H. and Mills, C.W. 1948, *From Max Weber* (London: Routledge)

Zimmerman, D.H. 1971, 'The practicalities of rule use', in Douglas, J.D. (ed.) *Understanding Everyday Life* (London: RKP)

Chapter 9 What Does Social Structure Explain?

Caplow, T. 1968, *Two Against One: Coalitions in the Triad* (Englewood Cliffs, NJ: Prentice Hall)

Gellner, E. 1973, 'Scale and nation', *Philosophy of the Social Sciences*, **3**

Granovetter, M. 1978, 'Threshold models of collective behaviour', *American Journal of Sociology*, **83**: 1420–43

Mann, M. 1986, *The Sources of Social Power; A History of Power from the Beginning to 1760* (Cambridge: CUP)

Marx, K. 1858, 'Trade or Opium?', *New York Daily Tribune*, September 20

Oliver, M.L. and Shapiro, T.M. 1997, *Black Wealth/ White Wealth* (New York: Routledge)

Piven, F.F. and Cloward, R.A. 1979, *Poor People's Movements: Why They Succeed and How They Fail* (New York: Vintage)

Sayer, A. 1992, *Method in Social Science: A Realist Approach* (London: Routledge)

Sulloway, F.J. 1996, *Born to Rebel* (London: Little, Brown)

Weber, M. 1968 (eds Roth, G. and Wittich, C.), *Economy and Society* (New York: Bedminster Press)

Chapter 10 Testing the Explanatory Value of Social Structure

Archer, M. 1979, *The Social Origins of Educational Systems* (London: Sage)

Ashworth, T. 1980, *Trench Warfare 1914–18: The Live and Let Live System* (Basingstoke: Macmillan – now Palgrave Macmillan)

Collins, R. 1979, *The Credential Society; An Historical Sociology of Education and Stratification* (New York: Academic Press)

Durkheim, E. 1952, *Suicide* (London: RKP)

Gellner, E. 1983, *Nations and Nationalism* (Oxford: Blackwell)

Gellner, E. 1996, 'The coming of nationalism and its interpretation: the myths of nations and class', in Balakrishnan, G. (ed.) *Mapping the Nation* (London: Verso)

Gellner, E. 1997, *Nationalism* (London: Weidenfeld & Nicholson)

Kabeer, N. 2000, *The Power to Choose: Bangladeshi Women and Labour Market Decisions in London and Dhaka* (London: Verso)

Mann, M. 1986, *The Sources of Social Power; A History of Power from the Beginning to 1760* (Cambridge: CUP)

Parsons, T. 1954, *Essays in Sociological Theory* (rev. edn) (New York: Free Press)

Chapter 11 Get Real: A Perspective on Social Science

Archer, M.S. 1995, *Realist Social Theory: The Morphogenetic Approach* (Cambridge: CUP)

Benton, T. and Craib, I. 2001, *Philosophies of Social Science* (Basingstoke: Palgrave – now Palgrave Macmillan)

Giddens, A. 1984, *The Constitution of Society* (Cambridge: Polity)

Parker, J. 2000, *Structuration* (Buckingham: Open University Press)

Weber, M. 1930, *The Protestant Ethic and the Spirit of Capitalism* (London: Allen & Unwin)

Chapter 12 Being Practical: The Uses and Payoffs of Social Explanation

Coleman, A. 1985, *Utopia on Trial: Vision and Reality in Planned Housing* (London: Hilary Shipman)

Flyvbjerg, B. 1998, *Rationality and Power: Democracy in Practice* (Chicago: University of Chicago Press)

Fried, M. 1963, 'Grieving for a lost home', in Duhl, L. (ed.) *The Urban Condition* (New York: Basic Books)

Fried, M. and Gleicher, P. 1976, 'Some sources of residential satisfaction in an urban slum', in Proshansky, H.M., Ittenson, W.H. and Rivlin, L.G. (eds), *Environmental Psychology: People and Their Physical Settings* (2nd edn) (New York: Holt, Rinehart & Winston)

Gans, H. 1972, *People and Plans* (Harmondsworth: Penguin)

Ignatieff, M. 1999, 'Less race please', *Prospect*, **40** (April): 10

Newman, O. 1972, *Defensible Space: Crime Prevention Through Urban Design* (New York: Macmillan)

Okely, J. 1983, *The Traveller-Gypsies* (Cambridge: CUP)

Rooney, J. 1995, *Organizing the South Bronx* (Albany: State University of New York Press)

Sennett, R. 1998, *The Corrosion of Character* (New York: WW Norton).

Glossary

Archer, M.S., Bhaskar, R., Collier, A., Lawson, T., Norrie, A. (eds) 1998, *Critical Realism: Essential Readings* (London: Routledge)

Craib, I. 1992, *Anthony Giddens* (London: Routledge)

Hume, D. 1888, (ed. Selby-Bigge, L.A), *A Treatise of Human Nature* (Oxford: Clarendon Press)

Mann, M. 1986, *The Sources of Social Power; A History of Power from the Beginning to 1760* (Cambridge: CUP)

Merton, R.K. 1982, *Social Theory and Social Structure* (USA: Macmillan)

Outhwaite, W. 1994, *Habermas* (Cambridge: Polity)

Parsons, T. 1968 first published 1937, *The Structure of Social Action* (New York: Free Press)

Runciman, W.G. 1983, 1989, *A Treatise on Social Theory*, Vols 1 and 2, (Cambridge: CUP)

Sheridan, A. 1990, *Michael Foucault: The Will to Truth* (London: Routledge)

Stouffer, S. et al. 1949, *The American Soldier, Vols 1 and 2* (Princeton, NJ: Princeton University Press)

Winch, P. 1990 (2nd edn), *The Idea of a Social Science* (London: Routledge)

Further Reading

Althusser, L. 1971, *Lenin and Philosophy* (London: Verso)

Anderson, E. 1999, *Code of the Street: Decency, Violence and the Moral Life of the Inner City* (New York: WW Norton)

Archer, M.S. 1988, *Culture and Agency* (Cambridge: CUP)

Archer, M.S. 1995, *Realist Social Theory* (Cambridge: CUP)

Archer, M.S. 2000, *Being Human. The Problem of Agency* (Cambridge: CUP)

Archer, M.S. and Tritter, J.Q. (eds) 2000, *Rational Choice Theory* (London: Routledge)

Atkinson, P. 1985, *Language, Structure and Reproduction* (London: Methuen)

Barnes, B. 1995, *The Elements of Social Theory* (London: UCL)

Barnes, B. 2000, *Understanding Agency* (London: Sage)

Baszanger, I. 1997, 'Deciphering chronic pain', in Strauss, A. and Corbin, J. (eds) *Grounded Theory in Practice* (Thousand Oaks, CA: Sage)

Boden, D. 1994, *The Business of Talk: Organisations in Action* (Cambridge: Polity)

Bourdieu, P. 1984, *Distinction* (London: RKP)

Brody, H. 1987, *Living Arctic* (London: Douglas & MacIntyre)

Bruce, S. 2000, *Fundamentalism* (Cambridge: Polity)

Calhoun, C. 1997, *Nationalism* (Buckingham: Open University Press)

Carrithers, M. 1992, *Why Humans have Cultures* (Oxford: OUP)

Cicourel, A. 1968, *The Social Organisation of Juvenile Justice* (New York: J. Wiley)

Cohen, S. 2001, *States of Denial* (Cambridge: Polity)

Collins, R. 1992, *Sociological Insight: An Introduction to Non-obvious Sociology* (New York: Oxford University Press)

Collins, R. 2000, 'Situational stratification: a micro-macro theory of inequality', *Sociological Theory*, **18**(1)

Cowley, R. (ed.) 2000, *What If?* (London: Macmillan – now Palgrave Macmillan)

Craib, I. 1997, *Classical Social Theory* (Oxford: Oxford University Press)

Davis, M. 2000, *Late Victorian Holocausts: El Nino Famines and the Making of the Third World* (London: Verso)

Douglas, M. 1970, *Natural Symbols* (London: Barrie & Rockliff)

Douglas, M. 1986, *Risk Acceptability According to the Social Sciences* (London: RKP)

Douglas, M. 1996, *Thought Styles* (London: Sage)

Douglas, M. and Wildavsky, A. 1982, *Risk and Culture* (Berkeley: University of California Press)

Durkheim, E. 1982 (trans.), *The Rules of Sociological Method* (Basingstoke: Macmillan – now Palgrave Macmillan)

Eagleton, T. 2000, *The Idea of Culture* (Oxford: Blackwell)

Flyvberg, B. 2001, *Making Social Science Matter* (Cambridge: CUP)

Gerth, H. and Mills, C.W. (eds) 1948, *From Max Weber* (London: RKP)

Gladwell, M. 2000, *The Tipping Point* (London: Little, Brown)

Goffman, E. 1983, 'The interaction order', *American Sociological Review*, **48**

Haberle, S.G. and Lusty, A.C. 2000, 'Can climate influence cultural development? A view through time', *Environment and History*, 6: 349–69

Hall, J.A. (ed.) 1998, *State of the Nation: Ernest Gellner and the Theory of Nationalism* (Cambridge: CUP)

Heritage, J. 1984, *Garfinkel and Ethnomethodology* (Cambridge: Polity)

Hughes, J.A., Martin, P.J. and Sharrock, W.W. 1995, *Understanding Classical Social Theory* (London: Sage)

Hutchinson, S.E. 1996, *Nuer Dilemmas: Coping with Money, War and the State* (Berkeley and Los Angeles: University of California Press)

Jackson, B. and Marsden, D. 1962, *Education and the Working Class* (London: RKP)

Lash, S. and Urry, J. 1987, *The End of Organised Capitalism* (Cambridge: Polity)

López, J. and Potter, G. 2001, *After Postmodernism* (London: Athlone)

López, J. and Scott, J. 2000, *Social Structure* (Buckingham: Open University Press)

McCrone, D. 1998, *The Sociology of Nationalism* (London: Routledge)

MacIntyre, A. 1999, *Dependent Rational Animals* (London: Duckworth)

Marx, K. 1964, *The Economic and Philosophic Manuscripts of 1844* (New York: International Publishers)

May, T. and Williams, M. (eds) 1998, *Knowing the Social World* (Buckingham: Open University Press)

Mills, C.W. 1951, *White Collar* (New York: Oxford University Press)

Morgan, E.S. 1972, 'Slavery and freedom: the American paradox', *The Journal of American History*, 59: 5–29

Mouzelis, N. 1995, *Sociological Theory: What went Wrong?* (London: Routledge)

Ozkirimli, U. 2000, *Theories of Nationalism* (Basingstoke: Palgrave – now Palgrave Macmillan)

Parsons, T. 1951, *The Social System* (London: RKP)

Parsons, T. 1968, *The Structure of Social Action* (New York: Free Press)

Parsons, T. 1971, *The System of Modern Societies* (Englewood Cliffs, NJ: Prentice Hall)

Porpora, D.V. 1989, 'Four concepts of social structure', *Journal for the Theory of Social Behaviour*, 19(2): 195–211

Ray, L. 1999, *Theorising Classical Sociology* (Buckingham: Open University Press)

Rueschmeyer, D., Stephens, E.H. and Stephens, J.D. 1992, *Capitalist Development and Democracy* (Cambridge: Polity)

Runciman, W.G. 1998, *The Social Animal* (London: HarperCollins)

Sahlins, M. 1999, 'Two or three things I know about culture', *Journal of the Royal Anthropological Institute* (NS) **5**: 399–421

Sayer, A. 2000, *Realism and Social Science* (London: Sage)

Smith, A.D. 1998, *Nations and Modernism* (London: Routledge)

Smith, D. 1991, *The Rise of Historical Sociology* (Cambridge: Polity)

Toman, W. 1996, *Family Constellation* (Northvale, NJ: Jason Aronson)

Turner, B.S. 1999, *Classical Sociology* (London: Sage)

Wright, G. and Kunreuther, H. 1875 Cotton, corn and risk in the nineteenth century', *Journal of Economic History*, **35**, September

Index